Divine Love Affair
An Akashic Journey

Dear Ray Richard!
Love & Be Loved

Nancy Smith

Divine Love Affair

An Akashic Journey

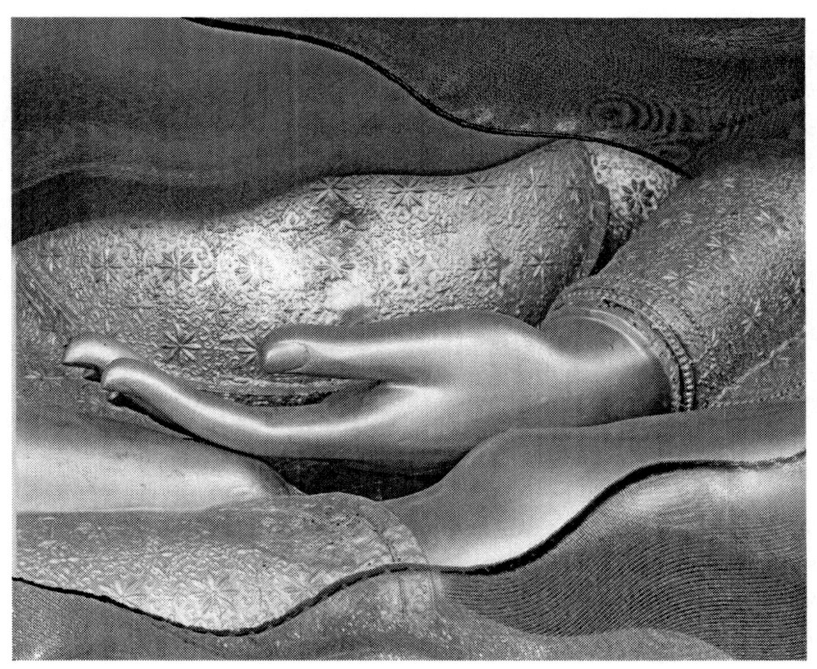

Nancy Smith

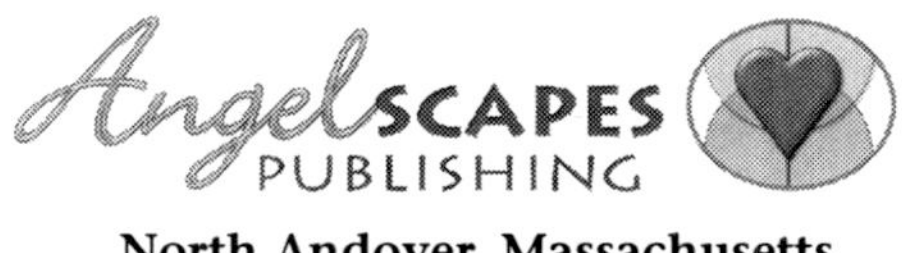

North Andover, Massachusetts

First published in 2016 by Angelscapes Publishing
A division of Angelscapes LLC
119 Blueberry Hill Lane
North Andover, Ma 01845

Copyright © Nancy Smith 2016

Contact Author Nancy Smith:
nancy@angelscapes.net
www.angelscape.net

Disclaimer: the information provided in this book does not constitute legal, psychological, medical of financial advice. Readers are responsible for their own choices and actions.

ISBN: 978-0-9906090-5-6
Ebook ISBN: 978-0-9906090-7-0

Library of Congress Control Number: 2016916487

Edited by Joan Schaublin
Cover Design by Nancy Smith
Cover images: Fiery Flying Silk ©Tatiana Grozetskaya / istock photos
              Hand of Buddha Statue © PJ66431470 / Istock photos
Cover type: In and Out with Onyx
Interior design and illustrations by ©Nancy Smith,
Chapter 7 tree by ©macrovector
Typeset in ITC Stone Serif Standard with Cafeteria and Wendy

POD through Ingram and Lightning Source

This book is dedicated to my family,
especially Cort, Deirdra, Ryan, Rowan, Jesse, David,
Collin, Liz, Mike and Nicha, and all my family members
on the way that I haven't met yet.

To my parents Jim and Yvonne Smith.

To my students and clients and to all those on their own
soul's journey.

May your path open wide with ease, grace and divine love.

With the Deepest Gratitude...

My Journey has been filled with many people who have traveled with me, influencing me, teaching me, inspiring me on my Akashic Path. Many people have helped me make this book into a reality. From personal friends, teachers to students and clients, I can't possibly name everyone, please know I am deeply grateful to all of you.

I thank the following people for their help in this book, for their influence and teachings, and for their pioneering efforts that paved the way for me. To my husband Cort who read every word of this book before it went to the editor. To my editor Joan Schaublin who did a magnificent job not only editing this material, but talking me through the many times I seriously doubted myself.

Special Thanks to my daughter Deirdra, my son Ryan, my sisters Jacki Smith and Patty Shaw, Juliet, Sandra and Rebecca, who inspire me. To Katie Malloy Ramaci, dear friend and owner of Women of Wisdom who believed in my work and allowed me to set up the *School of Akashic Soul Mastery* in her *Wisdom School* in North Easton. Thanks to Kristy and to ALL my students and clients who were my best teachers of all.

To the professional teachers that were like guides to me, whether they realize it or not, to Christina Cross, Rita Straus Berkowitz, Jose Louis Herrera, Lorna Dimeo, John Holland, Tony Stockwell, Janet Nohavec, Marcia Blair Goodman, Dawna Memont, Kelle Sutliff, MaryLee Trettenero, Anne Deirdra, Karen Paolino Correia, Kimberly Marooney, Cathy Burke. Thanks to all the authors, pioneers and teachers that have guided my path, especially Michael Newton, Larry Dossey, Linda Howe, Amit Goswami, Ervin Laszlo, Edgar Casey, Helena Blavatsky and many, many more.

Table of Contents

Introduction

How many times have we heard about self-love—self-care—only to be challenged by a world around us that wasn't supportive of our efforts at self-love and care? With so many conflicting ideas about love it's no wonder so many of us give up on it, or find the very notion ridiculous.

This book is about connecting to and living in the Divine Love we were created from. This Divine Love, once we establish a relationship with it, supports us, protects us, and sustains us throughout our lives. Divine Love is our birthright; it is your gift from the Creator.

As I embarked on a spiritual path, first as a healer and then as a spiritual medium, my first, and what I thought my prime objective, was to serve and help others—usually giving first to those in need. The pecking order was wife, mother, employee, friend, healer, medium—and bringing up the rear, me. I was always last. Then, unexpectedly, in my mid-forties I was struck with a health crisis. I had to pull from deep within myself to survive an infection that was on the verge of taking my life. I had all the right spiritual stuff—the prayers, the meditations, the gifts—but I didn't have ME. There were plenty of reasons I didn't have a sense of ME. The fact was that I had lost a connection with my Divine Self—my essence—and my life force was ebbing away. I thought I was okay with letting my life go; I had worked hard, given much, and done well. I was alone in the hospital for six days deciding that it was okay to go to Spirit.

But it wasn't okay; not really. I simply didn't have enough of a sense of my own Self to want to live. That's what giving without caring for Self does. It totally disconnects you from life, leaving you with no desire to continue. But when it came right down to the truth of it, I wasn't meant to leave my life like this.

I mulled this over while I watched TV from my bed (because that was pretty much all I could do), when a commercial came on with waffles covered in fresh fruit and whipped cream. I asked Spirit what I needed to do to heal my Self and get back on my feet as I watched this commercial repeat itself every ten minutes . . . for six days. I was too sick to eat, or even drink. I had no appetite. I didn't even care. But, as I watched the waffle commercial, I began to wonder—*What if I could taste again? Would it be worth living if I could enjoy food again?* Little by little I considered what I would miss about my life. I thought about what I wanted to see and *feel* again.

A one-time friend of mine once told me a story about a time in her life when she had hit bottom and had to rebuild her life. She examined every piece of her life; from her relationships all the way to the underwear in her drawer. She would ask herself, *Does this work for me now? Is this positive or negative?* She learned discernment and how to implement it. She showed me how to use it for my own well-being. Then our relationship ended. Her choice to walk out on me showed me how I had walked out on myself, and why that mattered so much. She had brought me a message from my soul that the only way back to life was to care about and for myself—there was no one else. That is what I realized as I laid, day after day, alone in that understaffed hospital.

So, little by little I began to consider all the things in my life that were not serving *ME*. For me, this was a BIG change in thought. I felt very awkward and unsure of myself. But what the heck else was there to lose? I made imaginary piles of *working, not working; negative, positive.* I also made piles of *pisses me off, makes me happy,* and *I wish this to be so.* As I let myself feel my feelings, I judged myself for not being spiritually and emotionally above all of these piles. I told myself I was being petty (plus a few more things I don't want to admit on paper). The biggest choice I made at that time was to decide to put that inner critic into the *not working* pile so I could retrieve the lost Self that had been buried alive.

Then the *next* big, awful, horrible thing happened. The voices from Spirit stopped. I had been hearing these voices and feeling their presence for most of my life. My best, best friends ever had *left* me! What replaced them was what I affectionately called my broken record. Every time I reached for those in Spirit, all I heard was, *"Who do you love?"* or the variation, *"Who are you in love with?"* It made me crazy! I was downright angry that this was all Spirit would give me. *"What are you talking about?!"* I would scream inside my head. (As well as a few more colorful things I'd rather not mention . . .)

I finally got better enough to go home. The IV antibiotics started working the minute I decided that I wanted to taste that waffle with all those strawberries. When I got home I reorganized my life. I left my mediumship circle. I began to sit with a small group in a meditation practice. (The group was only three to four people when it was crowded.) Marcia was the leader, and I love her more than I can ever say for this gift she gave me. For over a year I silently meditated and became calm and empty. I had nothing to offer anyone in the group. I simply sat in silence and enjoyed the music and the calm. I continued to pray. I learned to manage the new silence in my life. I only heard my own thoughts. (Well, with the exception of the *"Who*

do you love?" broken record in my head.) And that's a big deal when you're someone like me.

This is exactly where I began my true love relationship with myself and with the Divine.

During this dark night of my soul, I took a class about accessing the Akashic records. I had always understood the concept of records and libraries in our soul; that, I knew, was what I accessed when I read for clients. I knew I wasn't so much a psychic, as I was someone who could see the soul and divinity in others and help them to see that divinity for themselves.

The organizing principles of prayer and meditation to specifically open to the Akashic records gave my spiritual work a helpful and powerful direction.

I experience the Akashic presence as a loving, nurturing energy that supports me and loves me. The significant change to my work was that I was now accessing this loving, healing energy before working with others. This universal energy had a wise presence that gently brought me into a connection with Divine Love. It knew me, loved me, and showed me what was best for me. Where I had always worked to raise my vibration spiritually and to be open and receptive in my spiritual practices thus far, it was the Akashic work that really brought me home to myself. This practice taught me to love and care for ME. My spirit—my physical, mental, and emotional selves—began to open and blossom with substantial power.

Eventually, I returned to mediumship and began to train to speak and present mediumship from what is called the *platform*, which means, *in front of groups in church settings*. I had *huge* public speaking anxiety, and felt I was making a mistake by forcing myself into another draining situation. But at the same time I felt inspired and challenged to get beyond my fears, and to develop my skills and abilities. I wanted to be able to share my gift. I tried several times to deliver messages from the platform, spending hours, even days, anxiously anticipating each event. Finally, one evening I stood in front of the church preparing to connect with Spirit, with the highest anxiety I had yet to experience. I prayed. *I can't keep doing this to myself. Please, help me, God.* Internally I heard, *Step into the love.* I saw an internal vision of myself standing next to a pillar of light, and all I needed to do was step into it. I didn't have a second to deliberate. I followed my inner guidance. Immediately, I felt Divine Presence; my eternal love and friend. My anxiety was replaced with joy. I became aware of the mediumship connections with loved ones in spirit, and began communicating with ease and grace.

Integrating Divine Presence and Love into all my practices became the key to my growth and development. I had a habit, as many of us do, of compartmentalizing what I learned into boxes of experience. When I consider all the boxes we might make, I can see the friend box, the family box, the employee box, and the hobby box; I had personally made a few *spiritual* boxes. A friend of mine once said to me, *"It's turtles all the way down,"* meaning it's all energy, and energy is mutable, changeable. Allowing myself to integrate Divine Love into all I thought and all I did was an epiphany for me. I had heard many times that *we are all connected*. The realization I had had on the platform brought this loving connection home to me in a big way. We *are* all connected—in the divine energy of love.

About this book

In this book I will refer to this Divine Love as the **Akashic Energy**. I will teach you how to purposefully connect to this presence. You will learn techniques and protocols that will help you develop your own magnificent relationship with the divine power of love.

As you establish your relationship to the Akashic higher power, you will be guided through a series of lessons to help you know and understand yourself. These exercises are meant to show you your own unique Self as well as your soul's plan for your life. You will learn how to access and heal soul level wounds and the destructive belief patterns that trip you up. You are a magnificent being with a soulful plan for a rich, meaningful life. You are loved more than you can imagine.

The secret to letting divine, Akashic love into your life is to build a loving relationship with your true Self. In this book, you'll explore compassionate communication with yourself, which will in turn build your capacity to appreciate and love yourself.

You will learn to open your Akashic records in order to explore the rich landscape of your life. You will meet and work with angels, loved ones, masters, and teachers—your soul team in spirit.

How to use this book

There are three sections in this book. Each section takes you on a specific journey towards divine Akashic awareness.

The first section is about how to navigate your Akashic journey. This is your starting point, with all the skills and tips you'll need to begin. The

 Divine Love Affair

organizing principles behind the Akashic journey are also in this section. I suggest working through this section purposefully and in order. Then you can jump around the rest of the book as much as you want to.

The second section is about you and your relationship with your Self (or, more accurately, your selves). Here you will learn how to access your unconscious self. This section will take time to get through, as it will introduce you to all the emotional secrets that are driving in the backseat of your life. It's important to meet these parts of yourself. Take your time. Be patient, have a sense of humor, and know that you are not alone on this journey, and you are loved!

The third section of this book is a series of protocols that will take you deeply into your soul. In this section you'll find exercises to help you access past lives, soul contracts, and healing from the soul level. As you explore these protocols, you'll begin to uncover and understand your multi-dimensional soul purpose.

Each chapter contains a personal story, followed by the teaching of a principle of the Akashic journey. You will find meditations, exercises and journeys you can dive into in order to experience the teachings in this chapter. You'll want to have a notebook handy to work out these exercises and journal your experiences in. Don't skip the exercises! They will make this work real for you.

Enjoy your journey! With love and blessings,

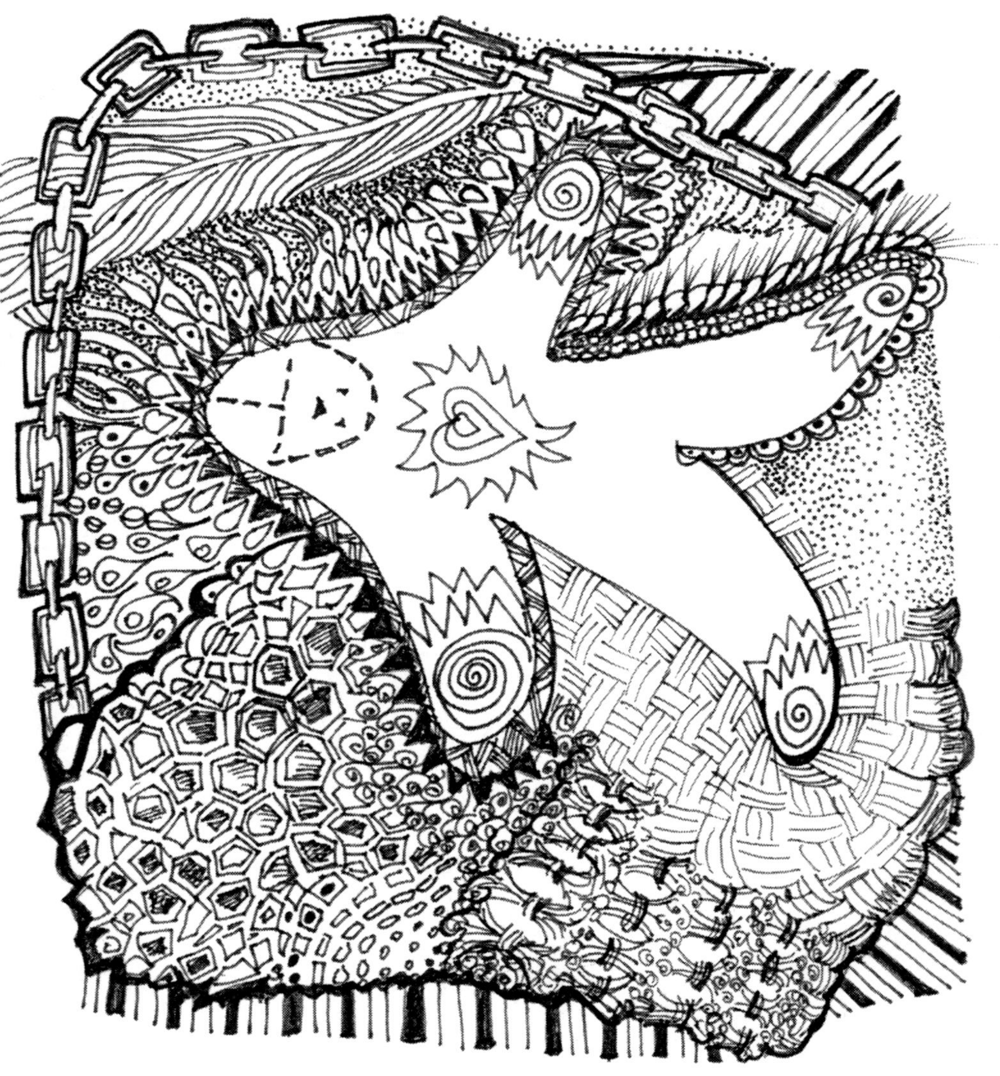

The Creation Story: A Brief History of Early Human Spirituality and Consciousness

The mystical power of creation is at the core of every religion and spiritual belief.

This *Creator* power is usually personified by the mindset and culture of the time. In some cases, the personification of this power becomes a communally agreed upon religious belief which supports the lifestyle of that culture.

Consistent throughout humanity's search for meaning and spiritual expression is the mystery of something beyond our individual self. Something within ourselves searches and imagines there is a beginning, a mind, or a presence that is greater than *ME*. Part of our intuitive being wants to understand and relate to, and even return to, the place *I* came from.

Is This Where I Began?

As tribes developed in different regions of the world, unique cultures and beliefs continued to develop. The following section is full of interesting descriptions of creation myths found throughout the world.

As you read these fascinating and simplified versions of creation, begin to consider the use of symbolism in each story. What could the symbolic elements be telling you about the beliefs from these various tribes and cultures? Our own intuitive and divine nature often speaks to us through symbols. What beliefs are these people working with? What are they trying to understand about themselves through these symbols?

Consider This ♡ Which creation stories resonate with you? Take some time to write down your observations and feelings around these myths and theologies. What do they mean to you? Begin to define your own sense of the *Creator*. How do you relate to a higher power? Is a higher power part of your life? How do you communicate with this higher power? ♡

Your beliefs were taught to you by your parents and guardians, and were reinforced by your culture, schools, peers, and society at large. Mass media subjects us to a myriad of beliefs and ideas that often contradict each other. You carry tribal memories of your beliefs in your physical DNA. You are also influenced by your past lives, and carry memories in what is referred to as *spiritual DNA.*

These creation stories are filled with symbolism and metaphors. As Micheal Caduto and Joseph Bruchas explain in their book, *Keepers of the Earth,* "Everyone's view of the world is molded by experience: a mix of fantasy, feeling, facts and faith. Each new event and experience affects our ideas concerning the nature of life and our surroundings, shifting the way we see ourselves, other people and our environment."

Knowing what has influenced and molded you is the first step on your journey to a soul-level understanding of yourself. In this book, you will be learning how to retrieve memories and work with deep-seated beliefs. You will bring them to your awareness in order to learn from them, so that you may grow into the power of your soul.

A Simplified History of Early Spiritual Beliefs: Where We Come From

Humans have tried to understand the origin of life and the source of their own being since the beginning of time. Spiritual beliefs and religions have been passed on by word of mouth descriptions and stories that explain the Creator and the beginning of the human race. The cosmology of a Creator—a *God*—is often personified based on that specific culture's earthly experiences. Most of these descriptions of life source energy are brief, sometimes vague, or not clearly documented. Ultimately, there is a consistency of reoccurring descriptions and references to a divine presence before all things were created.

The concept of *Creator* shifted from a female to a male over a long course of time. Archeological findings show that in the time before written language, the archetype of a female Creator seemed to prevail. As written language developed, The one God over all concept often assumes that a male deity is the highest God and Creator.

In most traditions there is a desire to obtain *spiritual wisdom* and a reassuring connection to the Creator. The archetypal belief is that this connection to the Creator will bring prosperity and relief from the sufferings of life.

Also present throughout most spiritual belief systems is the archetypal fear of having forgotten God and his commands. While some may have stayed true to the ways and faith of God, others fell to the ways of following their own worldly lusts, and neglecting or even forgetting God. If God has been forgotten, who is going to tell their children about the mysteries of God, the Creator, so that God will keep them safe? This archetype speaks to the yearning to nurture the human spirit and soul deeply embedded in humanity.

Immigration of Humans across the world

The continent of Africa is considered the birthplace of human evolution. The fossils of early humans who lived between 2 and 6 million years ago come entirely from the African continent. Three fossilized skulls unearthed in Ethiopia are said by scientists to be among the most important discoveries ever made in the search for our origins. They are considered to be the oldest known fossils of modern humans (Homo sapiens). What excites scientists so much is that the specimens fit neatly with the genetic studies that have suggested this time frame and part of Africa as the place where mankind emerged.

In the early days of human development, people began to migrate from Africa to the rest of the world. Once people began traveling from Africa, they populated the Middle East, and then moved on to Europe and Asia. These regions were all one land mass, and as cultures developed they were close enough to influence one another.

From the warmer southern part of Asia, immigrants traveled south to Australia and surrounding islands, then to Japan. The northern regions of the European and Asian regions were cold and often icy, and were sparsely inhabited compared to the south. The northern reaches of Asia were cold and formidable; these regions included Russia, with Slavic cultures, and Mongolians. People migrated from the northern region of Asia to the Americas through the Bering Sea. The northeastern part of Russia was thought to be full of glaciers during early human development. Anthropologists now say early nomads might well have traveled by boat along the coast from Siberia to North America, perhaps navigating arctic waters near today's Bering Strait. It is thought that the early people quickly became adept at sea travel and were able to travel easily down the coasts of the American continent.

Consider This ♡ More modern and controversial archeological theories have emerged about the population of the Americas. While there is no conclusive evidence, some feel the migration happened much earlier and under very different circumstances than previously assumed. As you read and compare the creation stories of each continent, what do you think could have influenced these stories? Do you feel the creation stories of the Americas could show a different kind of influence on these people compared to the Eurasian continent? ♡

Creation Stories of the African Region

Ethiopia

Wak was the Creator God who lived in the clouds. He kept the vault of the heavens at a distance from the earth and covered it with stars. He was a benefactor and did not punish. When the earth was flat, Wak asked man to make his own coffin, and when man did this, Wak shut him up in it and pushed it into the ground. For seven years he made fire rain down, and the mountains were formed. Then Wak unearthed the coffin and man sprang forth, alive. Man tired of living alone, so Wak took some of his blood and after four days, the blood became a woman whom the man married. They had thirty children, but the man was ashamed of having so many so he hid fifteen of them. Wak then turned those hidden children into animals and demons.

Ekoi

The Ekoi are a tribe in southern Nigeria.

In the beginning, there were two gods—Obassi Osaw and Obassi Nsi. The two gods created everything together. Then Obassi Osaw decided to live in the sky, and Obassi Nsi decided to live on the earth. The god in the sky gives light and moisture, but also brings drought and storms. The god of the earth nurtures, and takes the people back to him when they die. One day long ago, Obassi Osaw made a man and a woman, and placed them upon the earth. They knew nothing, so Obassi Nsi taught them about planting and hunting to get food.

Boshongo (Bantu tribe)

The Boshongo are a Bantu tribe of Central Africa.

In the beginning, there was only darkness, water, and the great god Bumba. One day Bumba, in pain from a stomach ache, vomited up the sun. The sun dried up some of the water, leaving land. Bumba then vomited up the moon, the stars, and then some animals—the leopard, the crocodile, the turtle, and, finally, some men; one of whom, Yoko

Lima, was white like Bumba.

Abaluyia

The Abaluyia believe that God created man so that the sun would have someone to shine on. He then created plants and animals to provide him with food, and gave man woman so that he would have someone with whom to talk.

Yoruba

Long ago, Olorun (OH-low-run), the sky god, lowered a great chain from the heavens to the ancient waters. Down this chain climbed Oduduwa, Olorun's son. Oduduwa brought with him a handful of dirt, a special five-toed chicken, and a palm nut. He threw the dirt upon the ancient waters and set the chicken on the dirt. The chicken scratched and scattered the dirt until it formed the first dry earth

Zimbabwe

Modimo was the Creator. He distributed good things, appeared in the east, and belonged to the water. He was a destroyer, a terrifying creature responsible for drought, hail, cyclones, and earthquakes. When these things happened he appeared in the west, and was part of the element fire. Modimo was also sky and light, earth and root. He was a unique being. He had no ancestors, no past or future. He ruled the whole of creation. His name was taboo, spoken only by priests and seers.

Zulu

The Ancient One, known as Unkulunkulu, is the Zulu Creator. He came from the reeds (uthlanga means source) and from them he brought forth the people and the cattle. He created everything that is—mountains, streams, snakes, etc. He taught the Zulu how to hunt, how to make fire, and how to grow food. He is considered to be the First Man and is in everything that he created.

Consider this ♡ Do you find these stories compelling? Do they bring up any thoughts or feelings? Is there anything here you can relate to? Can you see metaphors and symbols that are meaningful in your life now? Do you wish there was a Creator that would fix things in your life and bring you the tools and resources you need in this moment, so your life could be easier? What was the last prayer you remember saying? ♡

Creation stories of the Middle East and Europe

Ancient Egypt

In ancient Egypt, the pyramids were painted with the tales of creation. One translation reads:

> *In the beginning all was darkness, and there was nothing but a great waste of water called Nun. Swimming within this primordial deep were the mighty Ogdoad, or eight Gods. These primordial Gods swam within the waters, guarding the Great Egg that incubated the Creator. The power of Nun was such that there arose out of the darkness a great shining egg. From the egg arose a single blue Lotus. It rose high above the darkness of the abyss, and opened its great petals. Within its golden heart rested a beautiful young God, the Creator Amen-Re, with one single finger pressed against His lips in silence. He was all-powerful. He could take many forms. The secret of his power lay in his hidden name. When he spoke other names, that which he named came into being.*
>
> *Thus, He began his creation. In this He is known as Khephera; the God of Creation; the God of the Rising Sun. He brought order to the chaotic Ogdoad—setting them in their proper places—and it was thus the world came into existence. He accomplished this through the mighty power of the Divine Word, Thoth, and that power was yet another God—Ptah, the architect of the world and all of its creatures.*

Ancient Greece and Rome

In the warmer regions of Europe, the ancient Greeks and Romans have a creation story referred to as Hesiod's Theogony. The creative forces are etheric energies that give birth to Love, a creative energy. Love begins the creation of earth, the home that humanity knows.

> *In the beginning there was only Chaos. Then out of the void appeared Erebus, the unknowable place where death dwells, and Night. All else was empty, silent, endless, dark. Then, Love was born, bringing along the beginning of order. From Love emerged Light, followed by Gaea, the earth.*

Northern Europe

In the northern icy regions of Europe, the Norse people developed their own perspective regarding creation. The Norse traditions are believed to have their roots in a group of divine humans that migrated from Turkey.

The Norse speak of Muspelheim as the creative fire. Muspelheim impregnates the primordial ice to create life. The being created was the First Mother, who is a cow. She was birthed from this etheric energy. All other life was born from this mother. In the Norse myth, all things come from this fire. In the end, this fire will consume all things. The Fire isn't personified as male or female. Mulspelheim is fire, a creative etheric energy that started life.

In the Hebrew text of Genesis, the story of creation totally rejects all earlier mythology. The overriding conception of a single, omnipotent, Creator predominates; the one God that is above the whole of nature, which He Himself created by His own absolute will. The primeval water, earth, sky, and luminaries are not pictured as deities or as parts of disembodied deities, but are all parts of the manifold works of the one (male) Creator.

The book of Genesis, a Christian-Judeo expression of a story of creation, the beginning of creation starts with God. The book of Genesis seems to have its beginning in what is often referred to as the cradle of civilization, also called Mesopotamia; what we currently refer to as the Middle East.

In the beginning God created the heaven and the earth. Now the earth was unformed and void, and darkness was upon the face of the deep; and the spirit of God hovered over the face of the waters. And God said, "Let there be light." And there was light. And God saw the light, and that it was good; and God divided the light from the darkness. And God called the light Day, and the darkness He called Night. And there was evening and there was morning, one day.

~ Genesis 1, 1-5

Middle East

In the Middle East is a similar belief, written in the Quran (the Muslim Holy Book), verses 9 to 12, sura 41. God, being a male force with a personality, is at the heart of creation, as described in this passage. This belief was also embedded in the ancient Middle East.

Say. Do you disbelieve Him who created the earth in two periods? Do you ascribe equals to Him? He is the Lord of the Worlds.

He set in the (earth) mountains standing firm. He blessed it.

He measured therein its sustenance in four periods, in due proportion, in accordance with the needs of those who seek sustenance.

Moreover (tumma) He turned to heaven when it was smoke and said to it and to the earth, "Come willingly or unwillingly!" They said, "We come in willing obedience!"

Then He ordained them seven heavens in two periods, and He assigned to each heaven its mandate by Revelation. And we adorned the lower heaven with luminaries and provided it a guard. Such is the decree of the All Mighty, the Full of Knowledge.

The Christian—Judaic—Muslamic stories are some of the more influential cosmology stories spread throughout the world's cultures today. Many ancient cosmologies have been combined to create our modern cosmology. Threads of today's practices can be traced back to the earth-based practices (Paganism) scattered throughout the Middle East and later in Northern and Western Europe The wisdom and connection to a higher power came about through spiritual practices—practices that connected them to the natural energetic properties of the earth—finally making a connection to the higher power that created the earth. What would have happened to these creation stories from the diversified European regions, if Rome hadn't conquered Europe, bringing their Gods and Goddesses, and finally, their Catholic religion?

In early human development, each tribe of people was lead or influenced by a shaman, a leader and healer that had a strong connection with a spiritual power that went beyond everyday living. These medicine folks carried a higher level of wisdom, which they then shared through stories and rituals. The wisdom of the shamans was attained through spiritual practices that altered reality in order to commune with a higher power, often considered to be the Creator. Sometimes the higher spirit was female and reached through nature, other times it was referred to as male.

Some traditions eventually put aside the spiritual practices born of the altered realities of their healers and shamans, and relied mainly on the passing down of the old stories. The stories became theology and dogma, and the tribe or community strove to follow what they believed to be the essence of these stories. The dogma of these traditions were influenced and authored by those who wanted to hold political power over the tribe; the ruling belief of the tribe being that an obedient connection to a higher power would bring prosperity and relief from the sufferings of life. The definition of the higher power became more and more limited by the leaders that held the political power. Medicine people, shamanic seers, were placed further and further away from their tribes. Only kings and royalty, or the very wealthy, were granted access to the mystics.

 Divine Love Affair

Eventually, spiritual shamans were banished as leaders in these modern tribes, and replaced by kings and conquering rulers. At that juncture of human development, it became dangerous for individuals to show a talent for healing, prophecy, or other mystical gifts that suggested a special connection to a higher power.

Creation Stories of the Asian Region

Stories from the Slavic Region

From Northern Asia come the Slavic creation stories. Slavic mythology is full of ties to its original Indo-European roots, as well as Finno-Urgic, Iranian, and others. Like many other Indo-European mythologies, Slavic mythology contains a story about a golden egg.

In the beginning there was nothing but an old-dark, dark sea and sky. In the darkness was a golden egg which contains the Supreme God Rod. Rod breaks out of the egg and creates a helpmate, Mother Lada, goddess of love. And with this love he breaks through the darkness. He cuts his umbilical cord with a rainbow and straight away gets to work separating the oceans and seas from the skies. He builds all of creation from his own body. The sun is made from his face, the moon from his chest, and the stars are from his eyes. The bright sunrise is from his eyebrows, the dark nights from his thoughts, rain and snow and hail from his tears, and his voice became thunder and lightning. He then breathes life into his Son Svarog, who becomes the Creator of the earth with all of its life, including mankind.

The earth becomes submerged deep under the waters, and Svarog cannot reach it. In the distance he notices a little grey duck swimming above a dark hole in the water. He asks the duck if she has seen Mother Earth. The duck says that she's down at the bottom of the ocean. Svarog asks the duck to go get her. The duck disappears, and returns a year later saying that it couldn't hold its breath any longer and asks for help in retrieving Mother Earth from the ocean's abyss. Svarog calls for Rod's help, who then blows a mighty wind, stirring up the ocean, and the duck dives back down. Two years pass and the duck returns saying, "I got closer this time but still ran out of breath." So again Svarog calls upon Rod, who brings a storm upon the ocean and shoots lightning into the duck. The duck dives down and is gone for three years. After those three years the duck returns with a branch in her mouth. Svarog takes the branch, and rubbing it in his palms begins to command the forces of the world, "Make warmth, Sun! Light up, Moon! Blow, Wind! We must save Mother Earth, our nurturer." All the elements come together, the wind blowing the branch from Svarog's hands. As it falls into the ocean, the sun shines, heating the ocean, and as the water evaporated, the Moist Mother Earth appeared at the surface, and the moon quickly cooled her down.

Mongolia

Mongolia is found in the middle of the Asian continent. There is no singular Mongol account of the creation and the beginning of the world, but from a variety of accounts from Mongol tribes of Central Asia, a general outline can be made. The creation of the world is attributed to a lama named Udan, who is sometimes also conflated with God or Buddha Sakyamuni by the tribes influenced by Tibetan Buddhism. Here is a version of one of the myths:

A long time ago, the Mongolian creation myth says, Father Heaven had two sons, Ulgen Tenger and Erieg Khan. The first son became the lord of the upper world, and the second of the underworld. At that time, the earth was covered with water.

One day Ulgen Tenger asked the loon to bring up mud from under the water so he could create some dry land. When the loon could not do this, he was punished by having his legs broken so he would not be able to walk. The next one to try to create dry land was the goldeneye duck.

The duck created just a small piece of land; just enough for Ulgen to lie on. Seeing that his brother had fallen asleep, Erleg Khan tried to pull the land from under him, but instead the land stretched out in all directions.

The next task that Ulgen Tenger decided to take on was to create animals and humans to live upon the land, using the mud. He then created the dog to watch over the new bodies while he was gone. Erleg Khan was not happy at all to see the new creations, and decided to look at the new bodies.

The dog would not let him get close to the bodies. At first, the dog could talk, but had no fur. It was cold and snowing, so Erleg Khan promised him a beautiful fur coat. The dog agreed and was given a shiny, beautiful coat.

Erleg Khan then spat on the new bodies so they would have diseases and could die. When Ulgen returned, he noticed that the dog had new fur and that the bodies were damaged. As punishment, Ulgan made the dog's coat smell bad, took away his voice, and made the dog to follow humans to get his food.

Southern Asia.

Historical cosmologies that still heavily influence current spiritual cosmologies are the ancient Hindu and Buddhists traditions from **Southern Asia.**

***In Hinduism**,* as expressed through the Sanskrit language, nature and all of God's creations are manifestations of *Him*. He is within and without his creations, pervading the entire universe, and also observing it externally. Hence all animals and humans have a divine element in them. Here is a story from early Vedic thinking:

This is not the first world, nor is it the first universe. There have been and will be many more worlds and universes than there are drops of water in the holy river Ganges. The universes are made by Lord Brahma the Creator, maintained by Lord Vishnu the Preserver and destroyed by Lord Shiva.

Before this time began, there was no heaven, no earth and no space between. A vast dark ocean washed upon the shores of nothingness and licked the edges of the night. A giant cobra floated on the waters. Asleep within its endless coils lay the Lord Vishnu. He was watched over by the mighty serpent. (The serpent is also referred to as the Golden egg or The Hindu Cosmic Egg: Hiranyagarbha)

Everything was so peaceful and silent that Vishnu slept undisturbed by dreams or motion. From the depths a humming sound began to tremble, Aum. It grew and spread, filling the emptiness and throbbing with energy.

The night had ended and Vishnu awoke. As the dawn began to break, from Vishnu's navel grew a magnificent lotus flower. In the middle of the blossom sat Vishnu's servant, Brahma. He awaited the Lord's command. Vishnu spoke to his servant: 'It is time to begin.' Brahma bowed. Vishnu commanded: 'Create the World.' A wind swept up the waters. Vishnu and the serpent vanished.

Brahma remained in the lotus flower, floating and tossing on the sea. He lifted up his arms and calmed the wind and the ocean. Then Brahma split the lotus flower into three. He stretched one part into the heavens. He made another part into the earth. With the third part of the flower he created the skies.

When Brahma finished his creation, Brahma, the creator God, divided himself and became Vishnu, the preserver God, once again. At the end of time, he will become Siva, the destroyer God, and all will return to the Cosmic Egg where Vishnu will preserve himself once again in a lengthy, restful sleep. From here, he will be born again as a newer creation and begin the process all over again, a concept known as Reincarnation, which is the natural state of all life.

Another myth which began in late Rig-Vedic times is a story of the creation of the universe from the remains of the primeval cosmic male Purusha. Depending on the version, he either sacrificed himself, or was sacrificed by other primeval beings.

The Creator Man Purusha has a thousand heads, a thousand eyes, a thousand feet. He pervades the earth everywhere and extends beyond for ten fingers' breadth. The Man himself is all this, whatever has been and whatever is to be. He is the lord of immortality and also lord of that which grows on food. Such is his greatness, and the Man is yet greater than this. All creatures make up a quarter of him; three quarters are the immortal in heaven…From his navel the atmosphere was born; from his head the heaven appeared. From his two feet came the earth and the regions of the sky from his ear. Thus they fashioned the worlds.

The Hindu and Vedic principles (written in early Sanskrit) give us the concept of Akasha, the Etheric energy of the Creator. In Sanskrit, the word Akasha means primary substance; that out of which all things are formed. It is the first stage of the crystallization of spirit.

In Buddhism, there is no belief of creation. Buddhists explain that life is an eternal cycle of birth, death, and rebirth. If there was a beginning there would still be something that would cause that beginning. Every ending causes another beginning. In Buddhism, creation is just one part of the big, infinite cycle.

In the following excerpt from a blog on Transparent Language, Inc., a Thai Buddhist monk explains the beginning of the world to his student. This seems to be a combination of Buddhist and Hindu beliefs.

The world, as Buddha described it, began when the earth and stars spontaneously formed on their own. Water and air then collected and became seas on the earth. But life did not yet exist.

And then came what is called the Phrom; unfathomable beings from

what can best be described as another dimension beyond and above heaven, called Phromalok. These Phrom supposedly came first.

The Phrom are ancient beings that are the evolved form of that which resides in heaven (angels and whatnot). So where did the angels come from? That which is in heaven comes from humans that have reached enlightenment and nirvana. So where did humans come from? Humans came from both the creatures of Hell, and Phrom, who ate the dirt of the earth (because it smelled too good to resist, supposedly).

Explained in plain language:

The best way to describe Phrom is like 'light'. Heaven is 'light' to humans, and Phromalok is 'light' to heaven. Phrom have no emotions, but are capable of expressing emotions. They don't consist of matter or energy, and cannot be seen by people (unless they are psychic, traditionally). They exist beyond the concepts of good and evil. While humans can only live a few decades, and angels can "live" for thousands of years, the Phrom can "live" for millions of years before they "expire". What happens afterwards is unknown.

Consider This ♡ How do you feel about the Buddhist's concept of creation? Does it explain much about life to you? What else would you ask the Buddha if you could? ♡

Creation stories of Australian Aboriginals

The Aborigines of Australia are considered one of the oldest surviving cultures in the world. Many different creation stories exist among the different Aboriginal groups. These *Dreamtime* stories are considered to be a place where every person exists forever. According to the Aboriginals, the Dreaming era preceded our own, and was when spirit beings formed creation. It was believed that, before humans, animals and plants came into being; they were souls first, and knew that they would become physical, but not when. When that time came, all but one of the souls became either plants or animals, with the last one becoming human and acting as a custodian or guardian to the natural world around them. It is believed that a culture of heroes (gods) travelled across the land without form and created sacred sites and other significant places, giving the language to people.

In the Aboriginal world view, every event leaves a record in the land. Everything in the natural world is a result of the actions of the archetypal beings, whose actions created the world. The meaning and significance of specific places and creatures is wedded to their origin in the *Dreaming*. Certain places have a particular potency, which Aborigines call *"Its Dreaming."*

In Aboriginal tribes the name of the Creator is forbidden to be spoken publicly. It is also forbidden for women to see any drawings depicting the creator Baiame, or to go to any of the creator's sacred sites.

> *One of the legends describes only bare land existing in the beginning. There was no life on earth—no animals, no plants, no trees and no humans. Wandjina, the Creator, brought our ancestors from within the earth and over the seas, and life began. Some of the ancestors were like men and others were like animals. In fact, according to the myths, it is believed that our ancestors were able to change shape and become either man or animal. In some other versions, Wandjina was not one god but many gods, or spirit gods, which are depicted with big black eyes, no mouth, and a halo—certainly not representing human beings. Legends tell how Wandjina walked on earth and created everything from rivers and mountains to plants and animals.*

Creation Stories of the Liberated Continent of the Americas
The Southern Native Americans

The Mayans

The early Mayan established communities in 1800 BCE. In the *Popol Vuh* (or Popol Wuj in the K'iche' language) is the story of the creation of the Maya. Members of the royal K'iche' lineages, that had once ruled the highlands of Guatemala, recorded the story in the 16th century to preserve it under the Spanish colonial rule. *The Popol Vuh*, meaning *Book of the Community*, narrates the Maya creation account:

> *This is an account of the Beginning, when all was stillness, silence, and water. There was no light, no land, no plants, no people, no animals,*
>
> *Six deities covered in green and blue feathers lay in the primordial waters. There were the framer and the shaper, Tepew and Quetzal Serpent, along with Xpiyacoc and Xmucane. These deities helped Heart of Sky, also known as Hurakan, create the earth.*
>
> *Their spirit essence, and their miraculous power, gave the earth its creative energy. The land had a heart, they called it Heart of the Earth.*

 Divine Love Affair

To separate the sky from the earth, they planted a tall ceiba tree, making space for all of life. The roots penetrated deep into the nine levels of the Mayan underworld; the trunk was on the surface of the land, and the branches reached up to the thirteen levels of the Maya upper-world.

The plants were created next to live on the earth.

And then the animals were created. But the animals did not speak and they could not worship.

So the deities decided to create human beings from mud. But these first humans had no souls and were not good "Keepers of the Days."

The deities destroyed them in a great flood.

The deities tried again, and created humans from wood. But the wooden people could not worship either, so they were destroyed. Those that survived are said to be the monkeys in the trees.

The sky and the earth now existed, but there was no sun or moon, A vain bird called Seven Macaw claimed to be the sun and the moon. But this was not true.

Two amazing twins, Hunajpu and Xbalangue, defeated Seven Macaw by shooting him with darts.

The Hero Twins were conceived when their mother, Ixkik, spoke to the decapitated head of their father, Hun Hunahpu. He spit on her hand from a cacao tree, where he hung. Hun Hunahpu had been killed by the Lords of Xibalba, the underworld.

The Hero Twins became great ball players, and to bring their father back to life, they challenged the Lords of the underworld to a game in Xibalba.

The twins were permitted to play the ball games only after they had survived the dangerous trials set for them in the underworld.

Using great skill and cunning, the twins won the ball game, and this allowed their slain father to come back as the Maize God.

The Hero Twins left Xibalba and climbed back up to the surface of the earth. They continued up into the sky, becoming the sun and the moon. Now that the sun and the moon were in the sky illuminating the earth, the deities created the final form of human beings using white and yellow corn. Corn is the precious substance that ultimately succeeds in producing true and enduring humans.

The Incans and Quechus Creation Story

The oldest known tradition in Southern Native Americas is from the Quechua people. Long before the rise of the Incan Empire (1200-1572 A.D.), a beautiful and gentle people lived in the Andes of Peru known as the Quechua. For thousands of years the traditions and spirituality of these Andean people were passed down orally from generation to generation. Located in the surrounding areas of Qosqo (Cusco) and Machu Picchu, they were *Campesinos* (farmers) and lived closely connected to nature and the earth from which they came. They believed in a Creator god, a two faced deity called *Wirakkocha* or *Teksiwirakkocha*. The Quechua left no written records, but passed their traditions down through word of mouth. This tradition still stands strong into these modern times, and the ancient villages still remain intact high in the Andean mountains.

> *Creator God brought forth the Andean people from the caves of the mountains and the rivers and streams. The Quechua have a rich tradition of worshipping and communing with this god along with the feminine Pachamama, who is the earth and their mother.*

Incan traditions: The conquering Inkan people's mythology tells a creation story about the Sun God Inti, who created the first Inkankuna. Mankko Kkhapakk was the mythical founder of the Inkan Empire, which according to historians commenced in the thirteenth century. Out of several versions of this myth the most popular is about the Sun God.

Sun God and his consort, the moon Killa, had two children—Mankko Kkhapakk, and his sister Mama Okkllo. Inti sent his children to civilize the world. From their birthplace, which was the foam of the waters of Lake Titicaca, they founded the Cisty of Cusco, which was to become the center of the new Inkan Empire.

> *The Sun Inti gave his children a golden rod and told them that the site would be wherever the rod sank with one thrust into the ground, and was as soft and fertile as the human navel. The rod was thrust into place at Guanacaure Mountain. Cusco which means "navel" in the Quechua language, was born. The siblings Mankko Kkhapakk and his sister Mama Okkllo won the Quechua people over by teaching them a more advanced form of civilization.*

Another variation of an Incan myth and cosmology:

The Creator god made the earth, sky, and stone giants to inhabit the land. After some time the giants became violent and left the Creator

 Divine Love Affair

god no choice but to exterminate them. Some of the giants tuned back to stone, the rest were washed away by a huge flood. All except two of the giants survived. With these two giants the Creator god Viracocha pulled the sun and moon out of Lake Titicaca to use as light, so he could admire his newest creation, which was mankind.

With the arrival of the children of the Sun God into the Cusco area, the Incan Dynasty was created. Its rulers took over the territory and control of the indigenous people who worshipped Pachamama and all her earthly domain. Even still, the Quechua people continued to observe their own ancient ceremonies and offerings to Pachamama, Mother Earth. The strength of the Quechua's belief and love for nature influenced the Incans. Eventually, the Incans incorporated the Quechua practices into the new state religion of Qusco.

The Northern Native Americans

Northeast Woodlands Creation Story
The Onandaga, Iroquios, and Huron Tribes

Long before the world was created there was an island, floating in the sky, upon which the Sky people lived. They lived quietly and happily; no one was ever born and no one died or experienced sadness. However, one day one of the Sky women realized she was going to give birth to twins. She told her husband, who flew into a rage. In the center of the island there was a tree which gave light to the entire island, since the sun hadn't been created yet. He tore up this tree, creating a huge hole in the middle of the island. Curious, the woman peered into the hole. Far below she could see the waters that covered the earth. At that moment she slipped. As she grasped the tree to stop her fall, she came away with a handful of seeds. She fell through the hole, tumbling towards the waters below.

Water animals already existed on the earth, so far below the floating island two swans saw the Sky woman fall. Just before she reached the waters, they caught her on their backs and brought her to the other animals. Determined to help the woman, they dove into the water to get mud from the bottom of the seas. The duck tried first, but failed. One after another the animals tried and failed. Finally, a tiny muskrat tried, and when he reappeared his paws were full of mud. The animals took it and spread it on the back of Big Turtle. The mud began to grow and grow until it became the size of North America.

Then the woman stepped onto the land. She sprinkled dust into the air and created stars. Then she created the moon and sun. She sprinkled the seeds onto the bare soil. From those seeds the trees and the grass sprang up. Life on earth had begun.

The woman gave birth to the twins, and they were the beginning of the people who lived on the earth.

The Doina (Navaho) Southwest Creation Story

Before this world existed, there was a first world far below the world where we are now. In that world, everything was black. Within that darkness there were six beings. Those beings were:

Begochiddy – the child of the sun, was both man and woman, and had blue eyes and golden hair.

First man – the son of night and the blue sky over sunset
First woman – the daughter of daybreak and the yellow sky of sunrise
Salt woman
Fire God
Coyote

Begochiddy began to create many things in the first world; things as big as mountains and as small as insects. Begochiddy made the first plants. But there was no light, so everyone became unhappy in this first world and decided to leave.

Begochiddy told the first man, "Gather up all the plants and other things I made," and the first man did as he was asked. Then Begochiddy planted a big reed in one of the mountains. The reed began to grow and grow and everyone got on the reed. Up and up it went carrying everyone into the second world.

Begochiddy made even more things in the second world, like clouds and more plants and mountains. There were cat people and swallow people. The people in the second world began to fight the new people, but first man used his magic and overcame them. They tried to be happy, but it didn't work. Begochiddy planted another reed in a mountain that grew up and up and took them into the third world.

The third world was yellow, but it still had no sun or moon. Begachiddy made mountains that gave off light. It was the most beautiful of all the worlds. Begochiddy made rivers and springs, water animals and trees, birds and lightning. Then Begochiddy created all kinds of human beings. Everyone spoke one language and all beings understood each

 Divine Love Affair

other. They began to quarrel. Begochiddy told them if they didn't get along, a huge flood would come and wipe them out. Coyote went scouting one day, and found a baby with long black hair in the water of two crossing rivers. Coyote took the baby and hid it in his blanket. A great noise was heard around the third world. Begochiddy knew someone had done something wrong, and that the flood was coming to destroy the third world. Once again, Begochiddy gathered up all the beings and things created. Once again, the big reed grew up and up, lifting the beings up as the waters rose.

This time was not so easy. The reed stopped growing before they got to the fourth world. The beings of the fourth world tried to help them, but everything failed. The locusts made a hole for Begochiddy to climb through to the fourth world. She found herself on an island surrounded by water. Begochiddy saw that there were other beings that could help her. She called to them. They were the gods of the directions. The four powerful beings made the waters recede, leaving a world covered in mud. The winds helped to dry the world so all the beings from the third world could live there. Begochiddy looked back down the hole to check on everyone; the waters were still very angry and rising.

Begochiddy asked, "Who angered the water monster?" Coyote looked guilty and pulled his blanket closer. "Show me what you have," demanded Begochiddy. Coyote opened the blanket and Begochiddy saw the baby. "Give the water monster back its child," said Begochiddy, and Coyote dropped the baby into the third world and the waters receded.

Begochiddy went back to the fourth world and put things in order. The sun, moon, and stars were put into place in the sky. All was made ready for her creations. When they all arrived, Begochiddy taught everyone how to care for this new world so they wouldn't destroy it.

It was in the fourth world that changing woman came to be. She became a great friend to human beings and helped them. She gave birth to the Hero Twins who traveled throughout the world destroying monsters that threatened the people.

It is important to note that according to the Doina, this fourth world can be destroyed just like the others if people don't live the right way.

The Abenaki Northeast Woodlands Creation Story

After Tabaldak had finished making human beings, he dusted his hands off and some of that dust sprinkled on the earth. From that dust Gluscabi formed himself. He sat up from the earth and said, "Here

I am." So it is that some Abenaki people call Gluscabi by another name— Odzihozo—which means, "The man who made himself from something." He was not as powerful as Tabaldak, the Owner, but like his grandchildren, the human beings, he had the power to change things; sometimes for the worse.

When Gluscabi sat up from the earth, the Owner was astonished. "How did it happen now that you came to be?" he said.

The Gluscabi said, "Well, it is because I formed form this dust left over from the first humans that you made."

"You are very wonderful," the Owner told him.

"I am wonderful because you sprinkled me," Gluscabi answered.

"Let us roam around now," said the Owner. So they left that place and went up the hill to the top of the mountain. There they looked about, at all saw. They could see lakes, the rivers, the trees how all the land lay, and the earth.

Then the Owner said, "Behold here how wonderful is my work. By the wish of my mind I created all of the existing world; oceans, rivers, lakes." And he and Gluscabi gazed open-eyed at all that was.

Consider This ♡ How are the Native American stories similar? Can you see a theme of sacrifice? How many times is the Creator disappointed in the human beings? What were the different choices the Creators made when the humans were less than perfect? How do you treat yourself when you are disappointed in yourself? ♡

How many times was earth under water? What did the water symbolize? What about the darkness, or the creation of the sun and the moon?

Imagine yourself at the top of a mountain with the Creator. You are sharing a moment of deep appreciation. What would be your observations of the world? What would take your breath away?

The Modern Era of Creation Theories

The Creation Story of the Mystical Kabbalah

The Kabbalah is considered to be an inner and mystical aspect of Judaism, and predates any other known religions. It is not a religion, per se; it is more of a way of understanding the matrix of life.

 Divine Love Affair

Rabbi David Cooper, author of, *Kabbalah, God is a Verb*, writes that the Kabbalist views creation as an unceasing phenomenon. This does not preclude the fact that the physical universe—from our point of view—had a point of conception. In fact, according to Kabbalistic calculations, the beginning of the physical universe extends back over fifteen billion years.

The principle of continuous creation, without beginning or end, is based upon the idea that there is a source of life that eternally emanates the energy required for all existence. If this source of life were to withhold itself for but a split second, everything would vanish. That is to say, all humanity, all nature, all of creation is constantly being sustained each and every moment. It is as if creation were a light bulb that stays illuminated as long as the electricity is flowing. The instant we shut off the power, the light fades out. Now imagine that each time we blink our eyes we fall into a mind state of an isolated room. Each time we open our eyes we experience creation anew. Assuming we could blink thousands of times a second, creation would always seem to be beginning.

The Kabbalistic view of a continuous creation is in variance with modern theoretical physics, which currently is pursuing the Big Bang theory. The Big Bang concept is that something happened many billions of years ago that instantaneously expanded into a primordial universe. Following this theory, our universe continues to expand from an initial impulse.

The idea that creation occurred in the past leads to the assumption of a time distance between the creative act and our present experience. It implies a physical distance between our location in space and the creative force. Thus, the reality in which we live, as long as we surrender to the limits of time and space, leads to the erroneous belief of separation between ourselves and the source of life.

The belief of separateness often leads to the loss of hope, and feelings of isolation. This can manifest as alienation and despair. Almost all of the difficulties experienced in the spiritual quest are related to the sense of feeling isolated, different from other people, disconnected from the source of life.

Jewish mysticism approaches the issue of feeling alone in the cosmos by questioning our essential assumptions regarding creation. Once we realize and experience our intimate relationship with God, which is continuous and fills each moment, we can never again feel alone. The mystical perspective suggests that this relationship is indispensable for both sides—Creator and creation—unfolding simultaneously. For example, a parent is defined by his or her child. Without a child, one is not a parent and vice versa. There can be no giver without a receiver, and one cannot receive without something being given. Nothing is separate, except for the "sense" of separateness, a feeling which is readily disproven. Indeed, if we were separated from the source of life by even a fraction of a second, we could not exist.

The problem with the Big Bang is that it suggests something happened in the past, a burst of energy that continues on its own momentum for billions of years. But in the mystical realm of the Divine, there is no past or future as we know it. Moreover, the momentum of the Big Bang theory would be predictable, while Jewish mystics believe that creation is always uncertain.

Rather, the Big Bang is an ongoing creative emanation. The universe is constantly balanced upon a symbiotic relationship of Creator and creation, each integral to the continuation of the universe. If either part of the relationship fails to nourish the other, the whole thing comes to a screeching halt. On the other hand, the ongoing interaction between Creator and creation defines and nurtures each moment—and each moment is another Big Bang impulse.

One of the great Hasidic masters, Rebbe Levi Yitzhak of Berdichev (18th century), wrote: "The Creator's continuous radiation of creative force never ceases from the world; in every instant these [vital] emanations radiate to Its creations, to all the worlds, to all the palaces [realms of higher consciousness] and to all the angels."

~ Rabbi David Cooper

Another similar, but different view of the Hebrew tradition of the Kabbalah Creation, is known as *Tzimtzum*—creation out of nothing. It is believed that in the beginning there was only God, and nothing else. God is called *Ein Sof*—an all-encompassing divine presence or light. In other words, the Light of Infinity. When God decided to create something (Yesh) from nothing (Ein), God needed to *make a space or provide a room* for that which was not God (otherness). To make this so, God emptied Himself by contracting his infinite light to create a conceptual space for the creation of the universe. In a great cosmic flash, God then condensed into a point of infinite density and infinite energy, Tzimtzum (contraction), and then exploded out in all directions. In a sense, this self-imposed *contraction of the infinite light* is a picture of God sacrificing himself for the sake of creation. (Consider the

 Divine Love Affair

similarity to the earlier Southern Asia Hindu description of the late Rig-Vedic story of the creation of the universe (from the remains of the primeval cosmic male Purusha, who had sacrificed himself.)

Here is a description of the doctrine of Tzimtzum:

> *Prior to creation there was only the infinite, or Ein Sof, filling all existence. When it arose in God's will to create worlds and emanate the emanated, He contracted (in Hebrew, "Tzimtzum") Himself in the point at the center, in the very center of His light. He restricted that light, distancing it to the side surrounding the central point, so that there remained a void, a hollow empty space, away from the central point. After this Tzimtzum, He drew down form the Ein Sof a single straight line of light from His own light surrounding the void from above and below (into the void), and it dropped down like a chain of many links, descending into that void. … In the space of that void He emanated, created, formed, and made all worlds.*

> *~ Isaac Luria, Etz Chaim*

Science and an Evolving Story of Creation

The Primordial Egg and the Primeval Atom

In current time, and in more scientific terms, the concept of the primordial egg of the Hindu tradition is revisited to explain a new theory of creation. Modern science began this exploration in the 1930s, and it would continue to be explored by theoreticians for the next two decades. The idea came from a perceived need to reconcile Edwin Hubble's observation of an expanding universe (which was also predicted by Alexander Friedmann using Einstein's equations of general relativity) with the notion that the <u>universe</u> must be eternally old. Current cosmological models maintain that 13.8 billion years ago, the entire mass of the universe was compressed into a gravitational singularity, the so called *cosmic egg,* from which it expanded to its current state (following the Big Bang).

Georges Lemaitre proposed in 1927 that the cosmos originated from what he called the *primeval atom.*

In the late 1940s, George Gamow's assistant, cosmological researcher Ralph Alpher, proposed the name *ylem* for the primordial substance that existed between the Big Crunch of the previous universe, and the Big Bang of our own universe.

Consider This ♡ Which types of stories did you prefer? Describe the presence of the Creator in these stories. Some Creators in these stories were happy and pleased, and others were very disappointed. In your own cosmology, is your Creator happy or sad? Loving or disapproving? Take a moment to imagine, and then describe what your Creator is like. ♡

Your Akashic journey is about building a relationship with your Creator and your soul. What are the elements you would need to be able to create a viable relationship to a higher power? Where would you begin to create that relationship?

Later in Section One we will discuss how to create a reciprocal relationship with your higher power. Take your time now to do some myth-busting. Be curious about the belief systems that brought you here, right now, to your personal belief or disbelief.

 Divine Love Affair

Chapter 2

Putting on Your Inner Mystic
and a Brief History of the Akashic Concept

I grew up in the Midwest, the oldest child of nine in my Catholic family. My mom stayed home and raised us, while my dad worked long hours to support us. My formal Catholic training began in the first grade with the Sisters of Mercy when I attended a Catholic school in Connecticut. When I was in second grade, we moved to Detroit. I was placed in a public school, and had to continue my Catholic training on Saturdays in the basement of Christ the King Church, at what was called *CCD class*. I made my first communion that year; the same year my newest baby brother was born. He was my parent's seventh child, born in their eighth year of marriage. Every event in my life was underscored by faith and reverence.

In my early teens, shortly after my confirmation, I became intensely interested in what was called *The Catholic Charismatic Renewal*. This was a movement made up of devout Catholics who wished to experience the renewal of the gifts of the Holy Spirit, just as the Apostles of Jesus had on the holy day of Epiphany.

> *As the story goes, the apostles were huddled in a room a few weeks after Jesus died and then rose from the dead. They had been instructed to wait in Jerusalem until the "Holy Spirit came upon them." In truth, they were hiding, sure that they were going to be arrested and put to death. It was a series of intense days filled with "What now?" and "What have we done?" and probably "It was great while it lasted, but here we are, all freaked out and alone." The wind began to blow really hard, the windows rattled, and then suddenly the window shutter and door flew open in a great noise. The Holy Spirit blew into the room and filled each of the apostles with the gifts of the Holy Spirit. Some began to speak in foreign languages; others began to speak with great inspiration; while still others received the gift of healing. The apostles then went forth into the streets and cities to do great works and share the message of their Messiah.*

I studied with a group of Franciscan monks, sisters, and priests. This group diligently and prayerfully explored the gifts of Spirit. My religious training escalated into a full-blown spiritual awakening at the age of fifteen. I was taught prayerful meditation. I would sit in prayer and then in silence, opening to the *quickening* of spirit. It was in that silence that spirit gave me my gifts. I felt a deep connection of love and joy every time I prayed and meditated.

During my meditations I saw movie-like scenes, and later, they would happen! I felt a pressure in my throat as if I wanted to talk, but was too anxious to speak. I took a breath and tried again to talk, but it was coming too fast for me to understand verbally. I grabbed a pencil and paper and wrote down descriptions of the pictures that were flowing through my mind instead. I shared them in my evening study group, and the Franciscans listened with rapt attention and encouraged me; they wanted to hear more and more from me. I spoke every week in my group after that. They taught me how to do hands on healing. In one healing session, I watched a man's crooked leg straighten. I listened to members of the prayer circle speak in tongues; foreign languages spoken by people who didn't know the language. One night a woman spoke in an African language and a priest who had been a missionary in Africa recognized it and interpreted it for us. I was amazed and deeply moved by her message of love from God. I eventually learned to speak in tongues. My training in the Catholic tradition did a complete flip; from learning lessons from books, to hearing and experiencing Spirit in my heart and actually experiencing the mystical in my life.

Ok, it was weird.

I was quiet, curious, serious, and visually artistically talented. My parents had no idea what to do with me. I was not the kid they had planned for, or could have ever imagined.

So I learned to internalize and hide my spiritual side. Truthfully, this wasn't really a new thing for me. I had experienced Spirit—what I felt were Angels—and had had interventions from Spirit many times as a small kid. That was a secret; I told no one. And here it was again, in this group I belonged to. I was so relieved to learn more about what I had always experienced. I finally had a chance to sort these experiences out, with adults who seemed to know a thing or two. But I didn't mention much of this to my parents; only what I absolutely had to in order to get to the meetings.

I only put on my inner mystic when no one was looking. My parent insisted that I only read books approved by the archdiocese. I could only talk to the monks, sisters, and priests because they were safe, holy, and knew better. They were safe mystics. Privately I thought, *Okay then, what my parents don't know . . . can't hurt me . . .*

Then my time with the Franciscans came to an end. Most of them were being transferred to other churches, some to other countries. We had a going away party. I felt such a loss. My gifts once again retreated inward.

A year or so later, I left for college. Once at the university, I was free to read whatever I wanted. I studied Asian art history, which led to my learning about world religions. My Catholic bubble burst as I was exposed to the spiritual teachings of religions around the world. To this day, I have a love for world religions and the mystical spiritual paths within them.

I remember a vivid dream I had at that time. In the dream, I was talking to a dear friend of mine about my spiritual experiences with the Franciscans. She turned to me, and in a very serious tone, said, "It's not that you've found your faith, or Jesus, or even salvation in what you have read or heard. It's better that you seek the truth and find God in that honest journey." In that dream I felt I had been given permission to expand my spiritual path, and to continue my journey toward experiencing a visceral, feeling connection with *God*. ♡

Exercise 1

Exploring Your Inner Mystic

You will need:

- A quiet time without interruption
- A comfortable place to sit
- A journal and pen or pencil

Take some time to review your life from a spiritual perspective. Relax. Go through your life as far back as you can remember and make a note of anything that happened to you that went beyond the ordinary.

Here are some things to think about as you take your Inner Mystic inventory.

- Have you had any memorable dreams?

- Have you ever experienced a personal challenge that compelled you to draw upon a deeper part of yourself, or something other than yourself, to get through that challenge? This could have been an illness, the birth of a child, the death of a loved one, or even just a close call. It could be the result of a shock, trauma, or a deep fright.

- Have you ever experienced a *runner's high* after extreme exertion?

- When swept up in the exhilaration of a big win, have you ever felt as if something or *someone* was helping you or guiding you? (This could manifest as the sense of knowing something that you really had no reason to know at that time.)

- Did you ever have an encounter with a unique individual that had something extra special about them? Or an animal or place in nature that deeply affected you?

- Maybe you have experienced something that you consider to be *supernatural.* (Supernatural is anything you consider to be outside of your normal experiences of life.) As you learn and grow through your spiritual journey, you will eventually see *supernatural* as *natural.*

- You may have felt alone in your life, possibly grieving, when you felt or sensed something touching your heart or comforting you.

- Maybe you've felt something brush your face or hand, or you've physically felt a presence around you.

- Maybe you've broken out in goosebumps, but had no idea why.

- Have you ever felt a sense of peace or calm within you, even though your world is in chaos?

- Maybe you've lost someone in death and you feel their presence, or smell something that reminds you of them; or you hear a special song as you are thinking of them, or have lights blinking on and off.

Where in your life did you experience these things?

Where else in your life did you have similar experiences?

How did you feel about that moment?

Did this experience change your thinking or help guide you?

Once you start this personal spiritual inventory, and as you go through this book and do the exercises, continue to keep a running inventory of your mystical experiences. These experiences and revelations will show you where and when your soul is talking to you, and give you clues about how to follow your Soul's map for your life.

Modern Day Akashic Mystics

What I didn't discover, or learn even a tiny bit about in my early Catholic days, were the many modern day mystics and spiritual pioneers that had opened the doors for us to experience Spirit on a personal level. These early spiritual pioneers moved the spiritual connection from the control of the *high alter,* which only priests and ordained ministers could participate in, to a personal spiritual connection that everyone who chose to could have. These pioneers even helped pave the path for the renewal of the Holy Spirit in my Catholic charismatic group to take place.

The beginning of a spiritual paradigm shift took place in America in the 1800s. Looking at American history at that time, the promise of constitutional *freedom of religion* began to take root in unexpected places. One could argue that the Christian church is where the underpinnings and foundational blocks of slavery, prejudice, and the suppression of woman can be found. Their beliefs were the driving force behind the politics and laws of early America. The churches kept control of their flocks through spiritual fear (much like the European Christian churches did), so the laws of the government reflected these Christian influences.

Also during the 1800s, the industrial revolution was well underway. Hundreds of immigrants were making their way into the new states of America to find freedom, jobs, and hope for relief from extreme poverty. The situation in America was dire; full of hunger, low wages, poverty, and illness. These hardships, suffered by so many, seemed to light a spark. People wanted more for themselves and their families. Women wanted more for their sisters and daughters and were finding their voices. The institution of slavery became morally unacceptable and unpopular. The nation began to split apart, and not just from north and south.

The scene was set for new thoughts to set root—enough people were questioning their lives and beliefs—enough people were beginning to set out with new spiritual compasses. The time was ripe for brave souls to forge new pathways.

The gentle Quakers and Shakers laid a foundation in the new world of the American colonies for spiritual exploration and connection with the divine, as well as a deep respect for the people in community. The Shakers, by choosing celibacy, knew their time was limited, but predicted a new expression of spirit was to arrive. They passed the baton onto Spiritualism in the 1800s as the ones who would continue their work with Spirit.

Quakers, Shakers, and Spiritualists did a tremendous amount of work to influence and change the culture of the times, calling for women's rights and the abolition of slavery. Many brilliant pioneers came forward to challenge the Christian churches and the government beliefs and policies of that time. These pioneers expressed a spirituality that was very different from the status quo. They were being inspired by a higher power, often directly communicating with Spirit Guides or Spirits of deceased loved ones.

Helena P. Blavatsky: The Woman Who Dared

"Is it too much to believe that man should be developing new sensibilities and a closer relation with nature?"

~ H.P. Blavatsky

A notable mystic of this time was a woman from Russia, named Helena P. Blavastsky (1831- 1891). Born a rich aristocrat, Blavatsky's wealth and curiosity for, *"the mysteries of ancient and modern science and theology,"* led her to take many journeys to the sites of ancient cultures. Eventually, Helena started *The Theosophical Society*, for contemporary inquiry into world religions, philosophy, science, and the arts, in order to help people explore spiritual self-transformation.

While Spiritualism was blossoming into a full-blown spiritual force in the mid-1800s in the United States and spreading into Europe, Helena traveled the world studying ancient religions and cultures. Helena desired to reveal the amazing history of spiritual and theological thought that ran through the history of human development. She particularly sought out secret mystical doctrines that would illuminate human spirituality and the true nature of the Divine.

During her journeys, Helena discovered what is thought to be the oldest form of written theology in India. It is a pre-Vedic Hindu doctrine, written in Sanskrit, which claims to have its origins from an even more ancient culture of people. These people were lost when part of the continent fell into the sea. This ancient secret doctrine is said to have influenced Egyptian practices and beliefs, which in turn spread into the Greek and Roman culture and traditions. Meanwhile, this same influence traveled into the Middle East into what is now known as modern day Jerusalem, Syria, Iraq, Iran, and Turkey. The Norse tradition claims to have roots in ancient Turkey, before the nomads traveled north and west.

Blavatsky writes about a group of mystery schools—the Essenes, Gnostics, and Nazarenes—that were the basis of Jesus the Christ's training. (Yes, his name was actually a title, something an acolyte of these mystical practices could aspire to.) These mystery schools had their roots in in the ancient writings of Sakyamuni Buddha and the pre-Vedic Brahmans. Once the religion of Roman Christianity was established, these mystery schools were systematically destroyed, the teachers put to death, and the libraries burned. Helena, along with many modern theologians, hoped that some of the records went underground, hidden away, to be found at some later and safer date.

During her studies and in her writing, Helena teased out the meaning of *God's,* or the *Creator's,* essence. Paraphrasing the ancient cosmology, she says, "The aged of the aged, the unknown of the unknown, has a form and yet no form." It is described similarly in the Kabbalah, as well as in the Hindu esoteric cosmology, as "Him who is and Him who is not." The pre-Vedic ancient concept is a visual description of a trinity that births an egg in a universal womb called *Nara.* The father is the inexplicable primordial essence. Nara (also called *Prana*) is the Spirit that activates the primordial energy and together they create a child. Nara then becomes the womb that births the child.

Helena names this inexplicable primal power and essence the *Principle of All Life,* as expressed in the Sanskrit word *Akasha.* This is the divine astral light. This light contains things past, present, and yet to come. It's as though the rays of this light were focused on a mirror and then broadcast throughout the universe.

This boundless expanse of cosmic matter—ether, light, mist, Universal Life Force energy, the Akasha, whatever you call it—flows through all of creation. This creative principle formed nature; the sun, the stars, and the planets, with every form and quality of life upon them.

"All are but parts of one stupendous whole whose body nature is, and God the Soul."

~ Alexander Pope 1743

Creative power resides within in each one of us. The same creative power that is the Soul of God is also the soul of humanity. Blavatsky compares this influential presence to the pregnant women who impresses her thoughts and emotions upon her unborn child. She theorized that the mother gives off an electrical energy pulse (*energy* in *motion,* or *emotions*) that radiates to the child she is carrying. And so it is that God's pulse of etheric energy affects all of creation. This is the Electricity of Life Principle; another form of the Akashic Energy.

The Akashic Energy, like a universal ether, fills the world—even the very air we breathe. Imagine! Every breath you take is full of Akashic energy. You are full of this Akashic energy, from the instant of your birth! The Akashic energy becomes potential energy within your body, activated and used by your spirit and soul throughout your life. You can choose to consciously access and develop this energy as you gain higher awareness of your spiritual nature.

"All things that ever were, that are, or that will be, having their record upon astral light, or tablet of the unseen universe, can be known by the initiated adept, using the vision of his own spirit and soul."

~ Helena Blavatsky

Edgar Casey: the Sleeping Prophet and the Book of Life

Edgar Casey (1877-1945) was a Christian mystic and founder of the Association for Research and Enlightenment, Inc. (A.R.E.). Casey was the most documented psychic of the 20th Century. He is known as the *Sleeping Prophet* because he was able to put himself into a sleep-like trance or state of meditation. He would lie on his sofa, and give readings from the universal consciousness; what he called the Akashic records.

Cayce explained that he received information from two sources; the first was the subconscious mind of the individual he was reading, and the second source was the Akashic records. Casey describes the records:

"Upon time and space is written the thoughts, the deeds, the activities of an entity— as in relationships to its environs, its heredity influences: as directed— or judgment drawn by or according to what the entity's ideal is."

~Edgar Casey

Casey described the process for accessing these records as his sense of himself becoming a tiny dot, out of his physical body, surrounded by darkness. His tiny dot self would become aware of a beam of light and he'd move upward, following the light as his guide.

As he moved along the light path, he viewed various levels of activity. The first level he came to was vague shapes, then human forms, then grey, hooded forms that moved downward. Gradually, color would appear and grow rapidly lighter. Hazy outlines of houses, walls, trees, and the like would begin to form, and then slowly clear into normal cities and towns. He then became aware of sounds; that eventually became recognizable as music, voices, laughter, birdsong. More light would come in and the colors became increasingly more beautiful. The sounds made a wonderful music.

Quite suddenly, he came upon the hall of records. It is a hall without walls or ceiling. He saw an old man who handed him a large book, which contained the record of the individual he was looking up.

Once in the records, Casey would then select the information appropriate for the individual he is reading for. He then read the past, present, and probable future for his client.

In a series of readings, Casey explains that anyone can access the records of the Akasha. He stated that the clarity of the information received from the records could be misinterpreted due to an individual's belief systems and life experiences; *"Prompted to give their version according to the reaction upon their personal ideals."* Casey continued, *"To clearly read the Akashic records, the intent of the reader must be total selfless and desirous of being of help."*

The purpose of the Akashic Records is to assist each Soul's personal growth and transformation. Casey's cosmology can be summed up in this: *"God is essentially Love and the Universe is completely orderly…each individual is purposefully created, as a soul, to become a companion to the creator."*

After reading a few of Casey's transcripts, it's easy to see we constantly enter into our own Akashic records. The records are everywhere; we can access them in our dreams, through our imagination, meditation, through a competent reader, through deep creative thought, and artistic efforts such as music, writing, and painting.

The Akashic records and the energy they contain are the impulses that draw us to exactly what we need and where we need to be. This is the force that brings people together to learn from each other. Within these same records are also the tools that help individuals to be the best they can be. According to Edgar Casey, the Akashic records are beyond a philosophical concept; they are a real force and intelligence.

> *"The entity should know that the record is as real as it is that which may give off a light, for it goes on and on upon the etheronic energies and is recorded upon the film of time and space."*

> *~ Edgar Casey 871-1*

Modern Science and Ancient Akasha

A huge body of recent research has been compiled that points to a *non-local (beyond our physical mind)* source of consciousness. Whether it's referred to as non-local, collective consciousness, one mind, higher source, higher being, or higher power, this concept has had its doors blown wide open in the medical and scientific fields of study. A lot of scientifically based research projects have been published about past life memories, healing through prayer, near death experiences, mind body spirit connections, extra sensory perception, and remote viewing. These studies are challenging the materialist paradigm of science. But even with the tremendous about of information being gathered, these research projects have been dismissed or ignored by traditional scientists. Maybe these universal rules that lay at the root of current scientific understanding simply don't leave enough room to comprehend spirituality.

Conventional science is grounded in the idea that matter is the building block of all things. Life, mind, and consciousness are all secondary to the prime matter, according to current orthodox science.

The problem is that this materialistic model of causal mechanisms, predictable associations, and of universal laws that are the basis of all science, has been unsuccessful in explaining the emergence of life and consciousness that animates the material world. What brings consciousness to a functioning biological body? Material science can't answer this.

When new data and phenomena are brought forward that measures and validates consciousness, conventional science dismisses it. Materialistic science doesn't have the parameters to consider the data, falling back to the argument that there is nothing but matter.

Yet, in many areas of science, there are murmurs and quiet admissions of not knowing exactly how to measure or quantify consciousness. *"The nature of consciousness remains a mystery,"* wrote scientist Donald D Hoffman of the University of California. *"The scientific study of consciousness is in the embarrassing position of having no scientific theory of consciousness."* The best conclusion that the field of science can make is that they don't have the means to understand the invisible force of consciousness.

Nikola Tesla (1856-1943) invented and developed the use of electricity as we currently know it. Edison invented the light bulb, but Tesla figured out how to supply the nation with long distant power (called the AC system) so that everyone could light that bulb in their own homes. In 1895, Tesla

designed what was among the first AC hydroelectric power plants in the United States, at Niagara Falls. Buffalo and New York were the first cities to light up. The alternate current system (AC) still remains the worldwide standard for delivering electricity.

Tesla, much like Edison, was more of an inventor at heart. With his brilliant mind and curiosity, he created many patents for ideas we are only seeing developed today. Tesla invented the first concept of a smart phone; he described to his funder and business partner, J.P. Morgan, a new means of instant communication that involved gathering stock quotes and telegram messages, and then funneling them to his laboratory where he would encode and assign each piece of data its own frequency. That frequency would be broadcast to a device that would fit in your hand, he explained. In other words, Tesla had envisioned the smart phone and wireless technology.

Tesla published an article in the Milwaukee Sentinel on July 13, 1930 that discussed his thoughts about humanity. The article is called *Man's Greatest Achievement*. In this article he describes, allegorically, the development of a child from birth.

"This child is full of senses and abilities and talents, and is hitched to the wheel-work of the Universe . . . The little engine labors and grows, performs more and more involved operations, becomes sensitive to ever subtler influences and now there manifests itself in the fully developed being. (Hu)Man – a desire mysterious, inscrutable and irresistible: to imitate nature, to create, to work the wonders he/she perceives.

What has the future in store for this strange being, born of a breath, of perishable tissue, yet immortal, with his powers fearful and divine? What magic will be wrought by him in the end? What is to be his greatest deed, his crowning achievement?

Long ago he recognized that all perceptible matter comes from a primary substance, of a tenuity beyond conception and filling all space – the Akasha or luminiferous ether – which is acted upon by the life-giving Prana or creative force, calling into existence, in never ending cycles, all things and phenomena.

The primary substance, thrown into infinitesimal whirls of prodigious velocity, becomes gross matter; the force subsiding, the motion ceases and matter disappears, reverting to the primary substance."

Nikola speaks of a larger force that the child and humanity's mind arose from. The mind is influenced, throughout its lifetime, by a force that has a high degree of creativity. Is this the force that influenced and inspired Nikola Tesla in his brilliant visions and work? Do we have the intelligent Akashic field of energy to thank every time we turn on our lights or use our smartphones?

Tesla revived the ancient idea of an original medium that fills space and compared it to Akasha. When Akasha is activated by Prana, or cosmic energy, matter forms. When Prana action ceases, the matter goes back to the Akasha. This concept contrasted the popular theory that space is a vacuum, and in the early 1900s scientists preferred Einstein's theory of relativity. Today, the concept of an underlying medium, or dimension in the universe, is accepted, and the materialism theory Einstein held is being increasingly abandoned. *Matter,* it has been discovered, is actually rare in the cosmos, making up only four percent of the universe. The main percentage of the substances that make up the universe, are fluctuating energies and information. Physical quantities are more like incidentals, while information is present throughout space and time everywhere. (Ervin Laszlo, *The Akashic Experience*)

Sadly, Nikola's scientific philosophical work wasn't embraced during his lifetime. Tesla passed away in a lonely hotel room, in humble surroundings. A while back, I was lucky enough to stay in the hotel Tesla used to live in, in the heart of New York City. As I hung out in the room, my game of solitaire played itself on my smartphone. Was Nikola moving my Queen of Hearts to the King of Spades? I began to wonder who Tesla was. He made a remarkable contribution to the world. Taking into account his writing about the Akasha, was he accessing that very creative force? Is that what inspired his brilliant ideas? When we learn to access the Akasha, we have the opportunity to expand our minds and be brilliant in our own capacity. You can embrace the brilliance offered in connection to the Akasha. I invite you to be curious and brave!

In Section One you will learn to connect with this Akashic field of energy, in a conscious, purposeful practice.

Learning to Navigate Your Akashic Journey

Akashic Healing Love

Akasha is a Sanskrit word and means primary substance, that out of which all things are formed. It is the first stage of crystallization of spirit…This Akashic, or primary substance, is so sensitive that the slightest vibration any place in the universe registers upon it."

~ The Aquarian Gospel of Jesus Christ

For God So Loved the World . . .

The presence of God is Love. God is Love. Love is the energy of "stuff" used in all the Creator's creations. The **Akasha** is the essence of the Creator's source and IS the energy of Love.

As a young child, small enough to be picked up, I felt a tremendous love surrounding me everywhere I looked and explored. I felt a wonderful optimism and trust within me. I can still remember that feeling. It is my life's journey to return to that love.

Spirit, Infinite intelligence and love, has many ways of connecting and communicating with us. It's up to us, truly, to consciously accept and receive that connection.

In this section, we'll explore the Akashic concept of Divine love through prayer, meditation, and visualization in order to become aligned with the Creator's energy of Divine love. With practice, you can develop this love in your life and learn to create miracles. But the *biggest* miracle will be your return to love, to Source.

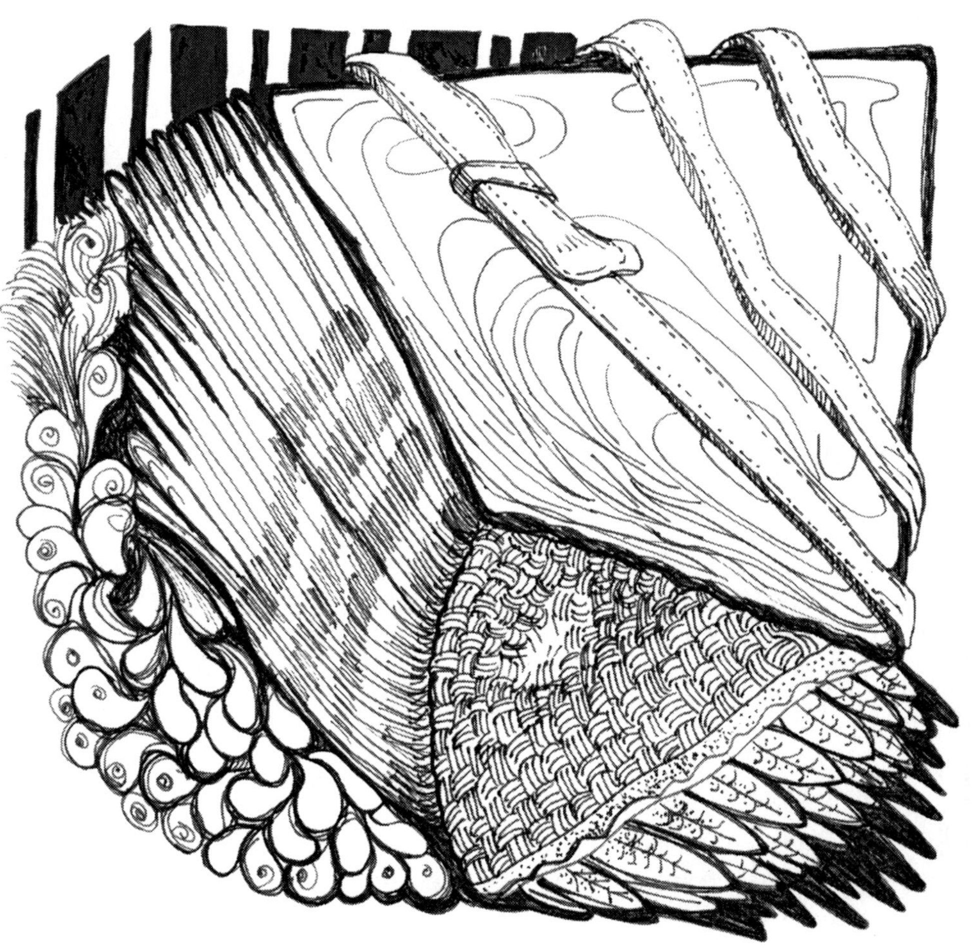

Chapter 3

The Akashic Principle of Love

When I was a tiny girl—still small enough to be picked up and carried—I had a sense of being loved in a large way. It was as if everything and everyone around me was made of love. I returned excitement and love to everyone and everything.

I was an affectionate child. I found a picture in an album of me as a toddler hugging the stuffing out of my little cousin. My mother had written: *We don't know what got into her.* I was nicknamed *Smiley* because I greeted every person and challenge in my way with a smile.

My parents took us to church as a young family. I watched with interest as the prayers and songs glowed in colors around the sacred alter. Sometimes I saw colors around people's heads. Sometimes I heard extra voices singing with us. Much later in life I learned I was seeing auras and energy, and experiencing clairaudience.

Influenced by my Catholic upbringing, I defined this joyful presence as God, the Holy Family, and my angels.

My expansive exuberance with the loving energies I saw all around was constantly bringing me to the edge of trouble. I learned that what I felt and saw inside myself was not always reflected, or *happening,* in the world around me. The world didn't always answer back with a smile. I quickly learned to back it off and move forward with caution.

I went to school in the strict Catholic traditions. Some of the Carmelite Sisters didn't share my joy. I found it difficult to keep up with the rules and to do all the worksheets and tests. I often felt anxious and my stomach hurt. The sisters introduced me to the concept of sin. They explained we were all filled with sin and not deserving of God's attention until we were forgiven by God.

> *"Lord, I am not worthy to receive you, but only say the word and*
> *I shall be healed."*
> ~A Catholic prayer to prepare for receiving communion.

When I learned this prayer, I instantly felt my heart squeezing shut. I hadn't known that I may not even deserve all the love I was feeling. I had to earn it, and I didn't know how. My mom was always angry, my dad was aloof, and based on what they taught me about myself, I felt I would never earn or be worthy of this awesome love. By the age of seven, as I neared my first communion, I began to confuse my parent's approval, my teacher's catechism lessons, and the love I experienced from my angels. It made for one hot mess. My spiritual enthusiasm took a nose dive. I escorted them all to the back of my consciousness.

After my tenth birthday, my mom gave birth to baby number eight, little Jackie. My mom bravely faced this pregnancy and new baby with optimism. She put her best foot forward, even though she suffered from post-partum depression. I was put in charge of Jackie, and called the second mom.

To celebrate Jacqueline's birth, our mom threw a big christening party, inviting all my aunts and uncles and cousins. The house was filled with guests, and my siblings and cousins were outside playing baseball. I was told to stay in and get Jackie up from her nap. I went upstairs, changed her into her beautiful white dress, and wrapped her in a delicate white blanket.

With Jackie snuggled tightly in my arms, I started down the stairs. At the top of the landing I heard a commanding voice I had never heard before say *STOP*.

"The angels," I thought to myself. *"I had better listen."* I stopped. I stood on the landing at the top of the stairs. I waited and waited and waited for what seemed like forever. As I adjusted the blanket for the tenth time, I squeezed my eyes shut and asked, *"When can I go?"*

In my mind's eye I saw a traffic light. The lights changed from red to yellow, and then to green. *"Okay,"* I said aloud, and continued down the stairs.

I had to walk past a bank of large windows to lay Jackie down in her bassinet. Just as I was about to step in front of the first window, a ball came crashing through it, shattering and spraying broken glass everywhere. The shards just missed hitting my baby sister and me. I knew that if I hadn't listened to the voice telling me to stop, we would have been badly hurt.

I hugged my baby sister and whispered, *"Thank you."* In my heart I knew my angels had returned, and they were keeping me safe. I promised I would try to listen better. I didn't tell anyone what had happened on the stairs.

From that moment on, my amazing journey with Spirit began to grow on purpose, by my choice. I could go to them when I felt lost and they would somehow convey comfort and guidance to me. I often think that the angels, in the presence of God, raised me. That was the beginning of my long journey back to remembering the presence of love in everything in my life, and the excitement that love evoked in my heart. ♡

Explore Spiritual, Divine Love in Your Life

You will need:

- A quiet time without interruption

- A comfortable place to sit

- A journal and pen or pencil (*I recommend you buy a special notebook to work in. A special pen might be nice too.*)

Set up: Find a quiet, comfortable place where you won't be interrupted. Create a safe space that you can return to whenever you want to. Make this place an actual spot in your home. Also create an inner space in your heart and mind using your imagination. Once you are quiet and fully present, begin some self-exploration using these guiding questions. Write your answers in your notebook.

- Where do you feel spiritual love in your life? How do you recognize this love? What does it feel like? Can you recognize it at all?

- Have you ever experienced divine intervention?

- Where and when do you feel a connection to something beyond yourself or larger than you?

- Where in your life do you show compassion and love freely without any expectation for getting anything back? Where in your life have you received love with no strings attached?

- How in your life do you give and receive love?

Journal ♡ How and when have you experienced Divine love in your life ?

My Own Version of Creation

In the beginning, there was Divine Consciousness.

This consciousness is LOVE. Unconditional Love.

Love wanted to express itself.

"I Am," said Love, and so it is.

Love became the creator with these words. Love desired to experience love, and continues to create.

Divine Love created little souls, just like itself. Each soul is unique and individual, ready to grow and learn. Love calls these little souls, I AM.

The creator, Divine Love, made light, space, and form for these souls to grow up in. They could experience their own nature and unique selves in everything the creator made. The souls took many forms as they grew and experienced themselves. The souls were never separate from the Creator Love, no matter what form they chose to take.

The creator's consciousness became full. All possibilities, all knowing, all thoughts, and all things created fill the consciousness of the creator. Not one thing is forgotten. Love and Creation are all one in the same.

This consciousness is what I call the *Akashic field* and the *Akashic records*.

You and I are the *I Am* souls in human form. While in our human forms we learn to create. We create light. We create our own version of space in our consciousness. We create all kinds of forms to help us experience our life. And we desire to be with Love. We've created many forms of love while being human. Love is our way back to the creator, to our true home, and to our truest essence.

The added bonus is that we're also granted the free will to choose and create what we want in our lives. Sometimes I think the creator, Divine Love, is holding her breath as she observes our progress.

Akasha is the intelligent, compassionate life force from which all things are created and to which all things return. Akasha is one of the many names for the creator energy, the Divine Consciousness. Akasha is also an organizational principle that we can use to understand and connect to the Divine Consciousness and Love of the creator.

Akasha is an energy that can be accessed. We are created and born to access this energy of love. As we access Akashic energy, our lives as humans are enhanced; we deepen the journey to our soul, to our *I AM*.

For God so loved the world . . .

The presence of God is Love. God is Love. Love is the energy used in all of the creator's creations. The Akasha is the essence of the creator's source and is the energy of Love.

When we return to God, whether during life as we live it, or as a result of transitioning from death to Spirit form, we return to Love. Illness, disease, and loss are often a call from our souls to redirect our lives. When we direct our minds, emotions, and Spirits to self-love, and accept a divine, loving, healing presence in our lives, miracles can happen. They aren't really miracles—we're meant to live our lives in Love—it's the natural way of being that brings us back to health and a sense of well-being.

The miracle is our return to Love, to Source.

Erich From, in his famous book The Art of Loving, presents love as a skill that can be taught and developed. He looked beyond the magical mystery of falling in love and becoming trapped or helpless to its power. He theorized that by engaging *"true humility, courage, faith, and discipline"* we could develop the capacity to create sustaining love in our lives.

Fromm describes the four basic elements within love as care, responsibility, respect, and knowledge. He also organized love into four distinct categories; familial love, which includes our first relationship with mother and father, Eros or erotic love, self-love, and agape love for God or creator. He posits that we experience all four of these different types of love in our lives.

Familial love is the first love we experience consciously. This love contains motherly love, fatherly love, and brotherly love. The first love in our lives is mother's love. We need maternal love to survive. Without some form of maternal love, human babies will not thrive. As a baby, our bond to our mother is probably one of the most powerful experiences of love we will have in our lifetime. The next level of relationship we are exposed to is a father, sibling, and extended family love. Brotherly love contains compassion for all, as well as social acceptance and group or tribal relations. It's possible to confuse our need for this maternal nurturing with the need for approval from our family or tribe. Maybe it was designed this way so that we would have to develop social relations that teach us brotherly love and compassion for each other.

Love is key to our emotional, mental, and spiritual well-being. As water is necessary for physical sustenance and even survival, so is love necessary for our mental- emotional balance and ability to thrive in our lives. Yet, with

The Akashic Principle of Love   43

our families, friends, and tribes, love is often outside of our reach. We negotiate and compromise for the closest thing to love we can get. We are social beings by nature. Our first inclination is to cling to our people, even in the absence of love. The absence of familial love can lead to heartbreak and imbalance, with a skewed perception of the world that could lead to physical illness and failure to thrive.

Eros or ***Erotic Love*** is exciting! It's filled with tension, passion, and physical connection. We're free to dream and fantasize with the emotions of this fantastical love. We see ourselves through the eyes of a lover, and imagine drinking in all the love that we've longed for throughout our lives. Erotic love has its ups and downs, as we find our way with our partner. We can choose to move from partner to partner in erotic love or we can choose to develop this love into a deeper partnership with a lifelong commitment. This type of love can lift us up or it can crash down around us depending on the relationship we have with ourselves and our partner.

Self-Love is a relationship you have with yourself. This love is about how you see yourself, how you care for yourself, and how you honor your being. Self-love is the connection between our conscious mind and our spiritual essence. Self-love begins developing as we are carried in our mother's womb. We feel the essence of coming into being in a safe environment under out mother's heart. As we experience others loving us, so we learn to love our self. If we don't experience love when we're small, we can still learn to love ourselves because we're smart, we're flexible, and we're alive. As we grow and mature into a sense of our own self and identity, we develop preferences and desires. We learn to recognize and take care of our own needs. Our ability to and skill level at caring for ourselves is in direct proportion to our ability to care about others outside of ME.

Children who are mistreated, exposed to trauma, neglected, or abused in some way develop tendencies toward guilt and shame. These emotions and thought patterns inhibit self-love. Internal beliefs about caring for self can become stunted or unrealistic.

The way we love ourselves is directly related to who we choose to love and who we allow to love us. This self-love is the key to allowing Divine Love into our lives. When I thought I was not worthy and had to earn that love from the angels, I lost my connection to Divine Love. To regain that angel love connection, I had to set aside what I was taught about myself in order to be available to listen to the higher voice. We are worthy of Divine Love, and we always have been. No questions asked.

Agape or Akashic Spiritual Love is about our connection to our spirits, souls, and the Creator (infinite intelligence, love, and light). This is a reciprocal relationship. This love speaks to a constant influx of spiritual energy that sustains our etheric, emotional, mental, and physical bodies which combine to create our Self in this life. This is not religious love; this love is the basis of the mystical essence of all religions, but in itself is not a belief system. It simply IS. This is the quantum field or the Akashic essence of creation, where all potential exists and all creation is born from.

We are mostly unconscious of this flow. Our thoughts and beliefs direct the flow of this spiritual energy throughout our bodies and our lives. We can become conscious of this flow, and then learn to direct it as a loving, healthy, and sustaining current in our lives.

We (our conscious and unconscious selves) are created to exercise free will concerning how we direct and conduct our lives. We're given the choice to connect or not to connect to this spiritual love and the guidance it contains. However and wherever we choose this love to flow, that's where it goes. Carolyn Myss describes the soul's energy like a trust fund.

Consider This ♡ Imagine you have a bank account that is filled everyday with 5000.00 dollars. Imagine you are only aware of 50.00 dollars a day and yet you manage to spend all 5000.00 every single day. You carefully budget the 50.00 on self-care and sustenance, the basic needs. It's all you imagine you can afford. In the meantime your unconscious self is spending 4950.00 a day on all the things running in the back ground like past grief, resentments, fear, anxiety, unresolved anger, loneliness, and insecurities. The enormous expenditure is on unresolved thoughts and emotions that you unconsciously allow to run unchecked day and night. What are you willing to do to consciously access your full bank account? ♡

Our self-awareness, and our ability to recognize our needs and care for ourselves, is in direct proportion to our capacity to open to and allow God's love and Akashic spiritual energy to sustain and elevate our lives.

Within the Akashic field of energy is a library of information and the wisdom of all creation. The Akashic energy is sensitive, and all events are impressed and embedded within this Akashic library of records. The records contain the macrocosm and microcosm of your life; the big picture of your soul's plan and the very personal information about your daily life are all retained in this Akashic field.

You have the tools and potential to access your own personal history and soul records within the Akashic field. You also have the potential to access the highest wisdom of your soul's group.

This ability is embedded in your energy anatomy. The potential is within you and the training is available. With this access you're able to retrieve soul losses. What has wounded your spirit and self in your lifetime can be reclaimed and healed as you access the Akashic field of infinite intelligence and love.

The healing capacity within the Akashic field is a flow that we enter in a relationship of give and take, deep respect, and humility. To enter onto this healing path you must take ownership of your path in your present life. The entrance fee is your willingness to be completely present in the moment as best you can. You own and learn to respond to all you feel, perceive, and choose to do. Blame, shame, victim guilt, and all those sorts of excuses will keep you grounded in lower vibrations. Curiosity, imagination, creativity, forgiveness, intuition, and a willingness to blend with Spirit elevates your vibration. This increases your ability to access Akashic healing and nurturing love, consciously and with purpose.

Journey to the Akashic Energy Field of Divine Love

Meditation1

Sitting in the Presence of Akashic Love, an Attunement

> **Set up:** Return to the quiet space you created earlier where you won't be interrupted.

> **Time:** 20 -30 minutes

> You will need:
> - your journal
> - pen or pencil

Make Some Agreements With Yourself:

You're journeying to a place that is timeless, so take all the time you need on your healing path. Blame, shame, guilt, or self-judgement is not welcome. Create an environment safe from inner criticism.

Set the intention that this is your circle of calm and connection to Akashic healing love.

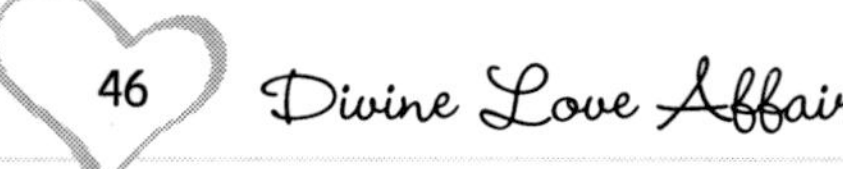

The best place to begin your journey is right where you are, just as you are. Open your awareness and your heart to YOU. You're in the perfect place at the perfect time. Take some deep, cleansing breathes, and with each exhale, let your body relax into the moment.

Begin the Journey:

Start by sitting straight up, feet on the floor, hands in an open, receiving position, palms up and resting on your knees. Get comfortable now so that discomfort doesn't distract you. Open to the Mother, Father, God, Creator of All, and the Akashic field of energy.

Breathe deeply in, hold and exhale deeply out, hold. Repeat this pattern until you are breathing deeply and evenly. When you're breathing slowly and rhythmically, you are telling your physical, mental, and emotional bodies that all is well. You are now free to be completely in the present moment. If you feel lost or your mind fills with thoughts, return to your breathing and relax. Focus on your mind and let it soften. Drop your awareness into your heart center.

Now imagine yourself sitting in the middle of an egg shaped sphere of gold that extends three feet above your head, three feet below your feet, and fits comfortably around you.

Focusing on your in breath, visualize it filling your heart with a golden light that spreads to surround you. As you breathe into your chest, imagine a bright crystal in the center of your heart. Notice as the crystal begins to glow and vibrate as it becomes active with light. Within this crystal is a cord that travels down towards your feet and up towards your head. This is your life-line—also called your *Hara* line—the energy thread that connects you to heaven and earth. As this thread drops down from your heart, it travels in front of your spine and down through your energy center, or chakras. Now imagine that there's a fine crystal at the center of your solar plexus just under your ribs (belly chakra) and notice it begin to glow and vibrate as it becomes activated. Continue to follow your life-line down past your belly button into your abdominal region (the sacral chakra) and then down through your pelvic floor area (root chakra). See the thread continuing down through your last energy center eighteen inches below your feet (grounding chakra), finally wrapping itself like a root deep into the earth.

Deep in the earth is a sustaining energy that nourishes the energy of your physical body. Imagine breathing this energy up through your life-line, through your feet, into your legs and body. You are anchored and grounded to the earth, your original mother. The earth is a conscious, living soul that nourishes and sustains life; your life and all life on the earth with you.

Breathe this energy into your heart. Allow your heart to be filled with this loving, nurturing energy. Allow your heart to be filled and expanded as you breathe in the energy of the mother.

Now bring your focus back to your life-line and follow this line up into the energy center of your throat chakra. Continue to travel up your life-line into the center of your brain. Imagine you can draw a line from the center of your forehead, between your eyes (the third eye center), to the base of your skull. Where your life-line intersects is the crystalline center, which is becoming activated in your energy body. Follow your life-line through this center and into the crown chakra at the top of your head. Imagine your crown chakra expanding and opening as you travel up, going through and beyond the top of your head.

You are now traveling beyond your physical body, yet you're still inside your etheric energetic body. There are two more energy centers you will pass through before reaching the edge of your etheric body.

Continue to breathe evenly and deeply, following your life-line to just above your head to the Akashic center of your personal life. This center contains your Akashic records, your book of life, your book of shadows, and all of your soul contracts. This center vibrates at a higher frequency then you are used to in your physical body. Allow your consciousness to expand into this center and adjust itself to this vibration. What do you feel? What do you see? Allow yourself to feel all the potential connections in this energy center.

Continue to your next energy center, eighteen inches above your head. This center is the seat of your soul. It connects you to non-local knowing. This center carries your soul's purpose and essence, the *I Am* of your soul. Your soul's essence may be slightly different than the essence of your current personality, although they are sympathetic to each other. This center vibrates at a higher frequency than your lower chakras. Allow your consciousness to expand into this center and adjust to the new vibration. What do you feel? What do you see? Allow yourself to feel all the potential connections in this energy center.

You're now ready to travel beyond your etheric energy body. Above your body are five stars that will lead you to the plane of compassion into the Akashic field of energy. Each star vibrates at a higher frequency than the other. Each star has a vibratory message and represents a plane or field of energy that has its own purpose. Your life-line travels through each of these stars all the way to the Akashic field of pure energy.

Follow your life-line to star number five. Allow yourself to expand and adjust to the higher vibration of this star. What color is this energy? What do you feel? What do you see? Allow yourself to feel all the potential connections in this energy center. Can you sense the essence of this plane of energy? Is there a message for you to receive in this star?

Follow your life-line to star number four. Allow yourself to expand and adjust to the higher vibration of this star. What color is this energy? What do you feel? What do you see? Allow yourself to feel all the potential connections in this energy center. Can you sense the essence of this plane of energy? Is there a message for you to receive in this star?

Follow your life-line to star number three. Allow yourself to expand and adjust to the higher vibration of this star. What color is this energy? What do you feel? What do you see? Allow yourself to feel all the potential connections in this energy center. Can you sense the essence of this plane of energy? Is there a message for you to receive in this star?

Follow your life-line to star number two. Allow yourself to expand and adjust to the higher vibration of this star. What color is this energy? What do you feel? What do you see? Allow yourself to feel all the potential connections in this energy center. Can you sense the essence of this plane of energy? Is there a message for you to receive in this star?

Follow your life-line to star number one. Allow yourself to expand and adjust to the higher vibration of this star. What color is this energy? What do you feel? What do you see? Allow yourself to feel all the potential connections in this energy center. Can you sense the essence of this plane of energy? Is there a message for you to receive in this star?

Notice star one is connected to a beautiful pink energy. See a pink staircase that rises up from this star. Your life-line travels up this staircase. Step up from star one and begin to walk up the pink staircase. Each step is higher in vibration. Allow yourself to adjust and expand into each vibration. Each step you take you feel lighter and lighter. You let go more and more of your body and your mind. You feel yourself blending with this pink light. We will count seven steps and you will feel lighter and lighter, blending in with the higher vibrations with ease. Seven, six, five, four, three, two, one . . . And now you are standing at the threshold of a beautiful white field. You know when you cross this threshold you will feel magnificent. You will easily blend with this white field which is a light, etheric energy that gently touches you.

Step into the white field and feel it surround you and bathe you. You feel cleansed of all that was heavy. You blend into this energy and feel safe, nurtured, and cared for. Stay in this white for a few minutes, allowing yourself to expand in the light.

Now it's time to return, gather up any feelings or messages you may have received, and know you will remember them when you return home. Bring your awareness back to your life-line. For the first time, notice it is a tube. Within this tube is a gentle pulse that directs a flow of white, etheric energy down toward your energetic and physical bodies. Remember this flow when you return home.

Retracing your steps, follow your life-line down the pink stairs. You become aware that the first star is denser now, and so you must adjust to the different vibration. Once you have comfortably adjusted, step onto the second star.

The second star is denser, and so you must adjust to the different vibration. Once you have comfortably adjusted, step onto the third star.

The third star is denser, and so you must adjust to the different vibration. When you have comfortably adjusted, step onto the fourth star.

The fourth star in denser, and so you must adjust to the different vibration. When you have comfortably adjusted, step onto the fifth star.

The fifth star in denser, and so you must adjust to the different vibration. When you have comfortably adjusted, step into your etheric energy body. You are home now. Begin to adjust to the vibration of each energy center as you travel back to the center of your heart. Take your time.

When you are ready to return to your room, tap your feet and roll your shoulders to begin coming into awareness.

Take some time and review your journey. When you feel ready, pick up pen and journal and write down what you remember and felt.

Journal ♡ What do I now understand about Divine Love and my own connection to this love? ♡

Chapter 4

Prayer and Meditation for Akashic Connection

Prayer and meditation are the gateways to spiritual connection and mystical practices. One could say that prayer is talking to Divine God, and Meditation is listening.

Prayer takes many forms—some are ritualistic and prescribed by religious doctrine or practice—some are heartfelt pleas of "Lord, Lord!" to a higher power that we hope has a resource we do not. The unconscious utterings of "Oh my God," may be reactionary, but they're still prayers. The key to prayer is to understand and consciously remember that these words are connecting you to a higher consciousness. Prayer creates a bridge—a connection through which to become one mind with higher awareness—a link to the creator's consciousness.

Prayers can be about setting an intention, and asking for assistance in reaching it. Prayers can be reminders to yourselves to make a higher connection before you do what you're about to do. The repetitive ritual of prayer can be comforting. This type of prayer can keep our attitudes and thoughts positive and faithful, reminding us that a higher power is here to help us.

Prayer is personal, based on our own mindset, energy, and vibration. Prayer can limit you or expand you, depending on where you are mentally, emotionally, and psychologically. Expand your prayer to include the Divine Love that is waiting to hear from you. A key to prayer is a listening state of self. Prayer is only one part of a dialogue. Your willingness to receive the other part of the dialogue is essential. Keep in mind, the answer from the Divine is an energetic answer, not always returned to you in the same language you are speaking. Your language could be based in fear, pain, or anger. The Divine's language is always love. A hurting heart doesn't always perceive the language of love. Love may be a new paradigm for you, a new language. The best you can do is live into the answer. Put your expectations aside and take baby steps towards the truths that are beyond you in that moment.

 Conscious entrance into the Akashic realm and its Hall of Records and wisdom is through prayer. We will talk about that later in the chapter. Right now, during this part of your journey, it's time to look at prayer in your life. What is your story? How do you speak to a higher power, The Divine, your creator? ♡

My Journey to Prayerful Connection

Here is my story. As you read this, examine your own relationship with prayer. Review your attempts to connect to a higher power. Do you feel connected to the Divine? Do you sense your prayers are answered, or do you feel your prayers fall into a void, with no response back?

Throughout my life, I've learned and implemented many styles of prayer. I've used the ritual prayers—Our Father, Hail Mary, The Gloria—and the rosary. As my life progressed, I practiced Buddhist mantras that touched my heart. I've prayed in tongues. I often ad-libbed prayers for special needs. I prayed in what my mom would call unholy ways, such as taking the Lord's name in vain when emotionally stressed out. On the other hand, Mom's favorite prayer was, "Jesus, Mary, and Joseph, God Almighty . . ." When up against the wall, she called in her whole team. Even though these names and words were said in an emotional outburst, as I said before, they are still prayers. Reaching out to a higher power in a moment of need is valid and accepted by our soul and our Creator. We are heard.

In my early mothering days, I changed up my prayer pattern to reflect my new lifestyle. I prayed for help and instruction on how to be a good, loving, and responsive parent. I prayed to be a loving, responsive wife, constantly asking for guidance in my marriage. I carried a sense of never doing a good enough job at either.

My husband at that time was chronically unhappy, which lead to mercurial outbursts that often took me by surprise. He would cycle between weeks of drinking and coming home late from work, followed by weeks of sober, cold, hard anger.

I saw a therapist, taking the baby with me in his little seat. We would sit in her office as I talked about what I was doing wrong ,and pondered how I could make our lives better, happier. I poured my heart out. How can I fix this? That was my prayer.

Every day and every night I prayed, Help me be better.

At some point, we crossed a line in our marriage. My prayers changed once again.

My husband was badly hurt at work and so was home on medical leave to heal. He urged me to cancel daycare and leave the children with him while I worked. He was on pain medicine and not able to do much physically. I tried to negotiate with him but he demanded that I do as he said. This was not in the best interest of our toddlers, so I stood my ground. "God help me," I moaned as I took charge. I prayed for a miracle. The answer I got back was that I was that miracle.

I managed my husband's acute care, juggled getting the kids to the sitter while I worked, and then got us all back home in time to make dinner. Within a few weeks my husband's health was improving, so he again insisted I leave the children with him while I worked. I reluctantly agreed. I came home to hungry and distraught children, diapers that needed to be changed and dirty faces. I gave hugs all around. When in my arms my children would cry for long stretches. These emotional outbursts angered their father, and so he would yell about the messes they made and he threw their toys around.

One day, at the end of a very long shift, I walked through the door, coat still on, brief-case in hand. I was greeted with a very angry and very hungry man. "Where's dinner?" he screamed. The children immediately began crying. My three your old went to his dad's toolbox and pulled out a screwdriver. As my husband moved toward me in rage, my little guy lunged at him in an attempt to protect me.

My husband had gone too far and my son was the one to deliver the message.

My prayers changed that day. "This is not working," I prayed. "Help me, God, to let go of what isn't working. Every day, dear God, show me one more step out of this mess. Show me for the kid's sake, and for mine, because I can't do this anymore. "

It took me two more years of hesitation to hear the answers to my prayers, and to clearly see what I was being guided to do. I was terrified. I negotiated all kinds of scenarios in my head, and prayed to last just one more day.

Finally, I got the message—there was no more waiting for the right sign, the best time, or my being at the best level of healing—I had to do what I had to do and do it now. The healing would be in the doing.

I took the leap, I filed the papers, I moved out of a house I couldn't afford. My estranged spouse gave me no child support for quite a while, choosing to be in contempt of court. He was angry. I was scared. He was not penalized for non-payment. I was getting food from the Red Cross. I constantly doubted my decision. My faithful trust in my prayers waivered.

Our young family fell into a pattern of daily living—going to school, doing chores and homework with me—with twice a month weekend visitations with dad. This meant that every other weekend I was alone. Being apart from my children that long was new to me. They returned home in various states; sometimes they were fine, sometimes they cried while I held them, sometimes they were sick. My anxiety was through the roof as I continued to doubt my decisions. I wondered, often out loud to God, whether if I had stayed in the marriage, I would have been able to protect my children better.

I began to experience insomnia, often waking up in the middle of a full blown panic attack, feeling unable to breath. My stomach ached in pain and nausea. After nights and nights of this, I was utterly exhausted. I would wrap up in warm blankets to relax my body and try to lull myself back to sleep. On one of these occasions, at about 4:00 am as I dozed off after a particularly bad episode, a woman's presence filled my consciousness.

She was kind, warm, and had a very loving presence. She was tall, hovering above me on a red-dirt hill. As I looked up at her, I also felt her by my side and in my heart. She had a strength and sternness about her. She lifted her arm and gently reached into my pain, into my stomach.

She said, *"Pray like this."*

She reached into my stomach (Solar Plexus) and seemed to blend with every thought and emotion I was feeling. She expressed my deepest pain and fear from the deepest part of my being. Every word she said was an honest and clear expression of me. We prayed together that way for quite a while; I felt a miracle was taking place.

As we prayed, I felt a heavy burden lift from my belly and heart. I felt a gentle light of hope. My lungs relaxed and I felt I could breathe deeply again.

And there was more. She took me to the hill she was standing on made of red dirt. We were in a kind of desert—the growth on the hill was scrubby, small, spindly bushes mixed with patches of short, dry grass. Not the New England landscape I was used to.

She walked me down the side of the red dirt hill. From the dirt she carved out the initials of my children.

She told me, *"You came together with your husband to create these children. Now you are apart from your husband. You must still raise these children in partnership with their father. Do not run, and do not doubt yourself. Do not raise your children in hate and fear. Do not lose yourself in your own pain and fear. Be strong and be present. Speak so you are heard. Listen with compassion. Divorce doesn't excuse your partnership as parents. The father is accountable for how he raises his children, just as you are accountable for your part."* She handed me the carved dirt initials. *"I put these children in your care. Pray to me every day as I have taught you. I will help you. Be honest and accurate. Don't pray to appease me; pray to show me your heart so that I may see you, love you, and heal you. I will be with you and you will be with me."*

Our time together ended just as quickly as it had started. My eyes flew open as if I hadn't been asleep. I could still feel her and I believed every word she had said. I felt lighter, and truly grateful.

I had secretly wished for help with straightening out my ex-husband in order to make my life easier. She had told me straight up to work with what I had and to do the best I could. She encouraged me to be strong, find my courage, and speak up. She made it clear to me I wasn't alone, and it was my own fault if I clung to the belief that I was. She called me out, and she brought me healing, nurturing love.

I eventually talked to my uncle, a Marianist Priest. He listened with sincere interest

 Divine Love Affair

to my story. He explained that I had experienced an apparition. The red hill told him it was Our Lady of Guadalupe who was helping me. He sent me a book filled with pictures and the story of Our Lady of Guadalupe. I immediately recognized the red hill and the landscape of the area we had walked together in my vision. I felt stunned and humbled by this validation. ♡

Consider This ♡ What would your prayer be, if you prayed as the Lady had instructed me to? Spend some quiet time, visualize your sacred place, and open your heart to the Divine. Allow yourself to pray from your deepest, most secret place inside. Let yourself express clearly and accurately what is within you. Trust that you are being heard. Let your words of prayer lighten your heart as you pray in your sacred place.

Sit quietly for a moment once you've finished your prayer. Place your hands on your heart and affirm that you are heard and that you are healed. You are loved just as you are. ♡

Accessing the Akashic Wisdom through Ritual Prayer

Meditation and prayer—quiet contemplation—can elevate us into a different state of awareness. Deep creative efforts, listening to music, or looking at art or nature can also elevate us into a different state of awareness. It's what we often call "being in the zone" or "following the flow". Or we may call it "Divine inspiration" or listening to our "muse". Sometimes we can receive a message, intervention, or an "intuitive download" that is way beyond our current life's reality.

Along this same idea, we are able to access the loving, healing presence of the Akashic energy through intuition and emotions. The Akashic vibratory energy also contains healing properties. Relaxing your thoughts, opening your heart with the intent of calming your body, is the formula for opening up to this higher consciousness of healing and love from the Universal Mind; the Akashic Field of energy.

We often need a boost to get to that creative place. At first, a habit needs to be set in place. Just like learning to play an instrument, when we are beginners we need to learn *how* to play, and then we need to practice until it becomes second nature. Once it becomes second nature, that's when the magic happens. The Akashic Prayer can be the vehicle to help you build a magical habit.

I had prayed long and hard, for many years, before my Beautiful Lady spoke to me. Were my prayers wasted; did they go unanswered? No, of course not; I had been building up the capacity to trust, desire connection, and then finally let go enough to hear Spirit answer. The ritual praying kept me in a sacred space and helped me remember where I was going, even when I felt so very lost.

Ritually designed prayer can be like poetry—words set to rhythm that help us remember to enter into a sacred place in our minds, and also in our intent. Words said in prayer can calm us. This type of prayer may even help us drop our guard to the Divine, so that we're more apt to open our hearts and share what is hidden deepest within.

When a prayer is shared by many people, such as the *Our Father,* or some of the ancient Jewish blessings and Buddhist mantras, the power of the prayer is multiplied. The Divine hears our every prayer, just as our souls always hear us. Remember—thought precedes reality—meaning we create in our lives what we focus on. When we come together in prayer, a creative energy builds between us that can be very powerful. Prayer can open doors, effect healing, and bring people together. Through shared prayer we enter into a *One Mind* connection with our souls, our higher power, and the one conscious mind.

The personal, heartfelt, expressive prayer, and the historical, traditional, ritual prayer, can both be powerful. The most important ingredient in any prayer is your presence as you say it.

The Akashic Journey Prayer

The following prayer is a ritual prayer done with purpose and presence in order to enter the Akashic Records for yourself or another person. The more often you repeat this prayer, the stronger your connection into the Akashic Records will be.

This is also the instructions for creating your own prayer to access the Akashic Energy flow and Records.

This chapter contains the prayer that I use, which you can borrow until you have created your own prayer of connection. Using your own language to communicate with the Divine is a process of growth and maturity towards your relationship with Spirit. This is YOUR Journey. Be your authentic self as you explore the Akashic Records and your soul. An honest open heart is the most powerful way to enter into the Records.

This prayer is broken down into an opening, the offering of a request, setting an intention, and a closing. Each part of this prayer has an energetic purpose. Once you understand and connect with this flow of energy, your journey to the Akashic Field will happen with grace and ease.

What you give is what you get: if at any time, in your mind, body, or emotional self, you disrespect the flow or use of this prayer, it will be difficult to connect. It is essential to be fully present in your prayer and this work for the flow of the Akashic Energy to be clearly received. The wisdom, grace, and healing of the Akashic Energy and their Records within can only be offered to you when you are available.

The first four parts to this prayer are the opening and offering, request and intention for the work. The closing contains a thank you and a resealing of the Records. Each part is an important component to the prayer.

The Opening

The first section of the prayer is about identifying who, what, and where you wish to connect. This important element recognizes the Divine Creator, the energy of love that is the source of all creation. This part also identifies how you are in relationship to the Divine: Your unconditional love fills me and surrounds me.

> *I call upon Mother, Father, God, Creator of all that is*
>
> *And the Akashic Energy of Compassion*
>
> *This Divine unconditional love fills me (us) and*
>
> *Surrounds me (us) in a sphere of protection and*
>
> *Guidance that sustains me (us) throughout my (our) life*
>
> *I acknowledge that this presence of love is the source of all creation*

Try This ♡ To understand the energetic power in the words of this prayer, stand with your hands by your side. Visualize a chakra or power center eighteen inches to three feet below your feet. Imagine you have energy tendrils, like roots, connecting you to this power center. Imagine this power center is connected to the minerals and crystals of the earth. These are the building blocks you are created from. Say Mother with an inward breath and imagine this breath is drawing that power up into your heart. Visualize the earth's power filling your heart.

Next, visualize two power centers above your head, filled with the light of the universe. This light pulses down through your crown chakra (top of your head) in time with the beating of your heart. Visualize your crown chakra opening and say Father as you breathe in—visualize the light of the universe coming from above, through your chakras and filling your heart— feel the loving mother and father energies blending together.

As you say, God, Creator of all that is, imagine your heart center expanding around you until you're sitting in the middle of your heart's energy.

As you follow with, and the Akashic Energy of compassion, imagine your expanding heart center filled beyond capacity with love.

Notice how you feel. ♡

When you're reading for someone besides yourself, use the word us, as you will be saying this prayer out loud. It's key to include the other person in this prayer. Your heart-filled energy or aura will surround and encompass the sitter. Your auric energies will blend with theirs to read their Records for the highest and best of all. Use your auric energy; not your personal energy essence. Do you know the difference?

The Offering

The second section of the prayer is the reciprocity back to Spirit. It is the statement of *I am present.* We must give and take to "seal the deal" or complete the connection with Spirit. Reciprocity with a higher power is an aspect of personal responsibility in a spiritual practice. The best gift we can offer to Spirit is an open heart and a willingness to commune, talk to, and be with our creator. We are loved and held in high esteem. When we show up in our requests, we are embraced in joy and love. It's not the olden days of sacrifice anymore. This is about our personal presence and power coming of age in connection to the Divine Creator.

> *I come to you with an open heart*
>
> *Filled with love and gratitude for all I receive*
>
> *I am fully present in this moment*

The Request

The third section of the prayer is asking for the connection. We MUST ask for connection in all communication to Spirit; this is a free-will human experience and we need to ask and be given permission for a connection. With that said, we also need permission to open the Records of anyone we read for. This is a reminder that from Spirit, all is love. Use this part of the prayer to affirm and build trust and faith.

> *Open the Akasha that I may enter*
>
> *Align me with the guides of the Akasha*

  Divine Love Affair

Open my eye, ears, and heart to see, hear, and understand

The council of angels, masters, teachers and loved ones of the Akasha

That I may communicate the wisdom of the Akasha and its Records

The Intention for the Work

This is the time to put your reason for opening the Records into words. Take time before you open your Records to consider what you want to do. This intention part of the prayer invokes the power of three. In sacred ritual, repeating an intention three time anchors the request into manifestation.

Intentions for Reading for Yourself and Others

In this part, you will say your name (or the name of whoever you're reading for) three times. For an extra punch, you can repeat this part two more times quietly to yourself.

Open now, The Akashic Records of (name)

Allow me to see the Soul and Divinity of (name)

That I may share clearly the messages and healing the Akasha

And its guides have for (name)

The following prayers of intention should each be repeated three times:

Prayer of Intention for Healing

Fill my body, emotions, and spirit with healing energy as I sit in this open state of love. Guide me, teach me, and fill me with your healing essence.

Prayer of Intention for Creativity

Inspire my spirit, body, mind, and emotions to create a solution to my desires. Show me, teach me, and align me with the highest and best possibilities as I do my work.

Prayer of Intention for Comfort

Hold me close as I journey through this pain. Teach me grace and comfort in my grief. I open my heart trusting the safely of your healing power.

Once your intention is spoken aloud, be sure to proclaim, "The Records are now open!"

The Closing Prayer

This part of the prayer brings the connection to a close. If you don't remember to close the session before moving your focus elsewhere, the connection will time-out on its own. When reading for someone else, it's in your best interest (and theirs) to disconnect your energy fields and purposefully end the session; both of you need to consciously return to yourselves. I recommend ending this prayer session with the line, *"The Akashic Healing Energy continues on."*

This assures both you and the sitter that behind the scenes, the energy work will continue. This line reminds us that there is a continuation of love and healing from Spirit, even when our minds are elsewhere.

With deepest gratitude

I thank Mother, Father, God, Creator of all that is

The masters, teachers, and loved ones

And the Akashic Energy of compassion

For their generosity, love, and guidance

I give you back to yourself and I bring myself back to me

This session and the Akashic Records are now closed

The Akashic Healing Energy continues on

So be it and so it is.

Amen

The Akashic Journey Prayer in Full

I call upon Mother, Father, God, Creator of all that is
And the Akashic Energy of Compassion
This Divine unconditional love fills me (us) and
Surrounds me (us) in a sphere of protection and
Guidance that sustains me (us) throughout my (our) life
I acknowledge that this presence of love is the source of all creation

I come to you with an open heart
Filled with love and gratitude for all I receive
I am fully present in this moment

Open the Akasha that I may enter
Align me with the guides of the Akasha
Open my eye, ears, and heart to see, hear, and understand
The council of Angels, masters, teachers and loved ones of the Akasha
That I may communicate the wisdom of the Akasha and its Records

Open now, The Akashic Records of (name)
Allow me to see the Soul and Divinity of (name)
That I may share clearly the messages and healing the Akasha
And its guides have for (name)

The records are now open

Closing

With deepest gratitude
I thank Mother, Father, God, Creator of all that is
The Angels, masters, teachers, loved ones
And the Akashic Energy of compassion
For their generosity, love, and guidance

I give you back to yourself and I bring myself back to me
This session and the Akashic Records are now closed
The Akashic Healing Energy continues on
So be it and so it is.
Amen.

Asking Questions While in the Records

Once you have opened you Records, the next step is to clearly state your query to the listening energy. When you're working alone, you can start to build your list of questions by opening your Records and, with a notebook or sheet of paper in front of you, begin writing what is on your mind and in your heart. Your Akashic Records know you and have been recording you since before you were born; be brave and inspired with your questioning.

When reading yours or another's (called a sitter) Akashic records, establish the intentions before opening the Records. This is different than a psychic or tarot reading, where the reader alone establishes the intent. In an Akashic reading, it's important that both the reader and the sitter are on the same page. Once the Records of the sitter are open, the sitter can then repeat and ask their question or state the intention for the reading. The reader can then proceed. These readings are best dome as one-on-one readings. Group readings can certainly be done, but not until you're a more advanced reader.

Exercise 3

Go Ahead and Ask

Set up: Return to the quiet space you created earlier where you won't be interrupted.

Time: 10 -20 minutes

You will need:

- your journal

- pen or pencil

- Your Akashic prayer

Before you open your Records ask yourself, *"What is Divine Love in my life? How do I experience it?"* Review your life and write down some notes.

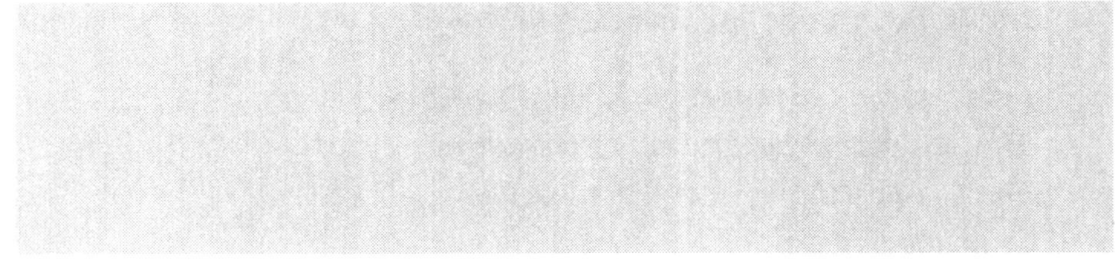

Now open your Records and ask the same question, "What is Divine Love in my life? How do I experience it?" Relax and allow yourself to hear the information, rather than thinking about the answer. Don't edit yourself: jot down whatever you sense.

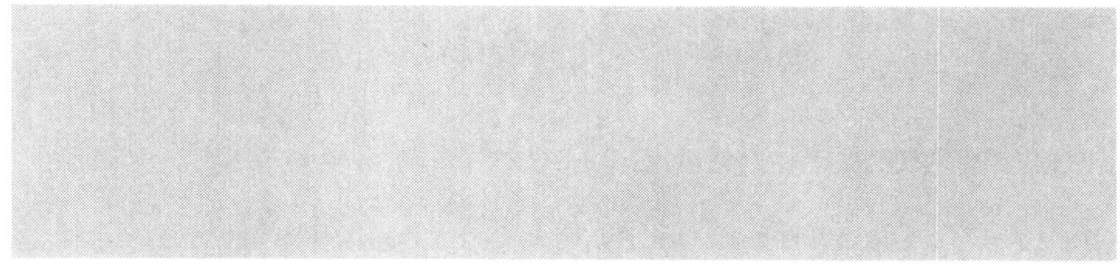

Is there a difference in the information?

Try this with a couple of different kinds of questions from your notebook.

Get into the habit of opening to the Akashic Energy and its Records once a day just to ask questions. Describe what you are feeling and thinking.

What are your biggest challenges? Write them down. Develop them into questions to ask your angels, guides, masters, and teachers as you work with your Akashic Records.

Here is a list of questions that may help you get different kinds of information than the questions you most commonly return to time and time again. Intersperse these with the questions that first spring to mind!

- How can I (and how do I) receive God's love?
- How do I block God's love for me?
- What are my soul's gifts in this life? How can I open to receive these gifts?
- What are my greatest gifts as seen by my soul in the Records?
- What is the best path for me to take right now in order to develop these gifts?
- How can I best access and nourish my spiritual self?
- How can I bring my spiritual self and soul into my daily life?
- How can I live a joyful life?
- What are roadblocks in my life that keep me from being happy?
- How can I transform my roadblocks?

- What do I need to know and do to have a happier and balanced life physically, mentally, and emotionally?

- How can I discover what my purpose is?

- How can I joyfully manifest living my life's purpose?

Receiving Information From the Records

Once you've asked your questions, the next step is to quiet your mind and receive the information and energy in whatever form it is presented to you from the Akasha.

Writing is a clear and helpful tool to use when first learning to hear and receive information from the Akashic Records and your Akashic team. At some point during your writing as you ask your questions, shift your thoughts and open your heart to really hear what you are saying. Begin listening for the new voice that may be developing as you write.

As soon as you sense something changing, write it down. Don't edit. Let yourself sketch out images, if you feel drawn to that. Don't try to understand. Simply go with it for as long as you can. When the energy fades and you feel the session is done, close your Records.

Try to stay in this mode until you've written a few pages; give yourself at least 20 minutes. As you return to this exercise on a regular consistent basis, you will start to see your progress.

You can certainly do this in a meditative state with great results as well. Having a partner to read with is helpful. You can say what is coming into your senses without editing it, with a witness to hear you and respond! At first you may feel disjointed with your words. Trust what's coming through you. As you speak aloud what you're receiving, whether you're writing it down yourself or relying on a partner, the flow of words and content will build. Practice will help a lot.

When working alone, writing will help make this process a bit more concrete. The thoughts and sensations you receive and don't understand may make sense down the road after a few more sessions. Having your communications written down will help you later when you return to look them over.

How you receive information depends on you and your particular way of perceiving things in your regular life. If you are a visual perceiver, you may

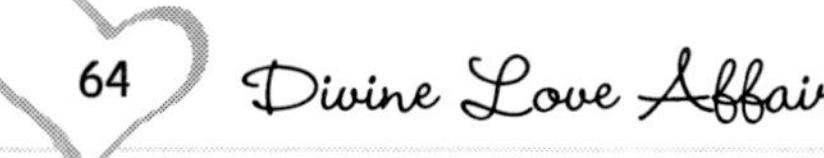

see images, as if in a daydream. If you are auditory, you may hum a tune or remember a song that contains a message. You may hear an inner voice speaking to you. Or you may suddenly know something that wasn't known to you before.

There are five basic ways we can experience spiritual communication. There are probably more, but the five *claires* (a French word meaning clear) are the most prevalent. You probably have bits of these extra sensory gifts already. As you work with the Records and communicating with Spirit, these gifts will begin to develop more fully. Observe yourself and how you receive (or prefer to receive) information throughout your day. Do you have to see it? If so, you may have a tendency toward *clairvoyance*. Do you often ask people to repeat themselves so you can hear it one more time? If this is the case, you may be *clairaudient*. Do you have to think things over before you can feel that you really understand something? That would suggest you may be *claircognizant*. Or do you have to feel an experience in order to fully appreciate what it's about? If this is your style, you could have a tendency for *clairsentience*. Noticing your tendencies can be clues as to which gifts you will develop naturally.

Clairvoyance is based in your third eye (above and between your eyes), and is the ability to visualize and receive information as an extrasensory perception. We constantly receive information as vibration through our bellies. This is a primal response; very much a part of our lizard brain. The vibration travels up to the heart and becomes language based. The heart then sends its pulses to our brain. Once in the brain, the third eye begins to envision the messages of the heart. I was taught this when I studied Andean shamanism. I often experience this vibration at the start-of a daydream. If this happens to you, allow the dream to unfold; don't analyze or think too hard about it.

Clairaudience is the ability to hear Spirit and receive extra sensory information through the sense of hearing. The sound you hear is usually internal, though rarely is actually coming from outside oneself. This inner hearing can manifest as a voice, a song, orchestral music, or just ringing in the ears.

Claircognizance is a sense of knowing something without having been given any reason to know it. You simply KNOW. This can be a challenging form of Spirit communication because your knowing may not match your logical thinking. As I suggested in clairvoyance, don't over-think things. Pay attention. You can test out your knowing by asking for the information to be presented to you synchronistic ally in other forms. I often have a precognition that gives me a heads-up signal. Then I start paying more attention to the signs and symbols I'm receiving to complete the message I am meant to get.

Clairsentience is a full body sense, in which you receive information through emotions and physical sensations. People most commonly sense an emotion around an issue or other person; some can even feel the energy and emotion left behind. Strong empaths can feel leftover vibrations, and can often describe what took place in a room before they enter it. As a medium, I often feel how someone died by the sensations I feel in my body; that is clairsentience.

Clairgustance (tasting)/ **Clairalience** (smelling) are the abilities to smell and taste in an extrasensory way. I've had the experience of tasting what my kids or my husband are eating even though I'm miles away. The smell of cigar smoke or a specific perfume often lets us know a loved one is close by.

Clairnunciate, a brand new term (I'm not sure of its origin), is the gift of communication from Spirit. This gift seems to be a combination of a few of the claires, combined with the ability to clearly communicate a concept and a teaching directly from Spirit. The reader/speaker connects in a special way with Spirit and begins to speak cohesively on topics they know very little about. This is often called channeling, but I feel clairnunciate is a more accurate term. When the reader is in the Akashic Records, he or she may find unfamiliar thoughts and ideas rolling off their tongues quickly and concisely, but the sitter completely understands what they are saying.

Exercise 4

Go Ahead, Ask Again and Keep Asking

Set up: Return to your quiet space where you won't be interrupted.

Time: 10 -20 minutes

You will need:

- Your journal and pen or pencil
- Your Akashic prayer

Open your records and ask, *"How do I receive information clearly from the Akashic Records? What are my gifts?"* Record what you "get" in your journal.

How Do You Know the Guidance is really from the Records and Not Just Your Mind?

As you venture into your (or another's) Records, continue to ask for clarity. Be aware of how you receive information, and trust the thoughts and images or feelings coming into your awareness. Don't edit or hold back. *DO* admit to whoever you are reading for that you're a novice reader. Choose people in your life who will understand this and are willing to work with you. You'll need some practice as you learn to differentiate the Akashic voice from your own.

At first you may feel that your words are disjointed as you share what you're receiving. Whether you are writing the messages down or speaking them aloud as you receive them, you will slowly begin to recognize the energy behind the messages. Your personal energy can be nervous, insistent, doubtful, or even willful. The energy, or senses, behind the messages from the Akasha are softer and can build up slowly as you engage with the Records. As you connect with, or link into this energy, a sense of well-being may come over you. Some people express getting goose bumps when connecting with Spirit; that's their validation, or signal, that they're with Spirit. I feel a sense that things have clicked into place; that I've made a connection to the flow of energy that then converts into a flow of words.

You will develop a personal code and a set of private symbols as you continue to work with the Akashic Energy. Trust that the potential to connect is always there. While you're a beginner, once the reading is done discuss the reading with the sitter to verify the information they received in their readings. You're not looking for approval; you're looking to find out when you were close to Spirit, and when you dropped into your own mind. You may find you were giving advice rather staying in the energy of the Records. You know you are in the Records when your message is the last thing you would have ever thought of saying.

What is your "Tell" when you are in the Akashic Records?

Learn to recognize your personal signs that let you know when you are in. Here are some of the more common signs you may experience:

- Tears welling up in your eyes and heart as you connect to a higher power

- Feel goose bumps or shivers

- Feeling a sense of relief and well-being

- Feeling the presence of a loving being

- Becoming aware of images or thoughts that are unique from any you've experienced before

- Words forming in your mind and flowing from your tongue that are only understood by your sitter

- Feeling a sensation of be present to profound truth

- Feeling a gentle resonance that you're moving toward something you know to be true

- Experiencing an inner *knowing* that you have no question is truth

If you are unsure of what you're "receiving", continue to ask for clarification and confirmation. Keep an open dialogue going, asking for deeper understanding. Ask, and ask again, then be still and listen with your entire being.

Working with Symbols

During a reading, you may receive symbols from Spirit as part of the message. There are two levels of symbols:

The first level is when you receive symbols that *you* understand, based on your life experiences. You may be reminded of something you've seen or done in order to clarify a part of the message you're receiving. That's just fine. It's a good idea to work with the Akashic Energy and your guide in order to build a library of symbols that you understand. For instance, car keys could be about taking a trip, whereas a map might mean planning a trip.

Consider This ♡ What are some symbols in your life? What does a rainbow mean to you? What about a dollar bill, or a teddy bear? Write a few more that come to your mind right away. Keep a record of your symbols. ♡

The second level symbols are decipherable to the sitter alone; you may not know what they mean at all. Describe the symbol or picture you're seeing in your mind's eye to your sitter. Help them to discover what it means to them. Don't suggest any particular meaning; it's up to your sitter to decide what it means to them. Often, an Akashic reading is about empowering and encouraging your sitter to understand and take ownership of their spiritual path. Creating or building personal symbols within the Akashic records can be a powerful experience for your sitter.

  *Divine Love Affair*

Which Akashic Records are Open to You

You are free to open your Records at any time, in any place. You may only open another's Records, however, with their permission. Children's and pet's records are opened through their parents or owner's Records. For you to read a person's Record they must be a conscious, legal adult and fully able to understand what the reading is about. They must be able to give you permission; comatose folks can't give you permission. You can open the Records of the caretaker of the comatose person. A young child isn't in a position to give you permission, but you can read then through the Records of their parents or legal guardians. You can open the Records of property you own, including the land and governing structures of the country you're a citizen of. One of my favorite readings is to open the Akashic Records of the United States on the 4th of July.

Using Tarot and Divination Cards in the Akashic Records

It's important that you do many readings in order to establish yourself in the Records before introducing another discipline into your practice. A good rule of thumb is to practice for thirty days before adding anything new. After establishing a clear connection to the Akashic Records, you may want to work with divination or oracle cards. This will not be a typical tarot reading.

Open the Akashic Records of your sitter, and verify for yourself that you are in their Records. Set the intention of the reading and pick a card. Everything is energy; we are energy, the cards are energy, and all energy is connected. As you choose the card, know and trust you are choosing the correct card. As you read the image and/or words, allow the Akashic Energy to give you the interpretation of the card for your sitter. Some amazing readings can be done with just one card!

In the next chapter, we'll explore how to create healing sacred space in the Akashic Energy. You'll learn to use your access to the Akashic to create Divine nurturing and healing love. An important part of your Akashic journey is self-care and nurturing. When you feel loved and cared for in the Akashic Energy, you will be more likely to return to it again and again. In order to establish and maintain a high level energetic connection to the Divine, you must establish a personal healing journey. You need to build your strength and spiritual capacity in order to do this amazing work.

Chapter 5

Creating Sacred, Personal Healing in the Akasha

Years ago I created a rich inner space I could retreat to; my sacred space. I would visualize myself in that beautiful landscape when I needed to get away. Through focused breathing I could calm my racing mind and sit in a sense of peaceful calm. Once in that calm, thoughts and worries could creep in, and I would thank them and let them go. At least that was the idea. Some days I had better results with this than others. Sometimes I was able to calmly let thoughts and feelings go; other times I had to firmly send them packing; still other times they would sneak in and take hold without me even realizing it. I would find myself twisting my hair around my fingers, a worry knot in my forehead, and a stomachache taking hold. There were times when I simply threw in the towel with an *'I just can't do this'* snort.

At one point, I had an epiphany. I learned a heart-centering meditation, with the main idea being that my heart, which is the center of my universe, was also the center of *THE* universe, following the spiritual law, *"As above, so below."* What's true in the macrocosm is also true in the microcosm. The Akashic energy of God's love that fills the universe also began to fill my heart. I loved this meditation, and I was able to do it with ease. Because I liked the visual component of the sacred space meditation, I decided to combine them. I pictured my beautiful landscape in the center of my heart and anchored it with my breath.

With each in breath, I imagined expanding my energetic heart encompassing my entire self and my sacred visualization. My landscape unfolded its magnificence with each breath I took. With each out breath, I released any pent-up energy I felt. I opened the center of my heart by visualizing that I was opening a crystal door to the heart of the universe. I invited the loving energy in along with my guides and angels to fill my heart space. I continued to breathe in and out slowly and with purpose until I felt the connection *click* into place. That *click* for me is a sense of deep physical and mental relaxation. As the universal energy expanded into my heart, I observed my sacred space continue to unfold. At times the images, colors, and textures would take on a life of their own as I opened to the universal life force and love. Other times, I experienced no visuals or sensations and simply focused on maintaining my relaxed breathing.

Then, as *THEY* crept in (the most insistent worries I was currently battling with), I would guide them into the center of my heart with my breath. Each breath in moved the energies into my heart; each breath out released resistance. I was mindful to keep my heart open, the heart of the universe, where all things are possible. Instead of repressing my thoughts, I allowed them to expand as far as they could. I went into an observer frame of mind and watched my worry expand. The key piece here is that I became an observer of this energy, not a participant. I was working with energy in the meditation, and energy is malleable.

I saw the energy change and transform into something new. Visually and symbolically, my worry grew wings, turned white, and began to fly in a beautiful dance. I had given my thoughts and emotions space to expand, to express   themselves. At first I cringed, thinking I would be overcome with emotion as they expanded. But instead of being overwhelmed, I felt freedom.

What I realized then is that I needed to work with my *whole* self in meditation. My conscious/unconscious selves would not let me block my emotions out with mental peace and calm; I had to work the *whole* me, worries and all. This meditation technique helped me feel safer and stronger within myself. I trusted myself more. I also discovered that I had more self-confidence in the outer, *real* world as I listened to myself in my sacred space.

When we don't address our feelings, we don't hear the messages they have for us. These feeling are energy left to languish. The disowned thoughts and feelings claim a kind of consciousness of their own. They become resolved to get the message to us at all costs, especially if they feel it's a survival message that we *HAVE* to hear. The heart meditation allowed me to safely face these difficult emotions and thoughts in a safe and sacred space.

Teaching Someone Else My Secret Sauce

Years later, while working with students, Katelyn began studying with me. She took a series of private session to learn to read the Akashic records. She wanted to be able to enhance her work as an intuitive reader. She was a compassionate, empathetic woman with a high level of intuition, but something just wasn't *flowing* for her. She couldn't get past an invisible barrier in order to trust what she was receiving intuitively. This barrier was causing her readings to be clumsy and hesitant, even though her information was spot on. As we worked in the records, I got the nudge that something in her life was bothering her, and she was reluctant to tell me. I began to intuit her home dynamics. She had young children, a demanding life. But that wasn't the exact source of her trust issue. A heavy energy was hanging over her life that she couldn't resolve. In fact, this heaviness was draining her.

I resonated with her struggle. When I opened her records and asked what to do, I felt guided to share my sacred space process with her. Together, in a guided meditation, we opened her Akashic records and healing energy so she could create a visual space that she could enter into during meditations. This became an etheric space, located in the center of her heart, where she felt comfortable and safe. Then together, as I guided her, she brought in her raw emotions and began to expand them. As her anxieties and fears expanded in her heart, she saw the other sides of what her emotions were telling her. Katelyn began to realize that she had more ability and skills than she originally thought she had. She began to trust herself to develop her inner talents and abilities.

Very reluctantly, very slowly, she allowed me to see her present life. She began to sort out what was going on with her invisible barrier. Two very important issues began to surface. She was afraid of her husband to the point she couldn't even talk about him. She did not have the skills to help herself out of this fear. Very slowly, through our sessions, she began to explore her emotions, as well as the inner treasure trove of skills that her emotions were revealing to her. She began to do this practice on her own, and expressed her relief at being able to do this kind of work. She trusted what she was experiencing in her meditations. She said she felt more confidence in herself as a person and as a young mother. She shared that she was taking more deliberate steps to express herself in her marriage. In this case, as she overcame the fears that originated both in her childhood and past lives, she found her husband to be receptive and happy to listen to her. Her life and her readings grew by leaps and bounds once she began to work with this sacred meditation on a daily basis. ♡

Creating Sacred Healing Space for Yourself

A foundational skill for your spiritual practice (and daily life) is knowing how to create and then navigate in and out of an inner place of peace and calm; a place where you can surrender the struggles of the day and relax. This inner sanctuary can be a source of inner power; the generator that recharges you and gives you a sense that life is safe; that everything is going to be okay. The sacred space and healing meditation is a two-part process.

The first part is to create a place within your heart that is joyful, recognizable, and safe. This is an inner visualization that brings you a sense of peace and calm. This space can be created in many ways.

When we're at peace and feel calm, our brain waves begin to shift to alpha waves, a higher, more creative vibration. As you embark on your journey of deep healing, start by creating an inner space that feels safe. What you choose to put in your inner landscape is often a clue to where your thoughts and emotions are in that moment. As you focus more deeply on your inner heart space, know that things can change; objects may show up that surprise you. That's when you know your unconscious self, your higher conscious mind, and your inner spirit have joined in your heart center. And that's a good thing.

How you set the scene of your own sacred space can vary. Wiccan tradition suggests using the icon of a tree, *The Tree of Life,* to focus on, allowing yourself to sink into the roots of the tree or to rise up the trunk into its branches. Some folks use landscape images, like the ocean or a garden filled with flowers, as their safe, rejuvenating place. Others build beautiful homes with luscious living spaces that look like they're straight out of the Architectural Digest. What images or landscapes in your life elicit peace and calm for you?

My happy zone is visualizing images that trigger peace and calm; that's how my brain works. Your brain may work entirely differently. It may prefer words, sounds, colors, or even simple sensations. You can build your space with memories. Katelyn built her space with her white cat and her feelings of love for her cat. Some of the most powerful meditations start from *nothing.* I often hear students say, *"I don't see or feel anything."* That's fine; nothing is actually something.

Try This ♡ Open your Akashic records with prayer. Feel into the sounds and sensation of your heart. Relax and imagine a happy place that is just right for you. Ask yourself, *"What relaxes me and brings on a sense of well-being and calm?"* ♡

The second part of this healing practice is to open your heart to the heart of the universe, the Akashic healing love. Once that intention is set, shift your frame of mind to that of an observer. Put your analyzing mind aside and simply watch.

Now it's time to invite your emotions or personal struggles into your sacred space with your breath. Use your in breath to encourage expansion, use your exhale to release pent up energy.

As these energies reveal themselves in the calmness of your sacred heart, encourage them to expand; let them reveal every detail they have to show you. They will expand to a higher vibration. Every emotion and thought is a vibration. And every vibration has a higher octave of healing and awareness. By bringing your emotions to your sacred space, you're giving them the chance to transform. As they transform, they'll reveal their *gifts* to you.

Try This ♡ Open your Akashic records with prayer. Feel into your worries and concerns. Ask yourself *"What is stressing me out and distracting me?"* ♡

The Akashic Sacred Space Heart Meditation

Set up: A quiet space where you won't be interrupted.

Time: 20 -30 minutes

You will need:

- your journal
- pen or pencil

Place pen and journal next to you, making sure they are easily accessible.

Start by sitting straight up, with your feet on the floor and your hands in an open, receiving position. Make yourself comfortable so that discomfort doesn't distract you.

Open to the Mother, Father, God, Creator of All, and the Akashic field of energy with your prayer. Consider the Akashic field of love and creation as part of your peaceful universe.

Take three deep breaths, inhaling through your nose and holding for a count of three, and then gently and deeply exhale through your mouth. Your first breath is to relax your body. Your second breath is to soften your mind and drop your focus into your heart. Your third breath is to bring you fully into the present moment, releasing the last bit of distractions from your mind.

Relax your breathing to a natural pace. Breathe deeply in, hold and exhale deeply out, and hold. Repeat this breathing pattern until you are breathing deeply and evenly. When you breathe in a slow and rhythmic way, you're telling your physical, mental, and emotional bodies that all is well. You're now free to be completely in the present moment.

Focus on your mind and let it soften. Drop your awareness into your heart center.

Begin to create a sacred, safe, personal space in the center of your heart. Breathe golden light into your heart and imagine this golden light expanding your heart's energy center with each breath, until you're sitting in the middle of your own heart's space.

Now imagine a crystal door in the center of your heart. This door leads to the heart of the universe and the unconditional love of the Creator. Open this door and invite in the energy of the unconditional love of the Akasha. Invite your teachers, guides, and angels to be with you.

Allow your heart to open to receive the Heart of the Akasha, the Heart of the Divine.

We will now create the setting of your sacred, healing space.

Imagine you're standing in the center of your heart, at the crystal door that's open to the universe of unconditional love. There's a path for you to step onto that will lead you to your sacred room.

Now imagine that you're walking on a long pathway, with woods on one side and the ocean on the other. The path winds up a steep incline. Take each step deliberately and carefully as you follow the path. With each step you take, count down from thirteen to one. When you reach one, imagine that in front of you is the entrance to your sacred space. Walk through the entrance and begin to imagine the perfect environment, made just for you.

Start counting back, thirteen, twelve, eleven, and with each step, relax and feel the peacefulness of this journey. Continue counting, ten, nine, eight . . . you're becoming more relaxed and aware of the path that you're walking on. You may smell the ocean or feel a breeze through the trees along your path. Seven, six, five . . . you're relaxed and feel at peace with your journey. You may even hear some sounds. You easily observe the surroundings on your path. Four, three, two . . . you're relaxed and feel you are in familiar surroundings that comfort you. You feel a sense of well-being throughout your body and mind.

And one . . . You're standing at the gateway to your sacred space. This space is exactly as you've imagined it, and feels just right.

Allow your imagination to fill this space with everything you want and need. Take time to create your perfect setting.

Bless this space with a connection to the sacred elements of your world.

Create a symbol for air. What does air mean to you?
How does air feel?

Create a symbol for fire. What does fire mean to you?
How does fire feel?

Create a symbol for water. What does water mean to you?
How does water feel?

Create a symbol for earth. What does earth mean to you?
How does earth feel?

Create a symbol for metal. What does metal mean to you?
How does metal feel?

Next, make a comfortable place in your inner space to sit, observe, and pray. You may want to create room for a guest to join you.

Observe the colors around you. How do you feel in this space? What do you need here to relax and be calm?

Continue to breathe slowly and deeply. Allow this space to continue to feel calm and relaxed.

If you're having trouble creating your space at this time, instead pick a color and focus on it. Breathe and relax. All is well. You are connected to the Divine through your intent. You are surrounded by love.

Pause for a few minutes to rest in your space.

When you feel ready, begin returning to your conscious self. Slowly walk to the gateway and step onto your path. As you begin walking back to full consciousness, count up from one to ten. When you reach ten, tap your feet several times, roll your shoulders and open your eyes.

Pick up paper and pen and make some notes about your experience.

Journal While Iin Your Records ♡ What is your sacred healing space like? After you journey to and create your sacred, heart-centered space, describe it in detail in your journal. ♡

Say your closing prayer.

Return to this space as often as you can to build on it. Each time you return, notice what's new in your space. Observe how you feel. Adjust your breathing and posture to create the perfect calm for yourself. Be sure to open with a prayer, and then end your session with a closing prayer.

Meditation 2 part two

The Akashic Sacred Space Healing Heart Meditation

Set up: A quiet space where you won't be interrupted.

Time: 20 -30 minutes

You will need:

- your journal
- pen or pencil
- your Akashic prayer

 Divine Love Affair

Place pen and journal next to you, making sure they are easily accessible.

Start by sitting straight up, with your feet on the floor and your hands in an open, receiving position. Make yourself comfortable so that discomfort doesn't distract you.

Open to the Mother, Father, God, Creator of All, and the Akashic field of energy with your prayer. Now it's time to gather up your heavy thoughts, worries, and situations in life you struggle with.

Take three deep breaths, inhaling through your nose and holding for a count of three, and then gently and deeply exhale through your mouth. Your first breath is to relax your body. Your second breath is to soften your mind and drop your focus into your heart. Your third breath is to bring you fully into the present moment, releasing the distractions in your mind.

Relax your breathing to a natural pace. Breathe deeply in, hold and exhale deeply out, and hold. Repeat this breathing pattern until you are breathing deeply and evenly. When you breathe in a slow and rhythmic way, you're telling your physical, mental, and emotional bodies that all is well. You're now free to be completely in the present moment.

Focus on your mind and let it soften. Drop your awareness into your heart.

Since your Akashic records can see all of your thoughts and experiences, ask to be led to the issue that is appropriate for you to work on right now. *Don't pick the biggest thing in your life for your first journey; you're still learning and need to master this before you jump into the deep end.* Once you identify what you're going to work on, observe your thoughts, issues, or feelings. Feel the textures, run the story through your mind. Feel where this issue lives in your body. Feel all that you can. Allow it to package itself up in a word, color, or symbol so that when you see it, you'll know what it represents.

Breathe golden light into your heart and imagine this golden light expanding your heart's energy center with each breath until you're sitting in the middle of your own heart's space.

Now imagine a crystal door in the center of your heart. This door leads to the heart of the universe and the unconditional love of the Creator. Open this door and invite in the energy of the unconditional love of the Akasha. Invite your teachers, guides, and angels to be with you.

Allow your heart to open to receive the Heart of the Akasha, the Heart of the Divine, and return to your sacred healing space. Shift into your observer mind.

Imagine that you can pick up your issue or problem with your breath. Breathe it into the center of your heart—the space of love—your sacred space. Breathe this issue into your sacred heart space, allowing it to expand. Breathe out all that you don't need in this moment.

Breathe in to hold the package within your heart, breathe out awareness that this issue is transforming. As you continue to breathe, observe how this package is changing and transforming.

Breathe out all that no longer serves you.

Continue to breathe as long as you need to. Use your exhale to release pent-up, emotional energy. Allow expansion with each exhale.

As you continue to breathe this issue into the center of your heart, affirm that you're breathing into the center of Divine Love.

Affrim: *I love myself, and God loves me more than I can ever know. I am in the presence of love.*

As you breathe in, allow this issue to spread and expand and transform into a higher form. Breathe out love and new understanding, and allow this transformed energy to fill you as it expands into its higher form. Ask yourself, *"What do I sense? What are the gifts?"*

Once you sense the transformation is coming to completion, create an affirmation that clears and sustains it.

As you feel the session come to a close, let your internal energy return to peace and calm. Bring yourself to full consciousness by counting from one to ten and opening your eyes.

Journal While Iin Your Records ♡ Describe and record what you experienced durign your meditaion. What is your sacred healing affirmation? Be sure to write down all your affirmations to support your healing. ♡

When you finish writing, say your closing prayer.

Working with a Partner

When working with another, the first step is to open their Akashic records with your prayer.

Using the Sacred Space Heart Meditation, guide your partner to create a heart-centered, sacred space. If it's the first time your partner has taken this journey, then stop as directed to allow time for them to write down the description of their sacred space.

Check in with your partner to be sure they are connecting heart to heart with Divine Akashic Love through intention. Be sure your partner's sacred space has a sense of well-being and peace. Confirm that your partner understands that they are to be an observer during the next step. There's no judgment at this time, no editing or controlling the outcome.

Now, ask your partner, *"What is blocking you right now from experiencing joy in your life?"*

Allow your partner time to answer. As the reader, you may receive information about what your partner will be working on. The most important thing here is to encourage your partner to identify the block they want to work on. Once the issue or concern has been identified and acknowledged, begin to walk your partner through the packaging exercise.

Continue on the journey, reading the script for the guided Sacred Space Heart Meditation to your partner. Observe what the issue/energy is transforming into. Ask for guidance and understanding from the Akashic field of healing.

Once you sense the transformation is coming to completion, create an affirmation with your partner that clears and sustains this transformation.

Journal This ♡ Take notes for your partner. Ask them, *"What is your sacred healing space like?"* After your partner's journey, note what they describe about their heart-centered space.

- Identify the issue your partner wishes to transform.
- Identify and describe all aspects of this issue.
- Message of Transformation
- Create an affirmation from the transformed energy. ♡

When you finish writing, say your closing prayer

Once you have completed this journey the first time, let the experience dwell in your consciousness. Wait at least a couple of days before repeating this exercise.

As you become more adept at recreating this journey, you can streamline some of the steps. I often take out the pause between steps one and two. Once I'm sure I have a heart to heart connection and I'm in a place of peace and well-being, I will go straight to the energy transformation in part two.

This practice is very helpful for resolving many-layered issues. You may feel that an issue you've *worked* on has returned. Don't be discouraged. Accept that you're working on something of complexity, and decide it's worth it. You are uncovering inner gifts, and the biggest one is your clear, uncluttered connection to your own divinity.

Chapter 6

Your Spiritual Team and the Akashic Journey

I woke up to Spirit while in a difficult marriage. I lived my life day by day; caring for my children, attending to my job, and dealing with my husband's mercurial swings, all while feeling a general sense of despair. I had become more and more exhausted. One night as I slept, I dreamt a beautiful light was shining down upon me, warming my face. The light was made up of brilliant colors and formed a mandala in a perfect circle. I could hear voices talking to me, encouraging me, and urging me to move forward. They asked me to consider looking at my life from a different perspective. I couldn't remember everything they said, and I had trouble understanding what I *did* remember! But most importantly, I could feel the meaning of their words and their encouragement. As I listened to them speak to me, I had a sense of myself being bigger than the woman who was going through her daily chores (and daily despair). When I woke up later that night to attend to a crying baby, I could feel the light still shining through my iced-up bedroom window. I was pretty much walking in my sleep so I didn't look clearly at the window, but I knew it was there. Early the next morning, I woke up as a dim, gray light was dawning. I remembered the circle of light. I went to the window; a perfect circle had been melted in the thick ice there. I was awestruck. That was the moment I began to look at my life as a much bigger picture. I realized that my life had meaning beyond the day-to-day sadness that I felt at that time. I also realized I was not alone. I had not just one, since I'd heard several voices that night, but *many* spiritual advisors and cheerleaders. ♡

People throughout time have experienced Divine guidance that redirected them on a soul level.

A well-known story about divine intervention originates with a man named Bill W., the co-founder of Alcoholics Anonymous. Bill Wilson suffered from acute alcoholism and had already been treated by several different hospitals. According to Wilson, as he lay in bed one night, depressed and despairing about his addictive drinking and the sad state of his life, he cried out, *"I'll do anything! Anything at all! If there be a God, let Him show Himself!"* He then had the sensation of a bright light, a feeling of ecstasy, and a new serenity.

Wilson described his experience to his physician Dr. Silkworth who told Bill, *"Something has happened to you that I don't understand. But you had better hang on to it."* As a result of this spiritual intervention, Bill did not drink for the remainder of his life. Bill's spiritual experience is the foundation of AA's spiritual growth program, commonly known as the 12 Steps. This program has helped countless people.

One of my clients told me a story about her beginning steps into recovery from drug addiction and alcoholism. During her darkest time, she described a spiritual entity standing at the foot of her bed. She said she knew that this was an important moment in her life. Before she went to bed that night, she had called a friend to pray for her; she had been afraid she wouldn't wake up. Even though she was dangerously high when she saw this apparition, she felt and knew that this was different than anything else she had ever felt or seen. She knew that she needed to somehow make changes in her life. The vision she had that night inspired her to begin her journey to healing, sobriety, and balance. I met her when she had been sober for a year. Together we worked in her Akashic Records to support her on her spiritual path. She is still doing well today.

Consider This ♡ These stories illustrate the presence and guidance we often receive from our soul and spiritual team. Look back on your life and remember when and where you experienced an intervention of guidance from a higher source. Consider the specific guidance. Did you follow it? Did you believe it was real and could be helpful? ♡

This experience would have been when you felt or knew something above and beyond what you had been thinking and feeling in the moment. It could have been an instance that changed your thought and direction. Maybe you took another course in your life because of it. It could have been intuitive information that kept you out of harm's way, or presented an opportunity you never expected.

These moments can be hidden from our logical minds, locked away in our protected memories. They may be labeled in your memory banks as unexplainable. You may not have considered these instances as real because you didn't know what to think of them or how to process them in your logical mind. Or maybe you think of these experiences all the time but don't know how to make sense of them, so they stay in a separate place in your mind, not integrated at all into your life. If this is so, that's okay; you're in the right place.

These experiences (and we all have them) are part of your spiritual guidance system. It's time to welcome your spiritual cheerleaders into your life.

Meeting your Spiritual Team

Making Trusted Connections with the Biggest Network Ever

The Akashic Field and its records are *HUGE*. The information they contain vibrates beyond what our minds can fully perceive. When we access the records, the information being downloaded into our conscious and unconscious mind often needs to be compressed, very much like a computer file that has been *zipped* shut. This Akashic information needs to be decoded into the language and vibration of our current lifetime. It has been said by many modern day mystics that as a collective consciousness, humans have reached the point in evolution of being able to receive more and more information from the highest source.

Multiple actions or steps must be taken when we ask for and receive a download (answer) from the Akashic Records. The first action must come from us, the petitioners. Through meditation we achieve a receptive state. Through prayer and intent we raise our vibration to begin to meet the higher vibrational information. The second action is from the Divine and those in Spirit serving the Divine. The information must *lower* its own vibration and decode itself to match the capabilities we are currently working with. In other words, the information is packaged for our highest and best in a way we can understand it from where we are now.

As we work on clearing our own energy field through meditation and active self-healing practices for our mental, emotional, and physical bodies, we'll be able to access more information; we'll be able to perceive the nuances in the messages we're receiving. We'll obtain a deeper and more robust understanding of our Divine connection.

Working with a spiritual team of angels, guides, teachers, masters, and loved ones is a powerful way to increase your ability to access the incredible information of the Akasha.

Ultimately, we're working as conduits, or tubes, to receive from the Akasha. We bring the energetic information forward and deliver it in message form. Once the information is received, we then begin to learn from it and integrate it into our conscious lives. So our spiritual teams work as messengers and interpreters. The most important goal our team has when working with us is to help us connect with Divine love and our soul. They encourage us and guide us to take responsibility for our own spiritual path, and to create a clear connection with *Mother, Father, God of all that is*. We are designed to be co-creators with our souls and the Divine during the course of our lives. This co-creation is possible as we become fully realized beings, incorporating our spirit and soul into our daily lives.

Our team wants us to succeed. They want us to grow into full realization of ourselves. This kind of success may not be what you currently think it is—this is *Divine* success—it's richer than you can imagine.

What Does It Mean for Me to Have a Team?

To have a team you know and communicate with in order to receive valuable information and support is a big step towards knowing you are not alone in your life journey. Your team is a part of you and always has been. But don't worry; they're not there to take over your life. As you become more consciously aware of them, you won't lose your free will, or turn over your own process. Instead, you'll be empowered to take more responsibility for much more of your life. Becoming conscious of the spiritual support in and around you augments your understanding of the many gifts and blessings you have going for you. You will also receive teaching and instruction that helps you to know how to access and benefit from these blessings. You truly have a dream team at your fingertips that want the very best for you; better than anything you can imagine right now.

Who Are My Team Members?

You have a **guardian angel** and **guide in spirit** who has been with you since your soul first dreamed of you. Our essence, personality, and spirit are born from our soul. Our soul ensures our path with a plan and map that is given to our spirit guide and guardian angel. The plan is also embedded into our unconscious ego self. This plan acts as a map that leads us to live our soul's purpose. We have designated appointments to meet certain people and have certain experiences that will stir us and compel us to choose the path our soul has designed for the course of our lives. You have the choice to open to your guides and guardian angel and work as a team—or—ignore them all together and make your own best attempt at your life. There are no wrong answers.

Loved ones who have known us and are now on the other side of life often choose to be part of our spiritual team. Some may be working silently in the background while others send us signs, signals, and messages throughout our lives. They often have a pretty good understanding about the specific patterns in our lives and can be very helpful. Loved ones are also on a journey of spiritual development; as they grow, heal, and expand into a higher awareness, you will benefit. I love bringing in grandparents from the other side into an Akashic reading. Often the grandparents who have been on the other side have an astute understanding of the ancestral patterns you inherited from your family that are affecting your life now. They bring awareness and healing into readings in a very personal way. They work closely with your spirit guardians. Readings with grandparents are often more helpful than parental readings. Grandparents often represent the unconditional love in a family, while parents can bring in the family issues and struggles that you're still beating your heart and head against. Grandparents have the advantage of distance and a larger perspective about your place in the family tree they can share through your family's Akashic Records.

Sometimes you'll receive unexpected guidance from Spirit. While I was going through treatment for cancer, I took time to open my records and draw in the spirits I felt around me. I was asking for support and healing from Spirit. I drew a portrait of a beautiful woman with a scarf on her head. I felt she had gone through what I was going through, and had ended up passing away from the cancer. She told me she was there to help me. Together we faced my fear of possibly losing my life. She gave me the courage to endure the pain of the treatments. Months later, I shared my sketch book with my students in a spirit art class. One of them recognized my drawing as her Aunt who had passed away from cancer. The student described her Aunt exactly the way I had felt her to be when I was drawing her. I was speechless; moved to tears. This woman in spirit had helped me gently, quietly, and with much love. Spirit is amazing, and often works in very unexpected ways. I feel so blessed when I am open and working with my team.

Masters and teachers come and go throughout our lives. They are here to help us focus on specific topics and learn what we need to in regards to what we are going through. When we were young and going through school, we had different teachers in different grades. The analogy is the same. Masters and teachers may or may not have had human lives. Ascended Masters bring wisdom and healing from a more non-personal level. They help us see our lives from a more global perspective. They inspire us to see ourselves beyond our personal pain, and into our magnificent potential. Ascended Masters have been there, done that, many times and have mastered, usually through lifetimes, the gifts and potentials life can hold. The presence of a spiritual master in your life is a tremendous source of compassion and healing. Ascended Masters can originate from any highly evolved aspect of life on this planet or another.

Angels in the Akasha

The Angelic realm has been in existence since before humanity showed up on planet earth. They have always been present with us. They did NOT originate from the Christian realm, although many Christian faiths have deeply embraced them. The New Age Movement has also embraced angels, and often resonates very closely with Christian communities. This can be off-putting to other faith-based communities. But in truth, almost every culture, tradition, and religion includes some form of angel who acts as an intermediary or messenger between the Divine and humans. The presence of angels has been with us since the dawn of recorded history. This history points us to the hidden truth that angels have been with us always, and some of us are even from angelic origins!

Angels appear to us in forms that we can recognize and receive. They must penetrate our cultural bias and beliefs to convey their messages. They vibrate at a very fast rate and exist and live close to the heart of God. Angels are in full service to God. Like humans, angels have many different jobs, skills, and qualities to serve their own particular mission. Some stay close to God and others specialize in working with different aspects of God's creation, including helping us. As angels help us, they serve the Divine.

Every human being is equally valued by God. The creator doesn't see race, religion, social status, or quality of our life. The Divine sees us as we are in our development as souls. The Divine plan for each of us is to perfect ourselves (sometimes over lifetimes) so that God may behold itself in us. The Angelic realm is in complete support to God and to us in this mission. God longs for us to be fully actualized in our spirits so that we may live at the side and in the heart of the Creator.

In the Kabbalah, it's said that the archangels' energy, along with all other angels, is so deep, so large and expansive, that we could hardly bear it if they stood next to us. No matter what, they will always find a way to answer our call, guide us, and sustain us. Each archangel and angel belongs to a ray or a throne that has a specific calling and discipline. In each of these rays are multitudes of angels that have specific jobs and skills that relate to the reigning throne or ray.

You need never worry that you are calling in the angels frivolously. Angels cannot intervene unless we ask and invite them. Each request is considered and responded to lovingly and intelligently with our best interest in mind. They deliver what we need better than we could ever think to ask for.

You Might be Angel Bound

Typically, angels have not had human lives. The one exception is Archangel Metatron. Born before the time of Noah, Metatron was called Enoch. Enoch had a calling to hear the word of God and understand the Mysteries of Creation. He wrote what is known as The Books of Enoch. (Enoch is also thought to be the name of four other persons—the oldest son of Cain, the son of Jared, the son of Midian, and the oldest son of Rueben. These men were born in different generations.) Enoch is said to have become the first fully realized human. It is also said that he ascended into the heavens instead of dying a mortal death, becoming Metatron, the Archangel of the Presence of God.

Metatron rules over the Akashic Records as its secretary and watcher. One of Metatron's great gifts to us is his understanding of human nature. He realizes how difficult it is to be human and undergo the challenges of the living world.

In Rose Van Eynden's book, *Metatron*, she asks a question to Metatron:

"How can I learn to trust my communication with my own spirit guides?"

Metatron replied to her in a channeled session:

"So many human beings believe in sacred writings that have been passed down but they do not believe the communication process continues today. Truth resonates in your heart. The truth is that God communicates to each of you.

He uses many means to do this, including guides and teachers and those of us in the Angelic Kingdom.

God is never separate from you—each of you is connected to God and thus you are divine in in your own right—you can never dislodge that sacred divinity within yourself.

Keep your energy vibration in a loving state. You exude a more loving aura and energy to everything around you. It follows that when you ask for guidance in this loving vibration, the answer will come more strongly and you will recognize the answer more easily.

Expect the answer to come in many ways. Never try to limit the ways. If you ask for guidance expect to receive it. Listen, look, feel, and open all your senses to receive the message."

As you open to the angels and attune yourself though your Akashic Records, you will also receive messages of healing and inspiration from them.

Aligning with the Angels

As you work in the Akashic Field, you will benefit from aligning and attuning yourself to the Angelic realm and energy.

A daily morning prayer will help you set the day. This type of prayer will train your inner self to align with angelic energy for the highest good and best possible outcomes. Here is the prayer I say:

Mother, Father, God Creator of all that is

And the Akashi Field of Compassion

Align me now with the Angelic Realm and its loving energy

To guide me and instruct me

To nurture and sustain me

In a circle I acknowledge and open to

Metatron *above me to guide my thoughts*

Michael *at my side to protect me and guide my deeds*

Gabriel *in front of me to light my path*

Raphael *at my other side nurturing my healing journey*

Uriel *at my back to sustain me through all things*

Ariel *beneath my feet that I may respect my environment*

And always find my way back home

*Be with me, my **guardian angel***

Whose God's love commits you here

And all the saint and angels

More than I can imagine

With gifts beyond what I now know

Thank you and I love you

Angel Attunement

What Are Your Angels Saying to You?

The following exercise will help you open up to connect and communicate with the many angels of the Akasha. Angels need to be invited into your life. Attune to your angels and invite them in! Make sure to write any observations about your journey in your journal.

Angel Attunement

Set up: A quiet place were you won't be interrupted

Time: 15-25 minutes

You will need:

- Your journal and a pen
- Clear crystal quartz point
- Music
- Your Akashic Prayer

This meditative exercise will help you to attune to the guides in spirit, especially your angels.

To Prepare

Select music to play while you are in meditation. Here are some of my favorites.

Metatron's Procession by Anela Strings

Calling in the Angels by Barbara Anne Keefe (In the Company of Angels)

Garador's Flight by Jo Blankenburg (Elysium)

Find a clear quartz crystal (it can have inclusions and surface patterns) that fits neatly in your hand. You will be using the crystal to help you attune to your guides and angels. The crystal will also carry the vibrations of your attunement for future use. Dedicate this crystal to your angel and your angel work. This crystal will become a vibrational bridge when you return to your work with the angels.

Review the heart meditation for creating sacred space.

Place a notebook with pen or pencil in front of you.

Begin by opening your Akashic Records. Hold your crystal in your left (receiving) hand with the point of the crystal facing you.

Make an intention about who you will be working with in the session. I recommend you start with your guardian angel. Your guardian has been with you since before you were born. They hold and know the map of your soul's plan for your life. This guardian will be your primary partner for all of your Akashic journeys.

At subsequent sessions, I recommend attuning to Metatron, then the Archangels—Michael, Raphael, Gabriel, Uriel, and Ariel. These angels will be your foundational team—protecting, guiding, and healing you on all six of your sides—right, left, front, back, above, and below.

Begin playing your chosen music, setting it to repeat.

Open your heart with your breath and enter into your sacred space. Once have settled into this space, invite in the angel you wish to attune to.

Sit quietly, listening to the music, and continue to breathe into your heart. Allow the energy to build and open to the messages for the angels. You may feel a gentle brush on your hand or cheek. Continue to keep your mind still as the energy builds.

Your invoked angel or spirit guide is now near and working with you to attune your vibrations. Sit for at least 10 minutes; 20 minutes is optimal. (You may want to set a timer.) As you feel the energy dissipate, you may begin to come out of your meditative state. Ask that you remember any messages you may have heard.

When you're ready, "come back" into the room, awake and present.

Journal This ♡ Write down your experiences in your journal. ♡

Close your records.

Try This In Your Records ♡ Once you are attuned, spend time every morning for a week or so opening your records to the angel or guide you're currently working with, and journal with your new associate.

Begin by writing a letter to your Angel or guide.

> *Dear __________,*
>
> *This is what is on my mind and in my heart: ____________________.*
>
> *What is your guidance for me now?*
>
> *Love, ___________*

Let you words flow from you without editing them. Allow yourself to hear the guidance you're getting and write it down without analyzing or editing it. Close your journal and don't read it again until your next session. ♡

Reading Your Crystal

After your attunement, hold your crystal in your hands and open the records of the crystal. Breathe in deeply and imagine the energy of the crystal is blending with your *auric energy*. Bring your crystal to your forehead, and breath is sharply three time times. Then bring you crystal to your heart and breathe in sharply three more times. Return to holding your crystal in your hands in front of you. Imagine you can journey into the middle of the crystal's center. Ask the angel of your attunement to communicate with you the message this crystal holds. Write your observations, and then close the records of the crystal.

**A note to the wise – as you work with these angelic spiritual attunements, you may go through healing episodes as your mental, emotional, and/or physical body begins to detoxify itself. Practice self-care, drink plenty of water, and get a healthy amount of sleep. Eat a healthy and balanced diet. Practice heart-centered meditations and use your breath to help you release any built up energies—keep the energetic flow going!*

Attuning a Partner or Client to the Angels

You may want to work with another person, or someone may even ask you to attune them to the angels. The procedure is the same; your partner holds a crystal and opens the records in a heart-centered, sacred space.

Remember—you are opening your partner's records and guiding them to open their heart into their own sacred space.

Once centered, play music and sit quietly with your partner or client as the power builds (often when two or more people are participating, the power can build more quickly). If the energy of the session becomes too intense, use your breath to expand the intensity, just as you did in the heart meditation. When you feel the session winding down (5 to 10 minutes), lead your partner out of their meditative state. Once they are fully present, lead them into a conversation about their experience.

Open the records of their crystal for them and ask them to tell you what they're experiencing or seeing in the crystal. Jot down any notes for them.

Give them the assignment to spend time every morning opening to that angel or guide and journaling with them. Recommend they do this exercise for at least a week or so.

Journal This ♡ Show your partner how to start a letter to their angel or spirit guide:

> *Dear ___________,*
>
> *This is what is on my mind and in my heart: _______________.*
>
> *What is your guidance for me now?*
>
> *Love, ___________*

Encourage the person you're working with to let their words flow out unrestricted. Suggest they work in stillness so as to more easily hear the guidance from their angel or guide. Instruct them to write everything down without analyzing or editing it. Be sure to remind them to hold their crystal as they journal. ♡

It's okay if they don't have the Akashic Journey prayer to work with, as they will be working with the angel's guidance that was given to them during the attunement.

Do use the Akashic prayer to facilitate the attunements. If your partners or clients want to go ahead and make attunements on themselves, they'll need to learn the Akashic prayer to get the best results.

Angel Readings from the Akashic Records

An angel guidance reading is as simple as opening yours or another's records and then intending and requesting guidance from the angelic realm (or from a specific angel, if you so choose).

It's best to be attuned to the angels if you want to pursue this type of reading. As you continue to attune and work with the angels, eventually you'll be able to feel their different energy signatures; you'll know which angel is drawing near.

Angels will come and guide you throughout your Akashic Journey readings. The attunements simply raise you awareness and your ability to connect with them clearly.

To do an angel reading, open your or your partner's records and ask for the angelic connection. Sit quietly and ask your guardian angel to draw near. Ask your angel to touch your hand, or give you some kind of sign that they're with you. Sit quietly and allow the energy to build. Once you feel the information begin to form, let the words flow. Ask that the words be clear and understandable. Don't edit or try to explain them; allow yourself to be the messenger.

Ask the angels to give you a description of themselves and their gifts. Get to know them and share what you sense about the angels with those you read for. This will help the reading to feel real to your partner of client, and can validate things in their own lives. This validation can serve as evidence that the angels truly are around them.

Try doing this a few times for yourself. Once you establish connection, write what you experience in your journal or workbook. The more you practice working with the angels on your own, the clearer you will be when you work with others.

Angels and Archangels You Will Want to Get to Know

Archangel Metatron – Metatron is the secretary and supervisor of the Akashic Records. He is known as *The Presence of God.* He works with your crown, ninth, and tenth chakras, as well as your third eye. Metatron will give you access (or not) to the Akashic library and records. He will ensure that you only receive the information best suited for you, and will also oversee, along with Archangel Michael, your understanding of and ability to use this information.

Journal This ♡ When attuning to Metatron, ask for descriptions of him along with the angelic message of God's grace to access your Akashic records. Ask Metetron to help you understand the information you receive from you records. ♡

Archangel Michael – Michael is *Like unto God.* He is the gatekeeper of heaven and a mighty protector. He will help you build trust in your practice. He protects us from our own fears and negative thinking, and helps us with the integration of our ego. He offers guidance. Michael works with the crown chakra and solar plexus.

Journal This ♡ When attuning to Michael, ask for descriptions of Michael along with his angelic message of protection and guidance. ♡

Archangel Gabriel – Gabriel is *The Strength of God* and also The Messenger of God. She is the bringer of light to show the way, and brings with her glad tidings and messages from God. Gabriel brings inspiration and reconciliation. She works with the third eye and heart chakra.

$Journal\ This$ ♡ When attuning to Gabriel, ask for descriptions of Gabriel's presence so that you will recognize her. Ask her to share her angelic gifts of clear seeing and Illumination of your Soul with you. Ask her to light your way. ♡

Archangel Uriel – Uriel is *The Light of God*. He is the minster of heaven, hearing and answering prayers. He is a mighty transformer of people's lives. He will help you with readings and delivery of healing messages. Uriel brings transformation and tranquility. He works with the crown, heart, and throat chakras.

$Journal\ This$ ♡ When attuning to Uriel, ask for descriptions of his transformational gifts and the signs and signals that he is with you. Ask him to clarify his angelic messages for you. ♡

Archangel Raphael – Raphael is *The Healing of God*. He brings healing and creativity. He will walk with you and inspire you on all of your journeys. He helps in disclosing pain that needs to heal. Raphael will inspire you and be your muse. He works with the sacral, hearth, and third eye chakras.

$Journal\ This$ ♡ When attuning to Raphael, ask for descriptions of his healing presence so that you will recognize him as he draws near. Ask for angelic messages of inspiration and beauty. ♡

Archangel Ariel – Ariel is *The Lion of God*. She assists Raphael in the curing of diseases. She holds the secrets of earth's magic, and knows how to rule the winds. She will help you to be in right relation to your environment, and to connect with nature. Ariel works with your root, sacral, eighth, and twelfth chakras, as well as the healing chakras in your hands and feet.

$Journal\ This$ ♡ When attuning to Ariel, ask for descriptions of her presence so that you will recognize her. Ask her to show you the many miracle of creation. Ask her to teach you the medicines and healing energies of the Earth. She will teach you to align your life style to balance with the well being if the earth you live on. ♡

The Sacred Mother – Mother Mary, the Queen of Angels, was asked to carnate on earth to be the mother of Jesus. She is the beloved of God. She has been seen in apparitions around the world bringing peace, hope and healing to the poor and suffering. She reminds us that we are all sons and daughters of

God. Call on her in your hour of need and she will reinforce you and protect you. You will be working with her in in your soul contractsinin chapter 11

Journal This ♡ When attuning to the Sacred Mother, ask for descriptions of her presence so that you will recognize her. Ask her to teach and train you to recognize her love as your mother. Welcome her healing as she trains you learn to love yourself with deep compassion. ♡

Archangel Azrael – Azrael means *Whom God Helps*. His main focus is reincarnation. He is known as the *Angel of Death*, as he is responsible for releasing the human soul from the physical body at the time of death. He also assists with the healing of grief. Azrael rules the eighth and ninth chakras above your head that contain your Akashic Records. He regulates your soul's development throughout your *lifetimes.*

Journal This ♡ When attuning to Azrael, ask for descriptions of his presence along with the angelic message of death and reincarnation in the Akashic recrods. Ask him to help you with your fear of death. Ask him for help in your mediumship work as well as past life journeys. ♡_

Archangel Asariel – Asariel means *Beatitudes of God*. He is earth based, and has the job of encouraging people to trust there intuition and act upon it. He is the champion of mediums, seers, and prophets. He is the teacher of self-dscipline. Asariel works with the third eye and throat chakra, as well as the creative energies of the second chakra.

Journal This ♡ When attuning to Asariel ask for descriptions of his presence so that you may recognize him. Ask for the angelic gift of knowing and understanding the information in the records as you read them for yourself and others. Ask this angel for the gift of mediumship. ♡

Archangel Zaphkiel – Zaphkiel (also Cassiel) is known as *The Knowledge of God*. He helps us to overcome long-standing problems. He teaches patience and serenity. Zaphkiel offers information from the Akashic Records in order to help humanity understand the deep knowledge available from the Creator.

Journal This ♡ When attuning to Zaphkiel ask for descriptions of his presence so that you will recognize him. Ask him for grace, patience and understandiing. ♡

Archangel Zadkiel –Zadkiel is known as The *Benevolence of God* He guards the power of the invocation and prayer that come from deep within the heart. Zadkiel brings with him the violet flame of alchemical and energetic clearing, and focuses on qualities of freedom, alchemy, transformation, forgiveness, and justice. Zadkiel tells us to use the violet flame to clear our heavy energy and transform our lives. You will be working with Zadkiel as you clear you soul contracts in chapter 11.

Journal This ♡ When attuning to Zadkiel ask for a descriptions of his presence so that you will recognize him. Ask to be empowered to use the violet flame for you own healing and healing of others. Ask to be taught true freedom from forgiveness. ♡

Archangel Haniel – Haniel is known as *The Glory and Grace of God*. In all matters of love, Haniel will intervene. He rules the planet Venus, and transported Enoch to heaven. Haniel will teach you the power of love.

Journal This ♡ When attuning to attuning to Haniel ask for descriptions of her presence so that you may recognize her. Ask Haniel to teach you to be in the presence of love in the Akashic field. ♡

Archangel Chamuel – Chamuel means *He who seeks God*. He rights wrongs and soothes troubled minds. He brings justice to the world, and teaches tolerance and understanding. Chamuel is adept at conflict resolution. His adoration for the beauty and balance of the Divine is infectious as he works with humanity. Chamuel is teacher of the *One Mind,* seeing the divine connection between everything. ♡

Journal This ♡ When attuning to Chamuel, ask for descriptions of her presence so that you may recognize her. Ask her to teach you tolerance and understanding for all your relationships. Ask her to teach you how to access the One Mind and Divine connections between all things. ♡

Archangel Sandalphon – Sandalphon means *Co-brother* and he is understood to be Metatron's twin. He hears the prayers of humanity and brings them to God's ear. He is known as the tall angel, because he can stand on earth and reach God's ears in heaven. Sandalphon has helped many great souls to be born on the earth in order to help humanity.

Journal This ♡ When attuning to Sandalphon, ask for descriptions of his presence so that you may recognize him. Pray to Sandalphon for strength and knowing that God is with you. ♡

Archangel Raziel – Raziel means *God is my pleasure,* and also *The Secrets of God.* He is often equated with Uriel. He brought a book listing all the medicinal herbs to humanity, so they might survive and live well on the earth. He also helps access the Akashic Records. Raziel inspires us to solve the mysteries and problems in our lives.

Journal This ♡ When attuning to Raziel ask for descriptions of his presence so that you may recognize him. Ask him to impart any secrets that may help you live your life in grace now. ♡

Masters and Ascended Masters to Get to Know

The masters work with us on many levels—seen and unseen. There are many masters, and many more souls slowly working their way towards mastery level. They're available to us whenever we're ready to learn what they're teaching. This is a short list of known masters; there are many more that you can research. Opening up to a master's teaching and influence can accelerate your path of learning and growing.

You don't have to worry about whether or not you should be working with a specific master or not; they'll come to you when the time is right.

Quan Yin – an ascended Buddhist deity, she is known to heal and release those who are suffering from physical and emotional pain. She is known as the goddess of compassion.

Siddhartha Guatama Buddha – dedicated his life to finding an end to suffering. He founded a pathway to enlightenment through meditation.

Red Tara – a female deity in Tibetan Buddhism. She is in attendance to the bodhisattva of compassion Avalokitasvre. She carries a bow and arrow made of flowers. Red Tara is the "Mother of all Buddhas," and the "Mother of Liberation." She helped Buddha overcome dark forces on his way to enlightenment. Sakyamuni Buddha taught her tantra (prayers) to his followers. Many practitioners have found relief of their suffering through Red Tara.

Melchizedek – is from the Hebrew tradition. His name means "the king of righteousness." He is the first priest of God Most High. Jesus was anointed into the order of Melchizedek. Some believe Melchizedek is Jesus, and a descendant of Noah. He is a great spiritual master of alchemy and sacred geometry, the building blocks of the creation of matter.

Jesus (also known as Sananda and Christ consciousness) – dedicated his life to the service of God, in order to help humanity. He is thought to have had many lifetimes as the Son of Man to show mankind the pathway to God's love. Jesus teaches compassion and forgiveness, and reminds us we are children of the creator. When called upon, he brings healing on all levels.

White Buffalo Woman – came to the Native tribes in North America to teach them peace and remind them of their connection to the sacred earth. She teaches peace and purity of mind. White Buffalo Woman promised to return some day to bring about world peace.

St. Germain – known as a master spiritual alchemist, he's believed to have had many lifetimes during pivotal times in history. His lifetimes include incarnating as both St. Joseph and Francis Bacon. It is said his last lifetime was as Le Comte de Saint Germain. His soul's drive is to instill spiritual freedom throughout humanity. He revealed the violet flame, and instructed us how to use it to free our spirits and ascend to our potential. You will work with St. Germain in your soul contracts later in chapter 11

Consider This ♡ Who are some of the masters or guides you would add to the list? You may be working with an entirely different set of names and energetic archetypes. The important piece to this is that you resonate with them within the Akashic Records. They must bring to you a sense of connection and clarity in your spiritual work. Don't work with a specific guide or concept just because it's popular or you were told to do so. Let your spiritual team connect with you in your heart; in your sacred space. Then allow the relationship to grow and become dimensional. Look for a presence that you are truly relating to. ♡

In Summary

The most important take away from this chapter is to realize you have a *huge* spiritual team to work with. This team will cheer you on at all times. You can receive guidance, protection, and healing from them. The only hitch is, *you have to ask!*

Building a relationship with your spiritual team is incredibly helpful as you travel on your Akashic Journey. Learn to talk to your team, but even more importantly, learn to *listen* to them. They will be there the very moment you reach out to them, because in truth, they are already with you.

Your Soul, Spirit, and Self

Moses was tending his flock at the edge of the desert, when suddenly the angels of the Lord appeared to him as a flame of fire, in a bush that didn't burn up. When asked to deliver a message to the Israelites, Moses asked, "Who shall I tell them sent me?"

God said to Moses, "I am who I am. Tell them I AM has sent me to you."

~ Exodus 3 (paraphrased)

Your Akashic Journey is about merging your consciousness with your Soul and Akashic or God consciousness.

So what exactly *is* consciousness?

To read your own records and understand how they work in your life, you need to know and understand your real self. To deeply know your self is to understand how you are designed to function. As you come to understand your authentic self and your motivations, you will realize how many tools you have at your disposal. Your capacity to live your potential will grow dramatically. In this section, we'll explore how to access and use inner tools to develop our innate talents and gifts.

The Three I AMs of Self Envision the consciousness of self, as we live our life incarnate, as three levels of "I Am" awareness. Using a tree as a metaphor, imagine three systems of consciousness working together during our lifetime.

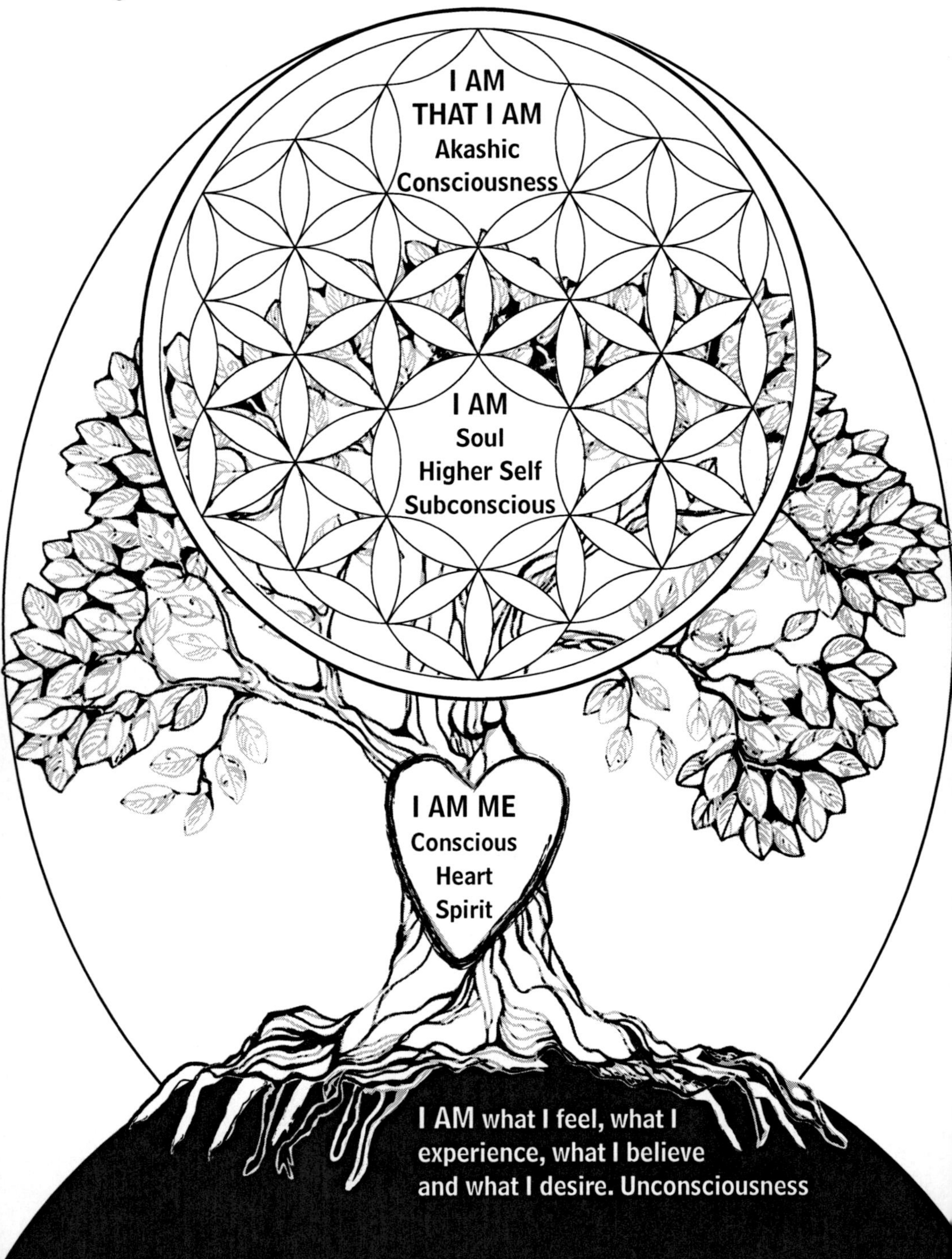

Chapter 7

The Three I AMs:
Your Complete Life Team

Integrating Awareness Between Soul, Sacred Self, and Ego

Understanding the concept of your mind and the many levels of consciousness is complicated. You can find all kinds of information about consciousness in the Theology, New Age, Self Help, and Science of the Mind sections of any library, bookstore, or on Amazon. Some information is helpful, some of it hard to understand. The information available about consciousness is full of conflicting concepts. One Buddhist teaching describes consciousness as having 54 states, while science refute most, if not all, religious or spiritual studies. Yikes!

One of India's contemporary philosophers, K. Ramakrishna, writes, "Consciousness is the light which illumines the things on which it shines." In essence, you are the light; whatever you shine your light (your thoughts) on, is what you'll see. To me, this concept makes consciousness a little easier to understand.

In the sacred teaching of the Kybalion, a study of Ancient Egypt and Greece, by three initiates of Hermes Trismegistus *(the Hermetic Philosophy)*, they write about the *Law of Correspondence*. This law is about the relationship, connection, and similarities between the planes (physical, mental, and spiritual) of existence. This law explains that there is a harmony, similarity, and agreement between these planes; *as above so below*. Simply put, if you want to understand a spiritual concept, study nature. We can also observe nature to better understand ourselves, since everything in creation comes from the same source.

I envision the consciousness of our Self, as we live our incarnate life, as three levels of *I Am* awareness. Using a tree as a metaphor and model, I see three systems working together during the lifetime of the tree, just as we have three systems of consciousness working in our lives.

Let's start with the roots as our model. What "roots" us in our lives is our underground consciousness. We often don't see all the richness and influence in this underground root system. Some of what goes on here is unconscious. This root consciousness exclaims, *"I AM* what I feel, what I know, what I believe, and what I desire."

The trunk of the tree is the heart of the tree. It's the trunk that keeps the energy flowing between the roots and the branches. As with the tree, our hearts direct the flow between our unconscious selves and our higher conscious Self; our Soul. The heart consciousness exclamation is *I AM ME!*

The branches that carry the leaves, the blossoms, and the fruit are a metaphor for the Soul. We're not always awake and aware of the growth and development of the Soul. The thoughts that emanate from the Soul are of a higher consciousness (vibration) than the rest of our "tree." The communication from this consciousness is often subconscious. The exclamation from our Soul is I AM!

The Akashic/God Consciousness exclamation is, *"I AM THAT I AM!"* meaning, *"I am all of this."*

Be the Tree

The tree is a magnificent example of using elements found in the environment around itself to live. The tree then returns the transformed elements back into the environment, which will sustain life beyond itself. Using the tree as a metaphor, when we function as we were created to, we have everything we need. At the same time, we become a gift to the world around us. When we "misfire" and don't function to our capacity, we have many options available to help us return to the flow of Divine life.

The first concept in the metaphor of the tree is the continuous and contiguous flow of energy through the tree. Sunlight baths the tree, the bark on the trunk, and the leaves on the branches. The trunk uses the warmth of the sun to modulate the flow of nutrition throughout the tree. The leaves turn the sunlight into food. The bi-product becomes part of the air we breathe.

The second concept in the metaphor of the tree is the interdependency and cooperation between all of the systems within the tree.

The third concept in the metaphor of the tree is about how water and minerals from the soil are collected from the root system. The root system then sends the nutrients up into the trunk, into the heart of the tree.

The nutrients travel up the tree trunk and are dispersed where they are needed. The bark on the trunk of the tree is responsible for monitoring the temperature of the tree, as well as the passage of light which creates the gasses that move the nutrients into the branches. The bark defends the tree against disease. The wood of the trunk supports the constant flow of water that supports the entire tree. If this process fails to provide water at any point to any part of the tree, the tree will die.

The branches carry the leaves that create sugars from the nutrients and water sent to them by the sunlight that surrounds them. The blossoms on the branches carry the fruit and the seeds that ensure there will be more trees. The greatest growth of the tree is in the branches. The branches are dependent on the rest of the tree for their growth.

Much like a tree, we need all our inner systems, including our levels of consciousness, to flow together. We need this not only to survive, but to grow and flourish. Consider that the nourishment from the roots of the tree travel up through the heart of the tree, and out to the branches which contain the leaves and the buds and potential seeds. The energy of the tree flows up. The integration and energy of our three levels of selves also flows up, from our roots through our heart to our higher mind. We may experience our consciousness flowing up and down and around our conscious body, with our final realizations and integrations happening within the vibrations of our higher Self.

Meditation 3

To Infinity and Beyond

Set up: A quiet place were you won't be interrupted

Time: 15-25 minutes

You will need:

- your Akashic prayer

This visualization meditation can be done standing up or lying down. Once you learn this technique, you'll be able to do it in any position, anywhere, and any time.

Open your Akashic Records and say a prayer and intention for healing.

Start by imagining the infinity symbol, which is a continuous Mobius strip that overlaps in the middle. This strip represents the flow of infinite energy that moves through the universe to you, and supplies you with continuous sustenance and guidance. Now imagine that the place the strip overlaps is centered at your heart.

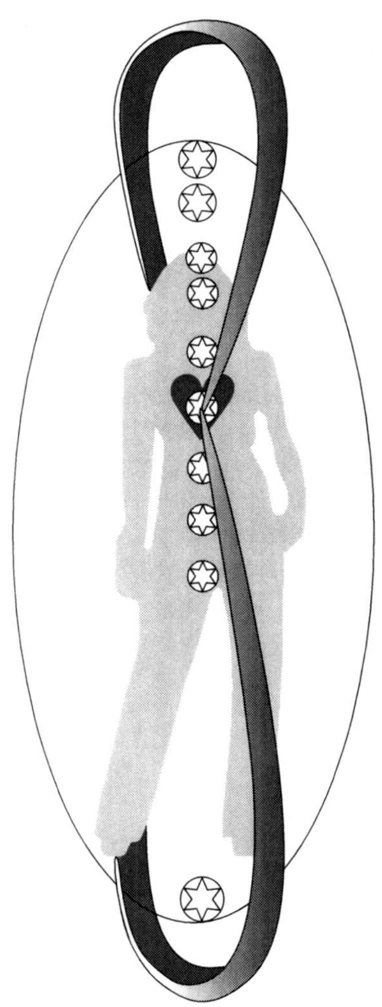

Imagine traveling up the strip from your heart, up the front of your body to three feet above your head, and into the star above your energy bubble. (We mentioned this star during the Akashic attunement in Chapter 3, Begin the Journey.) You may also envision the end of the strip going into the Akashic Field of energy, or into heaven. Once you pierce the star, imagine traveling down the strip behind your body and piercing through your heart.

Continue by traveling down the front of your body. Continue downward until you are three feet below your feet and into the chakra that reside deep within the earth.

Follow the strip as it turns to travel up the back of your body and returns to the center of your heart.

The strip will then continue up the front of your body until it reaches the star once again.

Once you get the feel of the motion of this energy, add a prayer.

Breathe in, pulling the earth's energy into your heart with your breath. Let this earth's energy fill your body as it travels upward.

Pray: *Mother.*

Release your breath slowly. Repeat again until you feel full.

Breathe in again, pulling heaven's light or beautiful sunlight, into your heart. Imagine your heart's energy center expanding with each breath.

Pray: *Father.*

Your heart's energy center continues to expand with each breath.

Pray: *God, Creator of all that is, and the Akashic Energy of compassion.*

Now imagine again the energy of your Mobius strip traveling through your heart, up and over your head, back through your heart and down your front to the earth, then traveling up your back and coming through your heart once again. Each new circumference shifts a little to the right (clockwise) until the Mobius strip has woven a complete sphere around you.

> **Pray:** *Divine, unconditional love fills me and surrounds me in a sphere of protection and guidance that sustains me throughout my life.*
>
> *I acknowledge this presence of Love is the source of all creation.*

Continue to envision infinite energy running through your body. Affirm that all is one and all is connected, and that you are filled and surrounded with Divine, nurturing energy.

Close your records.

(Trauma and our emotional/ mental reaction to trauma can cause disruption to this flow and create a closed energy circuit. Later in Chapter 9 we'll discuss how to recognize these closed circuits and how to heal them.)

The Roots of Consciousness

> *I AM what I feel, what I know, what I believe, and what I desire.*

The roots of a tree anchor it to the earth. Each tender root wraps itself around particles of soil and then draws out the water and nutrients contained in the soil. The soluble material travels up from the roots to nourish the tree. The roots also store some of this material as sugars and starches for a spring kick off when the tree comes out of hibernation. After hibernation, the tree starts to wake up, and the buds on the branches demand nourishment so they can bloom. The roots feed new growth in the form of branches, leaves, and blossoms, which turn into seeds, nuts, and fruits.. As the roots grow larger and dig deeper into the earth, the tree becomes more stable. The roots prevent the soil from eroding away from the tree, ensuring that the tree is well fed.

Our lower chakras—the root or first chakra, the sacral or second chakra, and the solar plexus chakra—make up the energy center of our belly. They function much like the roots of our life. They carry our base, *"underground"* consciousness. Much like the roots of the tree, they work in the dark. Another chakra, operates about eighteen inches below our feet. This chakra, while still part of our energy system, anchors us deep into the earth.

These lower belly chakras resonate energetically with the ancient part of our brain called the limbic brain. The limbic system of our brain contains the hippocampus, the amygdala, and the hypothalamus. Sometime referred to as the reptilian brain, this is a primary part of our brain that holds the ancient understanding of life and knows how to survive. Powerful drives reside here—our will to live and our prime directive to survive. Our fight or flight reactions live here. These primary drives can take over our conscious selves in an inkling if they perceive we are in danger and need saving.

Imagine stepping into a street full of traffic—you don't notice a car coming toward you; you're looking in the wrong direction—but an unconscious part of you is looking. Suddenly, you're jumping out of the way before you even realize it. As you recover, or become aware again, you may say something like, "Whew! That was a close call." You may not have even noticed that a different part of your consciousness had just kicked in and you had responded without "thinking it through."

We're often unaware of this reactionary center that informs us. We can be triggered by this center at any point in our life, and may not even know what is happening. The connection between our conscious Self and our unconscious Self is seamless. We often aren't aware of the exchange between these consciousness centers until the event is over.

Some disciplines consider this unconscious part of our mind to be the ego. This underground part of our Self contains our will to live, our beliefs, desires, emotions, fears, feelings, and reactions to *EVERYTHING* that has *EVER* happened to us, very much like our Akashic Records. As matter of fact, these patterns are recorded in our Akashic Records.

The consciousness center has a mind and imperative of its own—to stay in constant conscious awareness of all our activities— so we survive.

In order for our heart center to make choices, we must be aware of what our root or ego consciousness is telling us and motivating us to do. This root consciousness system is our secret motivation source. We may have very clear intentions in our hearts, but our deeper motivations can derail us every time if we're not aware of our deep inner dialogue. Leave no conscious part of yourself behind if you expect to make progress.

There are many hidden aspects and unseen personalities that live in our unconscious Self. (We'll look closer at this in the next chapter.)

As the roots of the tree are buried in the dark, lightless soil, so this consciousness is often buried. This unconsciousness is commonly called the Shadow Self. This is not to be confused with your sleeping conscious Self.

Nothing in your unconscious mind is sleeping. These thoughts can be less clear and harder to access because they are underground, and speak a different language than our hearts and brains.

The belly chakras connected to the brain centers have a language that is mostly vibration, texture, feeling, and reaction. They constantly feed input from the outer world into the limbic brain. For the most part, there is very little modern language here in this center. This is a reactionary center that contains early learning from childhood that we have stored away and often function unconsciously from. Everything we need to survive and live our lives is in this lower root area. Sometimes we need help up with a memory or emotional reaction we have relegated to this dark shadow.

Just as a root can get stuck around an unyielding stone, so our minds can get stuck around trauma or stubbornness and misunderstanding.

This unconscious part of our Self will believe and do whatever we ask it to, whether we realize it at the time of request or not. We will discuss how your heart can hear the messages of your unconscious mind, and interpret that information. The Soul also interacts through the heart to the roots. We will also discuss the life map that the Soul leaves in our unconscious mind before we're born

The Heart, Spirit, and Awareness of Self

I AM ME

The tree's heart is its trunk. The trunk connects the roots and branches. The tree's life story can be read in the rings formed in the wood of the trunk. Every year, a new ring forms and tells the story of that year.

Everything must pass through the trunk—from the nutrients and the water from the roots—to the light from the sun. The bark of the trunk protects the tree from disease. It monitors the temperature of the tree in order to keep the flow of nutrients moving. If this process fails, the tree will die.

Let's talk about our heart center; the center that exclaims, *"I AM ME!"* Our heart, like the trunk of the tree, connects our root center (or our ego, our unconscious) with our branches of growth and manifestation (our Soul, which is also our higher consciousness and our subconscious.) Our heart consciously makes decisions and judgments that impact the flow of energy between all the consciousness centers. Our heart center integrates all it knows in order to captain our ship.

Our heart is our awareness, our inner center that is alive and capable of making choices that determine our direction in life. Our heart is our living consciousness.

Within your heart lives your essence, your personality, and your sense of Self. Your heart contains your imagination, creativity, and wisdom. Within your heart is the ability to access all of the gifts and talents you have at your disposal for this lifetime. The heart is an actively energetic center of creativity. The root, ego place is a place of memories and old knowing. Can you see how these energy centers could help each other? Can you see how these energy centers could be at odds with each other?

Exercise 5

Recall a Challenge, Who Was Talking?

Set up: A quiet place were you won't be interrupted

Time: 15-25 minutes

You will need:

- your journal and pen

Imagine a scenario in your life when you wanted to learn or try something new (mine was learning how to ski at the age of 50).

Remember all your reactions and the considerations you had as you decided whether or not to do the activity (for example, I am too old for this, I am not agile, I will hurt myself and heal slowly, It will be fun, Great exercise, Meet new people . . .)

Now recall all the emotions and reactions you had as you engaged in the new activity.

Now recall what you thought, how you felt after the activity.

Write down what your heart wanted to do. Now write down all the considerations and opinions your inner voices mention. Can you identify the differences between your root ego voices and the voice of your heart? What choices did you make at the time? Which voices had the most influence?

All of your consciousness centers are equally important. Check in with everyone inside you and leave no conscious part behind. Consider yourself and your consciousness from a holistic point of view. Conquering your fear must start with checking in with that fear. In the next chapter, we'll learn how to check in with our emotions to get the real deal about what's going on.

Your heart center is receptive and sensitive in nature. At its weakest point, the consciousness in your heart center can get overwhelmed, and check out or go to sleep. When the heart consciousness goes to sleep, what happens? The flow of essential life energy could stop running through your life, or the unconsciousness in your root ego, with its will to live, could take over the driver's seat of your life. It takes over to ensure your survival. Unfortunately, the ego root system has a lousy navigation system. It's not a good listener because it already knows everything. It usually isn't so flexible because it lives in the past. But it will make sure you survive. It knows how to do that.

The problem is that the flow of nutrition and energy to the branches of growth and manifestation *stop* flowing. Root ego is only interested in surviving and it uses what it already knows. It hunkers down. Growth and development on a spiritual and Soul level stop. Manifestations of your Soul's purpose stop. Creativity stops. Things stop in your outer life as well; you no longer have a sense of well-being.

Your heart center is compassionate, wise, and a good listener. Once your heart is open and awake, listening to your emotions speaking up and explaining things to you, the healing begins. Your heart doesn't have to do what the emotions tell it to do. The heart only has to listen. Creativity kicks in, and what you thought you *SHOULD* do evolves into an action of compassionate Self-love.

Once you observe yourself in sacred Akashic space—the higher vibration of your Soul entrains the lower vibrations of your unconscious to reach it's higher potential. Review Chapter 5 on creating sacred heart space. Have you tried the meditation yet? Go to https://angelscapes.net/meditations/ to hear a recorded version of the meditation. When you're working with expanding the heavy energies in your heart, ask yourself – Where did this feeling or thought originate?

In the next chapter I will explain how to open your records to order to create a safe inner place for your unconscious to express itself. You will learn to observe from a non-judgmental, neutral position to listening to your inner voices. Your inner voices have a lot to say to you!

The Heart and the Analytical Mind

The Age of Reason as reigned for hundreds of years. It was designed to help humankind go beyond the reactions, fears, and superstitions that were informing humankind from the limbic brain, the root consciousness. This Reign of Reason, which is meant to give credence to scientific method and logic above all else, is now a passing trend. Slowly a new trend is establishing itself toward integrating thought with body, heart, and Soul.

Many of the beliefs and understandings of the mind can be tracked to the root level. You may find yourselves logically, mindfully, supporting a concept that is ego based, rooted in your unconscious mind. You may also find yourself running in circles with this belief until you're willing to take a look at the roots from where this concept originated.

The Heart is the champion of discovery and creative thinking. The Soul feeds that energetic thinking with more inspiration and more information. Heart and Soul consciousness are behind science all the way. When we're tirelessly curious about something, we are usually being guided by our Souls to dive deep. When we open ourselves up to knowing and learning, we will eventually be rewarded.

Dmitri Mendeleev is the author of the periodic table of elements. He was a scientist and chemist, and his self-appointed task was to create a table of chemical elements known to scientists. He created flashcards of each element, and would spend hours in a day over many years trying to organize them, according to their qualities. One night Mendeleev had a dream. The cards that represented all of the elements that he'd been studying began to organize themselves into the table of elements. The organization of the table also included elements that were not yet discovered. Blank boxes positioned themselves in specific order next to certain elements he already knew. When he woke up, he quickly sketched out what he saw in his dream. The reconstruction of his dream became the periodic table of elements that scientists currently use today. Since his revelations of the periodic table, newly discovered elements he predicted now fill the blank boxes of Mendeleev's table of elements.

The attitude, or energetics, around a story or informational discovery, need to be a continuous flow of energy; very much like a dance. This allows the body of information to grow and manifest into whatever form it naturally takes.

A realization about a hypothesis or a theory isn't an end result. This is not the time to clamp down and make rules. Realization is a doorway, not

 Divine Love Affair

an end or a wall. When we make it a wall or a rule, we stop the flow of the thought energy and its inspiration. When we root our Self into believing this end result, and ask our unconscious mind to hold that rule and belief as real, the energy stagnates. Once we create that energetic belief, our unconscious mind will defend this belief, no questions asked, until we choose to change the belief and release the defense.

In summary, the Heart is capable of wondrous thought. When a thought or idea is defended and limited in scope, then it's time to check out the root source and motivation behind it. When the idea or thought is free flowing, inspired, and you have a sense of growth and development, then you're energetically aligned for the best possible outcome.

The *Akashic Journey to Soul Contracts* is designed to help you discover beliefs and rules that you are unconsciously defending. Through observation and listening to inner dialogues while working in sacred space, you will open up closed energies. Once your consciousness is open, you will be free to explore your life's purpose, learn, and grow. Your personal vibration will increase and you *will* feel a sense of well-being.

The Soul

I AM

The Soul and higher consciousness are represented by the branches, leaves, and fruit of the tree. This level of consciousness can be difficult to discern. We connect with this center through intuition and inspiration. Creative endeavors can open us up to our Soul's higher consciousness.

We can also be driven to this higher awareness by frustration when we find ourselves exclaiming, "Wait, there's got to be more!" It's the search that brings us to our Soul.

Faith and Hope can lead us to this center of Soul's consciousness. The Soul's higher consciousness vibrates to I Am that I Am – the Akashic God consciousness. This vibration is about a state of being that is connected to all consciousness. What does that mean? It means that this part of our consciousness goes beyond our lives as we are living them now.

When we begin to access the Soul's conscious center, it can feel like the unconscious mind of the root. The language is different and we have to work to understand it. Communicating with the Soul can feel like waking up. This higher Self communicates through our subconscious mind. It speaks to us through symbols and extra sensitive senses.

This consciousness is always with us, always speaking to us, and guiding us. It's the journey of the heart to learn the Soul's language and respond. While the Soul's presence in our life is less personal than our root consciousness, our Soul knows us intimately. Our Soul is our creator. Our Soul dreamed us into being.

We are created from our Soul's inception of our Self. A plan was laid out before we were born. Other Souls were contracted and agreed to participate in the plan of our life. We were designated with abilities and gifts that would help us in our life. We were totally aware of this plan. We helped make this plan. We were given a map, imbedded in our etheric energy body, in between our first and second chakras and in our 8th chakra above our head. This energetic map is multidimensional through time as well as through our physical space. Our Soul interacts with us through this map. Our Soul desires to experience our life with us. Our map contains experience and relationships timed like appointments that we are meant to keep. These specific encounters guide us and influence us to keep us on our soul's desired journey. What we feel, what we learn, what we accomplish are all connected to our soul's learning and accomplishments. Michael Newton, in his books *Life between Lives* and *Journey of Souls,* records many Soul's descriptions of how the Soul plans the next life, and what it wants to accomplish in that lifetime to help the Soul accomplish a specific challenge.

Our Soul, our higher consciousness, is always with us to guide and sustain us. Our Soul is constantly communicating with us through a constant flow of the Creator's healing, loving Akashic energy. Whether we are conscious of it or not, we are wealthy with this love.

Scientists talk about different levels of brain waves and levels of consciousness that allow us to receive and access information. Dr. Rex Jung of the University of New Mexico is able to detect alpha waves at an unconscious level that are active behind the scenes of our conscious mind. Alpha waves are associated with divergent thinking which is associated with creative and cognitive abilities beyond the mundane. In this sense, he felt we are constantly receiving energy and information at a higher level; it's simply a matter of accessing it. Consider these alpha waves are originated from a higher energy source, as in the Akashic Records.

The information in the Akashic plane is energy that vibrates at a different rate than our everyday minds. Through prayer, intention, and meditation we are able to access this vibratory library of information from the universal mind, or the Akashic Records, much like Dr. Jung's alpha waves.

Along the same idea, we're able to access the loving, healing presence of this Akashic energy through intuition and emotions. The Akashic vibratory energy also contains healing properties. Relaxing your thoughts, opening your heart, with the intent to calm your body, is a formula for opening up to this higher consciousness of healing and love from the universal mind; the Akashic Field of energy. When you open up to this vibration, you begin a process of vibrational entrainment. The higher vibration will affect the lower vibrations within your consciousness. The law of vibration teaches us that vibrations naturally harmonize with each other, seeking to harmonize with the highest vibration.

When we meditate or pray to open to that higher consciousness—the Akashic Consciousness—we invite a higher vibration of love and guidance to blend with us. This blending heals us, informs us, and opens us up to our greatest capacity. Please understand that higher consciousness is always there, it never leaves us; we don't have to *go out there* to find it. We only have to open to this higher power through meditation, prayer, Self-love, and inner calm. When you're open to your higher mind, it's possible to develop your own higher awareness. You can develop your sensitivities to hear, receive, and be aware of this Soul level consciousness. When you relax your willpower and align your thinking and feeling along with the flow of the Soul, you open yourself to the highest capacity of your life. You're able to receive and develop the gifts your Soul has given you. You will have access to a huge, loving network of the One Mind, the Akashic Consciousness, which connects all Souls to the Creator.

Chapter 8

Meeting Your Team of Experts

Inner Resources: You Have More Than You Ever Bargained For

In the early 70s, a transition happened in in the field of psychology. Some therapists developed an energetic, spiritual approach to treatment. Brugh Joy, Carolyn Conger Hall Stone, and Sidra Winkleman began to move beyond the traditional practices into what they called transformational psychology. It claimed to be a more humanistic approach to an aware consciousness.

"Transformational psychology reflects integration of spiritual as well as physical, emotional, and mental aspects of health and disease. Access to expanded states of awareness is the major criteria which differentiates transformational psychology from other more conventional modes of approach."

~ Brugh Joy

During the New Age spiritual explosion of the 80s, and in many spiritual practices, a goal was set to reach spiritual actualization through depriving or overcoming the ego. The Akashic Journey has an organizational principle of full integration. This principle teaches that all the parts of our Self, including our *"ego"* are integrated together to become enlightened. All parts of *"self"* reach enlightenment. The Creator made no mistakes. Our Akashic connection can guide us to a clearer understanding about our self. Your Akashic Journey will help you build a solid practice for your spiritual life while you are here on earth as a human.

The key to deep Soul awakening is being able to listen to and integrate all parts of our diverse selves. When we listen to our inner *Self* with compassion, we create a connection that flows through us, just like the tree and it's three systems of nourishment. Through compassionate living, we allow Akashic loving energy to flow through us physically, mentally, emotionally and spiritually, to nurture and sustain us throughout our life.

According to Hal and Sidra Stone, consciousness is not an entity, it's a process. (It's a verb, not a noun.) Consciousness is not a static condition of being, nor is it a state to strive for, or attain. Consciousness is a process to be lived out, from one moment to the next. Happily, the practice of psychology strives to put some spiritual and energetic aspects into treatment. The challenge for any spiritual discipline is to put human experience back into their practice for a more balanced view of living and healing.

The organization of consciousness in transformational psychology is similar to our allegory of a tree. Three levels of consciousness are identified in this communication system. The first level is a witness of our life, a non-judgmental aspect that collects data, facts, and details. The second level is much like the roots of our tree. This level contains many aspects of our personalities and belief systems which operate in our unconscious. The third level is referred to as the aware ego—the sense of *I* or *Self*—the part that makes the choices in our life. This third level is similar to the heart of the tree.

The word ego and the concepts attached to it have been tossed around quite a bit in spiritual circles and psychological studies. In some teachings, the ego is something to be overcome. Ego is seen as the source of many sorrows. In psychological terms, a healthy ego is something to strive for. The term ego has so many preconceived ideas about it that I'm going to use the words awareness and consciousness in its place. The development of consciousness and awareness about the choices we make in our lives is a huge milestone on the path to living an enlightened life.

The three levels of consciousness are very much like three steps towards a healed and whole, integrated Self.

The First Level - Sacred Witness

The first stage, or steps, toward conscious living, is to practice awareness of your inner selves, inner voices. Develop a witnessing, observant Self that is willing to see and observe without judging. This observant Self is also the sacred witness. Opening sacred space in your Akashic Records will sustain and nurture your sacred witness. Your own Akashic Records are already functioning as a sacred witness.

This capacity to witness life in all its aspects without trying to control the outcome is funded by your Akashic Records. This observing is done as pure insight with no judgment. The witness doesn't react, doesn't do anything, it just observes. This is a silent mode and needs to be unattached to whatever is taking place. It is not rational or emotional. This state of awareness isn't aligned or attached to an agenda or influence from any part of the Self—no agenda, baby—simply a collection of data.

The witness Self's job is to observe the many selves in our unconscious within our lives. The expression of these selves is the next level of awakening.

The Second Level – The Experience of Our Many Selves

When we're born, we get an imprint from our Soul. It's unique and specific as to our abilities, talents, purpose, inclinations, and genetic make-up. The Spirit of the baby has a unique psychic imprint, like a fingerprint. The baby is vulnerable and dependent on an adult world. The individual that lies inside the baby needs to establish a way to begin in the world. She protects herself by learning ways to deal with the unpleasantness of life for her own well-being. She must develop a control style that suites her. This is the beginning of developing her unique personality. She will learn to become more powerful as she interacts with the people and world around her. She learns that smiling brings more attention and nurturing. She learns that crying brings attention as well, but maybe not the kind she wants.

As the baby grows into a child, she develops aspects of her personality that relate to the input from the world around her. She develops understandings and expectations from trial and error and reward and punishment. As her personality develops, aspects of her Soul imprint will flourish and grow, while others will be repressed and not develop at all. Many smaller, sub-personalities will develop along with her main personality. Some of these "selves" will have nothing to do with her original intent and Self she was born with. Other sub-personalities will develop because of her Soul's imprint. Her Spirit and Soul will have some influence on her personality as it develops. Her personality and sense of Self will also be highly influenced by the way she is nurtured in the environment around her.

As the child grows into an adult, she's already filled to the brim with inner *"selves"* and belief systems that will inform, influence, and control her. She has probably lost sight of her original Self; her authentic or essential Self. She now operates under the influence of the many voices within her unconscious Self. Every single aspect of her personal Self has her best interest in mind, only it comes from a skewed perspective, depending on who, what, or where her learning came from. Each aspect of sub-personality holds a gem—a piece of her Soul's origin. There is a little truth in everything she's ever been told. The only way to mine those gems and sort them out from the mistaken beliefs is to observe each personality and listen to the messages they have for her from an objective point of view.

The Third Level – The Awakening of an Aware Heart Center

This third level is the key to integrating our unconscious voices with our Souls. Once the messages and sub-personalities are viewed objectively, they no longer have the unconscious pull on her ability to make choices in her life. The center of her power and ability to choose is an aware sense of Self. Without awareness of authentic Self, her ability to see and choose freely will be taken over by the controllers from her sub-personalities, i.e. inner voices.

Our task in life is to become aware of the fragmentation or multiplicity of our Self, so that we can make more consciously aware choices. Our original set of primary selves will serve as a functioning ego until we embark on the journey of awakening our consciousness. As we make more consciously aware choices, we will begin to uncover our Spirit Self which contains all the gifts our Soul intended us to use in this lifetime, as well as our Soul's purpose for sending us here.

Here are some definitions to go with the terminology we'll be using.

The parts of our consciousness that form our root or unconscious Self are referred to as voices, selves, sub-personalities, energy patterns, archetypes, belief systems, and primary Self.

The primary Self is an expression of Self that is clearly developed. This is a very important voice and can be in charge of other minor and less developed sub-selves, personalities, or voices. A primary Self could be a protector, a pusher, a critic, or a controller.

Voices, selves, and *sub-personalities* are all expressions of parts of our consciousness that haven't grown or developed to maturity. They are frozen in time at a certain age and maturity level, usually due to unresolved hurt or trauma.

A belief system is a belief that a group of primary and sub-personalities agree upon and support. Often sub-personalities are developed in the unconscious to specifically support a certain belief. For instance, a belief that you aren't smart enough may be reinforced by a voice that constantly tells you that you're wrong, or that you won't understand what you're learning.

Archetypes are models of behavior that reflect our beliefs about how life works and how things should be. Archetypes are based on role models we have experienced or fantasized about in our lives. Some common archetypes are mother, father, sibling, priest, prostitute, victim, and saboteur. Each archetype will have at least two sides; a dark side with negative attributes, and a light side with positive attributes.

Energy patterns are thoughts and beliefs that have their own individual vibration. They can be disconnected thoughts or emotions that aren't following the natural flow of our etheric body. They can cause blockages in our etheric body, which leads to a block in the energy flow in and around us.

Disowning Yourself isn't Good for You

Rejecting parts of our Self can make them more powerful. When they're driven underground into our subconscious due to our unwillingness to accept them, they're free to operate beyond our control. We need to honor all our selves by listening to them. As we develop awareness (an aware ego) and embrace all those diverse parts of ourselves, we grow in the capacity to respond to life and choose consciously. When we listen objectively we can recover our inner gifts. Our personal power grows and our moments of self-sabotage decrease. We become more conscious and able to respond as we listen for and learn from the information revealed by our inner selves.

Who Are You Really?

Our minds are often buffeted back and forth between conflicting ideas and feelings. We ask "Which part of me do I believe?" Since we are creating the conflict it's hard to figure out which "belief" to be loyal to. In this exercise your will learn to dig for the true voice that will unite your inner conflict.

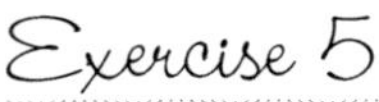

Exercise 5

Mind Map of Feelings and Personalities

Set up: A quiet place where you won't be interrupted

Time: 20 minutes

You will need:

- loose sheets of paper

- colored pencils or pens

- your Akashic prayer

Open your Akashic Records with the intention of having a clear connection to your unconscious.

List all your personality traits on a sheet of paper. Write down whatever you recognize in yourself; good, bad, or neutral. Put the paper aside.

On a clean sheet of paper, in a column down the middle write down, in

colored pencil, a list of compelling characters from literature, movies and television series. Include "real life" popular figures. With a different colored pencil, on the left side of your paper, write down personality traits you *like* about these characters. On the right side of the sheet, choose another color and write down what you *don't like* about these characters. With yet another color pencil draw a circle around all the traits you recognize in yourself.

Every personality trait you've written on this page is you. The aspects you have not circled are you as well, but they're the underdeveloped or suppressed parts of you. Every character you listed on your sheet is an aspect of yourself. You wouldn't have bothered to remember them if you had nothing in common with them. Compare these personality traits to the first list. Do you see a deeper layer of your inner-self beginning to appear?

Consider this ♡ Every person in fiction and in the news and in your life that you have a strong reaction to is a reflection of your inner, often unconscious, self. When you HATE some one and they are affecting you to the point of distraction, you must find that aspect within yourself and bring it out into your consciousness. That is the only true way to be free of the emotional reactions you are experiencing. ♡

For extra credit...go a little deeper

Choose a character from your list that you strongly react to. The reaction could be love, lust, or really anything. I chose annoyance.

Write down the character's name and describe the characteristics that you are reacting to.

> *My "I can't stand" character is Minnie Mouse. She's squeaky and, in my eyes, only does what Mickey wants.*

In sacred space ask yourself where these characteristics live inside you. What are these characteristics telling you about yourself? Allow yourself to listen to your feelings concerning this reaction —in my case— annoyance.

> *As I worked with my "inner Minnie," I realized that I see myself as more likely to agree with whoever I'm with and less likely to speak my own mind. I judged myself as squeaky and unappealing when I am so "agreeable." I judge myself for NOT being assertive. Whew!*

How we feel about our traits and gifts determines whether or not we let them develop. When we judge ourselves, there's usually some self-repression going on.

Close your records.

Recognizing a disowned Self can be difficult because that part of our Self is hidden. A good way to recognize a lost part is to think of someone you hate. Describe the traits they have. What makes them worthy of your disgust? Once you're finished with you description, *Bingo!* You have just described your lost Self.

Describe someone in your life that hits your hot button. List all the aspects about them you detest. Honestly ask yourself, "Where do these aspects exist in me?" Are these traits you've repressed, only to have them pop up during an argument or in stressful situations?

Finding your lost Self and recovering those illusive parts can be tricky.

 Every disowned Self has an opposite energy that is accepted in the personality ring of sub-personalities. The primary Self has gone into partnership with the inner critic (with a good dose of shame) to exclude that energy pattern from your life. (These team members spend a lot of your psychic energy doing this.) The energy patterns you disown are not destroyed, they simply move into the unconscious mind, along with the underdeveloped parts of your life. ♡

Exercise 7

Mining for Lost Treasure

Set up: A quiet place were you won't be interrupted

Time: 15-25 minutes

You will need:

- your Akashic prayer
- your journal and pen

Open your Akashic Records with the intention of having a clear connection.

Think of something you have always wanted to do or someone you have always wanted to be.

Now, list all the reasons you can't do that or be that. Dig deep; don't just stop at "it wasn't meant to be." Somewhere in this world, someone has proven you wrong, I am sure.

Once you're done with this list, take a long look. You are now meeting your sub-personalities who are colluding to keep you from realizing your dreams.

What people on your list do you blame? Is it Mom, Dad, a sibling or teacher? You now have an idea of your inner archetypes and how they're influencing your sub-consciousness.

Take notes. You will connect with these selves in a later exercise.

Close your records.

These unconscious parts of ourselves drain us of our energy. It takes a LOT of effort to keep you down! It takes a lot of psychic energy to keep these energy patterns running in the background of your life. They are always awake and aware. Imagine a parking lot full of school busses that are all running, engine on, throughout the school day. How much energy would that burn? That's most of us on a good day.

Can you begin to see how uncovering and owning these lost parts of yourself will increase your spiritual energy and physical vitality? You'll recover gifts and feelings you'd forgotten you had. You'll also be allowing for more of your Spirit and Soul to be part of your life.

Meeting Your Team

The first sub-personality, or inner voice, to develop in your life is a combination of *Protector/Controller*, otherwise known as *The Boss of you.* This is the Self that watches over you; your bodyguard that constantly searches for dangers that lurk in your life and determines how best to protect you.

Your inner protector absorbs the models, rules, and regulations set out for you by parents and caregivers in your community as a child. The protector then creates a list of rules and regulations you must follow to keep yourself safe. Your protector decides how emotional you can get, and makes sure you act in socially acceptable ways.

This protector is a far cry from your guardian angel. Your guardian angel, spirit guides, and Soul know your spirit and higher Self and support you and all your gifts. The protector will tell you to hush up and repress your inclinations if he feels you aren't safe. Your guardians in spirit will help you walk your path and speak your truth.

It's your inner controller that watches over and directs your inner selves. He tells them when they can act, and when they should disappear. When we're led completely by our controller we lose the essence of our original Self. We forget who we really are. Our controller is always concerned about our impact on others. He always has a goal in mind. The controller is quite rational and convincing, and determines what we perceive and how we think and behave.

You will identify more inner selves as you observe your life. You might meet *uncertainty,* or *joy,* or *grumpy,* as different aspects of yourself. These aspects are familiar, they've been with you before; you're simply meeting and greeting them consciously. The Disney/Pixar movie, *Inside Out,* illustrates this concept perfectly. I highly recommend watching it if you haven't already. The seven dwarves in *Snow White* are another good example of inner selves at work.

Your inner dialogue throughout the day can give you fabulous clues about your inner selves. Statements that start with *I should, I can't,* or *I'm afraid,* can show you your inner limiting selves. Thoughts like *You shouldn't, You always, You never, That's not the way it's supposed to be, That's not fair, You're not allowed,* can show you your inner judgmental Self, or maybe an angry inner child.

When you find yourself in a flow of criticism towards another person, *listen up!* The negative statements are coming straight at you. Those comments are more about you than the person you're criticizing. It takes one to know one. Refocus yourself away from your target and invite yourself into a conversation about the content of your criticism. You'll learn a lot about yourself.

When an inner voice becomes emotional (and they will), use your breath to release your emotions. Emotion is energy in motion. When you release the energy, you'll return to calm so you can hear what your inner Self is telling you.

The best advice I ever got was from author and friend Karen Paolina Correia. She instructed me to imagine blowing up a balloon with all my feeling and emotions. Then, once it was filled, letting the balloon go. Blow up as many balloons as you need to until your inner calm returns!

Remember, your aware heart, your *I* Self, is always in charge. When you notice you're not making the best choices, ask yourself, "Who is here right now? Who wants this? What are you saying? What is your message to me right now?" As you listen to your inner voices, you'll expand your awareness of what is *really* going on in the moment. You'll be able to make more self-aware choices. You don't have to do what you are being "driven" to do. By listening to your inner selves, you may choose to nurture and care for yourself in a more meaningful way.

The Akashic Plan

To balance our inner controller, our Soul and Spirit's authentic (heart) Self is embedded in our etheric and energetic bodies. These energies are contained not only in our eighth chakra, they're also embedded between our root and sacral chakra, and act like a map of our intended Soul journey. This map contains "appointments" intended to keep us on our path. These appointments can be relationships, events, illnesses, or some kind of outside influence that turns us in our tracks.

Two energetic crystal centers exist within our etheric body; one in our heart and one in our pineal gland in the center of our brain. When these crystal centers are activated, our consciousness opens us to our Soul.

Our Akashic Records also contain our developmental plan laid out before we were born. Your Soul and you laid out this plan together. In *Journey of Souls,* by Michael Newton, there are many, many regressions explaining just how this takes place. We are able to access these levels of Soul consciousness any time we enter our Akashic Records. Through our records we can become aware of how our sub-personalities are interacting with us.

When we observe and listen to our sub-personalities in the sacred space of the Akashic Records, we heal. We integrate life experience with heart and Soul wisdom. We expand our own personal awareness. Contained in each personality or energy pattern in our unconsciousness is a pearl; a tool or skill that will enhance our lives. Inviting these parts of ourselves into sacred space activates their growth, and expands them into the higher vibration they were meant to be in. In shamanic terms, they are Soul parts that are retrieved and returned to the self. These energies contain maps and instructions to our Soul's path in this lifetime.

Also contained in the records is our developmental journey in this lifetime, as well as all the lifetimes of our Soul. We access these levels of our consciousness any time we enter our records. Through our records we can become aware of how our sub-personalities are interacting with us and operating in our lives. By working with these energy patterns we can uncover our true Self. These sub-personalities offer us practical life tools that can help us. These personalities also contain maps to help us understand our motivations. They can reveal our Soul's path in this lifetime. Connecting with a sub-personality can activate inner growth and release gifts and abilities from our shadows.

When we connect to our Soul through our Akashic Records, we are in the presence of *Soul Energy.* Soul Energy has a *high vibration.* The energy patterns that lead us *unconsciously* operate at a *lower vibration.* When we open to the higher vibrations in our Soul while working with our unconscious, the law of vibration is activated. Vibrations all want to vibrate at the same frequency. A higher vibration will naturally bring up the lower vibrations.

Everything in creation has a series of octaves it resonates with—lower, middle, and higher octaves. Becoming aware of a part of your Self while in the Akashic presence brings the opportunity to "sing" that part into a higher octave, a higher vibration.

Our healing journey calls us to experience ourselves in all the octaves of creation. Once we reach the higher octaves of an energy pattern in our sub-Self, all of our perceived experiences begin to vibrate at that octave. The telling of the story changes; the story itself can change. The influential players change. The archetype within us shifts to a higher octave of itself. For example, the victim can become the wise arbitrator, and the fool can become the courageous adventurer. This all happens at a natural progression and is not something you can control or force. That's why repressing part of yourself is not in your best interest. What's in your best interest is to become conscious of Self so that you can see clearly and feel fully aware.

The Journey of Inner Dialogue Begins

This inner conversation exercise is designed to speak to the unconscious inner selves that direct our lives and intend to keep us safe. These voices generally have our well-being in mind. Should any inner voice express violence or plans to hurt you or someone else, STOP IMMEDIATELY. In the case of inner violent tendencies, this exercise is not for you to do alone. Return to the sacred space meditation and find a healer or therapist that can help you resolve your violent inner conflict.

What You Will Need to Participate in this Journey

To prepare for this journey, begin to acknowledge the existence of your different selves. Spend a day or two observing yourself. Observe your different states of thinking, reacting, participating, or retreating throughout your day. Take yourself shopping and observe how you negotiate the store. Which part of you figures out the budget? Which part of you chooses what to purchase? Who decides it's time to go home?

Become comfortable with this work. Have fun exploring all the parts of your Self that help you. Laugh at yourself and your antics. Be willing to cry with your hidden sorrows.

Understand that this is a communication tool between you and your secret Self. This Self has been waiting to talk to you for a long time.

Look forward to learning about and experiencing the whole you! This is a gradual way to learn and experience the totality of yourself.

Put aside your self-judgment and condemnation. Strengthen your observer, your sacred witness. Become familiar with shifting into your witness self.

Getting Ready for a Dialogue Session

You will need your journal or notebook, a pen, and your Akashic prayer. You may want to have more than one chair to sit in. When you shift into a new voice or back into your integrated Self, it will sometimes be helpful to sit in a different seat.

The intent of these sessions is to step back consciously and allow your inner secret selves to talk. Your goal is to separate out the energy patterns you carry within your unconscious Self and allow them to talk.

Begin Your Session

Open your records with your prayer.

Ask your inner judge and critical Self to step back. Insure them this is a safe, non-judgement place.

Invite your sacred witness, your observer Self, to be present. Ask her to hover just above your right shoulder, and to observe and record in her memory all that takes place.

Prepare your inner sacred space. Imagine a calming, comfortable space with two chairs—one for you, one for your visitor. If imagination isn't enough for you, use the two outer seats you have set up. Once a guest has stepped in, be prepared to give over the reins. Allow your guest to speak in the first person. When the voice has completed the session, thank him or her and then resume using the voice of *"first person"* or *"I"*.

Bring yourself into a relaxed state. Breathe deeply 3 or 4 times, in through your nose—hold—then out through your mouth. Relax your entire body, starting at your feet, moving up your spine, over your head, to your chest, abdomen, and back down your legs to your feet.

When you feel relaxed, open your eyes and return to this page.

Invite Your First Guest into Your Sacred Space

I recommend that the first guest you invite to speak is your protector and controller, the Boss.

When you feel that your Boss has come forward, shift aside and allow them to take a seat.

Welcome your Boss. Begin a conversation. Here are some questions to get you started:

- *How long have you been with me?*
- *What is your name?*
- *Tell me about yourself.*
- *What is important to you?*
- *Who is the one who runs things in my life?*
- *How do you keep me safe?*
- *What would you like to tell me?*

As your Boss speaks, write down what you hear. Capture as much as you can. If you are comfortable doing so, you might want to record your session.

Don't judge or try to fix, argue with, or explain anything your Boss is saying. Simply *LISTEN.*

When you sense the Boss is finished, thank him or her and then let that personality fade. Shift into your aware, integrated Self. Resume using the first person *"I."*

A new voice may naturally show up for the conversation you just had. Invite that voice in and welcome them.

Once a primary Self (an inner voice) has been recognized, invite them to come forward. Welcome them, and ask any of the following questions:

- *Can you tell me who you are?*
- *What is your name?*
- *Please tell me more about yourself.*
- *How long have you been with me?*
- *How do I know you?*
- *What is your job?*
- *What would you like me to know?*
- *Is there anything else you want to say?*

You may decide to invite a specific voice to join you. Some personalities may show up during your first interview with the *Boss.* Have an ear out for any voices that push you and won't let you relax, criticize you often, or are

Divine Love Affair

anxious and concerned with every decision you make. These personalities may limit you in some way. They may strongly believe in something that is holding you back. Certain words and phrases are cues and clues that there's an inner belief, or personality, lurking in your unconscious Self that needs to have a voice. Some of these words are *never, always, should, you're supposes to, I expect,* and *you can't.* Emotional responses can also be cues and clues. We'll examine them in more detail in the next chapter.

Once you've heard from three voices, you may decide to end the session. Thank your inner selves and their voices for coming to speak to you.

Return to the center core of yourself, your aware *"I"* self in that reside in your heart. Breathe deeply three times.

With the help of your observer, your sacred witness, record who visited you. Describe them in your journal.

When you are finished close your records, and then close your journal

Do not analyze or judge your experience. Simply let it be. Give yourself 36 hours or more before you review your journal.

Inner Voices Exercise for Two People

The following exercise is designed for two people; a facilitator and a participant.

Participant: Your goal is to separate the energy patterns you carry within your unconscious Self and allow them to communicate with you.

1. The facilitator opens the participant's records

2. You, the participant, will be asked to identify your witness Self by the facilitator. You will be guided to place this observer above and to the side, where she can observe clearly who comes forward and what is said.

3. Your aware I Self, the first person, will be identified. Your aware Self will be asked to step aside to allow your inner Self to come forward.

4. As the facilitator asks you questions, they will invite an inner Self to come forward. Shift yourself into a new space and allow that primary Self to speak in the present I. Don't edit or judge what is being said. Allow the voice to speak freely.

5. Continue following your facilitator's guidance and answer questions from your inner Self's perspective. Allow your inner Self to speak from the I point of view, in the first person.

6. Allow yourself to go deeper into an expanded state. You are safe.

7. Your facilitator will invite more inner selves or personalities to come forward. Allow them to come in just as you did the first one.

8. After two or three inner selves have been met, the facilitator will invite your aware I Self to return. They will report to you who they met and what they heard and observed during your session

9. Discuss what you learned and experienced. Stay in this space to relax and come back to yourself.

10. The facilitator will now close the participant's records.

Facilitator: Your goal is to interview the participant's primary personalities.

1. Open the participant's records.

2. Help participant AND the personalities feel comfortable and safe.

3. Facilitator and participant must have no hidden agendas; all thoughts, feelings, and concerns need to be expressed before the session gets underway.

If there are concerns, express them clearly to each other. Write them down. Ask the participant what they think might solve their concerns. Write down any solutions. Make an agreement that all concerns will be put aside for now.

For instance, a material concern might be:

"I am concerned I will get a call while I am in session."

A solution might be:

"I can return the call when I am free."

An emotional concern might be:

"I am afraid I won't like what I will hear from my inner voice."

A solution might be:

*"I will not judge myself and I am ready to listen to all of my inner voices." ***

4. Invite the participant to identify and place their witness Self above and to the side. Remind them that no judges or critics are allowed in this space.

5. Invite the participant to recognize their aware *I* Self. Ask their aware *I* Self to stay present while listening to and observing primary selves.

**If the participant cannot put aside their fear of listening to their inner voices, you will need to discuss and decide if the session should continue.*

6. Invite the participant's *I* Self to move to the side. You can even have a chair ready should they choose to move to a new location when a new inner Self comes forward.

7. Assist in separating primary selves by recognizing body language, facial expressions, and language clues. Invite the primary Self into the room and ask them to shift to allow other personalities in.

8. When a new personality comes in, assist in recognizing the shift, thank the previous personality, and invite the new voice in. Help the participant to shift again as they embody the new voice. Help the new voice to identify itself.

9. Repeat until you have talked to two or three voices.

10. Protect the participant from outside influences as they will be in an altered state of consciousness. Do not let anyone else comment or intrude on the session. Do not answer any queries, take phone calls, or answer the door. If you absolutely can't avoid an interruption, let the participant know and very gently bring them back to their I Self.

11. Once the session is complete, invite the participant to return to their aware I Self. Share with the participant which inner selves came forward, and what they had to say. *This report should be neutral observations only. NO opinions or advice. Do not attempt to change, advise, or heal the primary Self.*

12. Invite the participant to come back to their *I* Self to discuss what they felt or heard. (It is also perfectly okay if they choose to remain quiet.)

13. Close the participant's records.

Preparing to be a Facilitator

1. Energetically move to a neutral place within yourself, calling up your inner observers. Place the inner judge aside.

2. Be aware that your inner selves may be triggered. This trigger is meant to show you what or who is beginning to come forward in the participant. Allow your sensations and inner Self to inform you as to what is happening energetically with your participant.

3. Remain neutral and calm. You must NOT offer advice.

4. Find your inner calm. Ground yourself often while in session by repeating part of the Akashic prayer, and saying, "I am fully present in this moment."

5. Make yourself available mentally, emotionally, and intuitively.

6. Be aware and responsive to the needs of the participant as they shift in their internal space from personality to personality.

Interview Questions to Draw Out Inner Selves

Once an inner Self has been recognized, invite them to come forward.

- Hello and Welcome, can you tell us who you are?
- How long have you been with _______________?
- Does _______________ know you are there?
- What is your job?
- What would you like _______________ to know?
- Is there anything else you want to say?

The Boss or Controller/ Protector

- Who is the one who runs things in _________ life?
- Who keeps them safe?
- What is important to you?
- How is your relationship with _________?
- Common themes of the Boss or Controller: *"You should" statements… or not now, or directives of what you can and can't do, shows impatience and uses demeaning words, a sense of knowing whats best, better than anyone.*

The Pusher (Willpower)

- What needs to be done in _________ life?
- What needs to be done around the house?
- What are _________ goals in life? Do you approve of them?
- Did you help make them?
- How is _________ doing with them?
- Common themes of the Pusher Self: *I don't have enough time, or "There's so much to do . . ."*

The Critic or Inner Judges

- What is your opinion of _______ life?
- Are they making good choices?
- Do they know what they're doing?
- Common themes for the Critic or Inner Judge: *I don't know enough, I am too fat, or other statements that promote a diminished sense of Self.*

Create a chart, or use this one, to fill discreetly while in session. This will help during the feedback stage of the conversation.

Personality Interview Questions	
Name:	**Date:**
Voices in order	**Key words, descriptions, observations, body language**
Participant's observations	

Chapter 9

Energy in Motion – Feel It and Heal It

Curiosity Triumphs over Fear

A couple of years ago, I took a trip with my husband to Thailand to visit my stepson. The three of us took a side trip to Cambodia. One of our tours was deep into the jungle of Cambodia, to a gun range of sorts. They had a collection of weapons, bombs, bazookas, and a variety of rifles leftover from the Vietnam war. We were directed to choose and weapon we wanted to shoot. My husband chose an M16 rifle, and was taken to a shooting gallery. No one spoke English and all of our interactions were translated through our guides.

My nerves were on edge the whole time. All I could think of was the history of this place. The Vietnam War was horrible, both for US military troops and for the starving families of Cambodia, especially the children. I observed no anger or resentment in the men around me. These guys were children when that war took place. I was a child watching it through a television set. I was fearful of them and they were ambivalent of me.

My husband handed me his iPhone and asked me to take a video of him shooting the M16. I stood behind him, a little off to the left, to get the best view. I pressed the video button and said *Go*. The Cambodian men came up behind me and watched with awe. Apparently they had never seen an iPhone before. When we were done, they circled around me to see the phone up close. They stared at the small, thin rectangle that could do lots of amazing things. Our guides had wandered off, so I had no translators. We had no spoken language in common. I showed them the video I had taken with the phone. Then I showed them some of the apps and how they worked. At first they were confused, until I played Angry Birds. Then they got it. They laughed hysterically. I encouraged one of the men to play the game. He gave it his best attempt.

My visit with these Cambodian men was a watershed moment for me. My fears and doubts gave way to kindness and curiosity. The final breakthrough was our mutual curiosity. That was the emotion that brought us together, over a game of Angry Birds. I felt amazement and deep respect for what I had just experienced. ♡

The Energetics of Emotions

Emotions are energy in motion. Our emotions can be like flairs, rocketing up into our awareness to say, *"Pay Attention! This is important!"*

The typical busy life is full of mental and physical jobs and tasks. Rarely have I heard anyone say, *"I have to spend more time feeling."* I've heard them say, *"I have to spend more time at the gym,"* or fixing the house, or working longer hours . . . These kinds of "chores" are measurable in visual ways, but as a culture we're taught to hide our emotions. That is, until they snag us into feeling something we can't avoid.

We subdue our feelings with judgment, criticism, and rationalization. Then we ignore them, hoping they'll just fade away. But feelings *don't* just fade away. The principle of energy dictates that our emotions don't stop; they simply take another form, in another place in our consciousness. Energy is a never-ending cycle. And so are our emotions. Unexpressed emotions often express themselves as physical ailments or mental pressure or psychological struggles. Unexpressed emotions can be projected onto other people, places, and things. Blame, shame, guilt, prejudice, and jealousy are all forms of unexpressed emotion. It's all energy in motion.

The purest form of our internal energy is our emotion. Emotion speaks a language we understand the best. Across all cultures, humans recognize and understand emotions, even when there's a huge language barrier.

Feelings, emotions, and emotional reactions are multi-layered. When we finally connect with our feelings, we often feel a sense of confusion. Our feelings are clear, but our minds tell us conflicting stories about our feelings. As clear as our feelings are, our logical mind (probably the *Boss*) may react by pulling away from the emotion and trying to analyze and figure out a solution. This disengagement or misunderstanding caused by the mind can cause even more conflicting reactions. The whole communication process within our neurons and brain can break down into a hot mess. Your emotions and feelings may go underground, to the roots of your tree. Your conscious Self is then lulled into thinking your feelings are resolved. Truthfully, your emotions have only just begun to vibrate in your life. The resolution to this hot mess of emotions cannot found through analytical reasoning.

The Closed Circuit

A pure energy from the Divine Creator, the Akasha Energy, flows through us constantly. Like the beat of our heart, this energy pulses into our etheric and physical bodies.

Our entire bodily system—etheric, physical, emotional, and mental—absorbs, uses, or transforms this energy as needed. This energy is a continuous flow throughout our bodies that connect us to the higher Akashic heaven. This energy is love and is the source of all healing and creation.

Our own energy system aligns with this flow, for the most part, until something happens. That something could be a trauma, an unplanned influence, something that stops us in our tracks emotionally, mentally, or physically. If this event is not integrated or understood throughout our energy system, a disruption in our energy flow takes place. This disruption can cause what I call a closed circuit in our energy system. The energy continues to flow, but it no longer integrates with our consciousness as a whole.

The broken energy flows in a cycle from our root and lower chakras to the point of disruption and then back again to the root chakra. A closed circuit of energy can happen anywhere in our chakra system, but since we need our lower root system to survive in life, at least one lower chakra is usually involved.

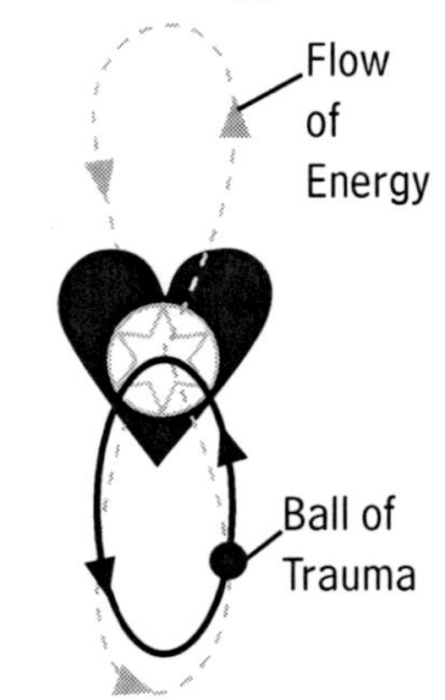

The energy flow is closed in that it no longer receives sustenance or guidance from other sources, including our Akashic Soul source. These closed circuits can create misplaced belief systems, unresolved grief, or anger that feeds off of itself and perpetuates never-ending pain in our lives.

You can recognize when a closed circuit exists within you when you have reoccurring themes in your life that don't resolve. Anger without forgiveness is a closed circuit. Fear without courage, grief without resolution, or blame without compassion are all closed circuits. Mother issues, father issues, or issues with authority almost always stem from a closed circuit in your consciousness.

It's possible to resolve a closed circuit through meditations such as the Sacred Heart Space meditation in Chapter 4, or the To Infinity and Beyond exercise in Chapter 7. Sometimes we need to hear from the emotions that are holding the circuit closed.

In the next exercise, *Mapping Your Emotions,* you will allow your emotions to have a voice. Your emotions will tell you who they really are. Once you work with your emotions in this way, you may see a big difference in how the energy flows in your life!

 Divine Love Affair

Exercise 8

Mapping Your Emotions

Set up: A quiet place where you won't be interrupted

Time: 15-25 minutes

You will need:

- sheets of paper ((8.5 x 11 or larger))
- markers, assorted colors
- your Akashic prayer
- your journal and pen

Consider an emotion that repeatedly shows up in your life—anxiety, a fear of some sort, grief, anger, boredom, restlessness, nervousness, crankiness, or even joy, excitement, anticipation, or calm—you name it. Somehow negative emotions work a little easier in this exercise, but choose whichever one feels right. Mapping a positive feeling is a great idea, too. Do both! But, please, do one at a time.

Open your Akashic Records.

Invite your emotion to step forward, just as you invited your inner Self to step forward. Ask your emotion, *"Who are you?"* Circle the answer.

For example, I worked with fear. Once I wrote *Fear,* I circled it.

Ask yourself, "What is this emotion telling me?" and "How am I reacting to this emotion?" Draw a line from the circle and write your answers on that line. These answers reflect your feelings and reactions to this emotion.

For Example: *What is this emotion telling me?*

The first answer I perceived was, *"You're not smart enough to do what you want to do."*

I drew a line from the circle and wrote down the message.

Then I heard more:

- *You are wrong*
- *You are not capable*
- *Life isn't safe enough to do what you want to do.*
- *You have no courage.*

I kept writing each phrase on a line connected to the circled word *Fear*

What Am I Feeling?

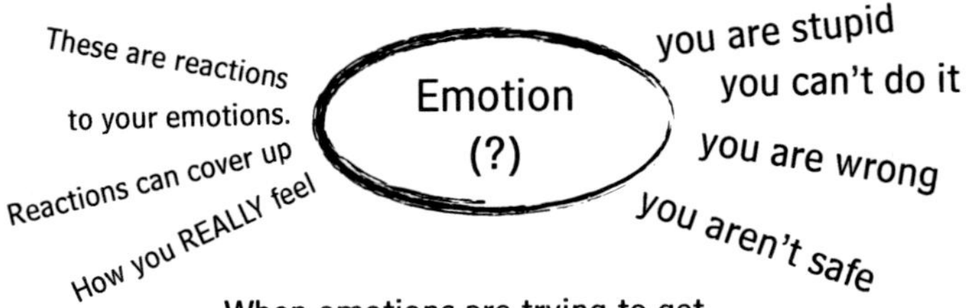

When emotions are trying to get our attention, our reactions to the emotion can cover up the emotion. When that happens we can become overwhelmed with limiting thinking.

Keep writing until you feel you've covered everything. What you're hearing are threads of beliefs related to this emotion. The information written on the lines under your circled emotion are the threads of your inner belief systems that are triggered by that emotion.

When you are finished, ask the next question:

(Emotion), what are you really telling me?

Listen for the answer. Once you perceive an answer, draw a dotted line from the first circle and write down your answers. Write down everything you sense and feel without editing. When you're finished, circle the list.

For example, I asked:

"Dear Fear, what are you really telling me?"

I wrote:

- *You're going in the wrong direction*

- *Stop looking outside yourself for the answers*

- *Listen to you inner guidance*

- *The answer isn't "out there"*

When you're finished, ask the next question:

(Emotion), who are you really?

Take a moment to breathe into your emotion. Allow it to expand into your sacred space. This is very similar to the Sacred Heart Meditation where you breathe into any heavy feelings of energy to allow them to expand and transform. This time, you're communicating to your emotions, and they're responding to you.

For example, I asked: "Fear, who are you really?"

Divine Love Affair

What is This Emotion Telling Me?

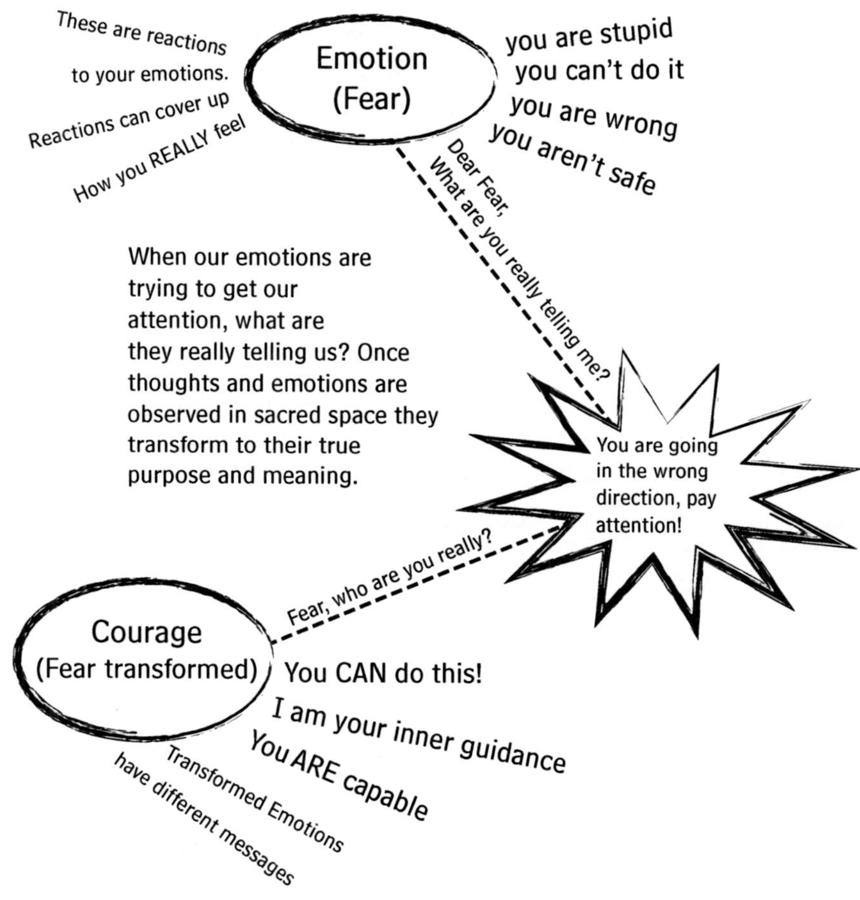

And intuitively I wrote:

I am courage, and I love you.

Ask the next question:

(New Emotion), what are you telling me?

Write what you hear on lines drawn from the second circle.

For example, I wrote:

- *I am your inner guidance*

- *You are strong*

- *You are capable*

- *You CAN do this*

The information written on the lines under your circled new emotion, are the new threads of belief from the higher essence of your original emotion. Once you connect and communicate with your emotions, they follow the law of vibration. They respond by growing and expanding towards their highest essence. When your emotions expand in this way, the closed circuit that has been informing your conscious mind of limiting beliefs is broken.

If, in the second circle, you're still receiving negative input, then create a second dotted line from your original emotions and ask the emotion, *"How are you serving me?"* Write your list down. When you're done with the list, circle it. Draw a dotted line from this new list and ask, *"Who are you really?"* and proceed from there.

It may take several sessions working with an emotion before you can transform it. Don't force the communication to go the way you think it should be. Trust the healing power of the Akashic Energy and your Soul. Remember to ask your guardians, angel masters, and teachers for help and guidance.

Once you're finished, close your records with your prayer.

The Journal Version of Mapping Your Emotions

Instead of a mind map, you will journal your dialogue with emotions. This exercise will take you a little deeper into your Akashic Records for healing. You may pose each question in your notebook, and then answer them through a written dialogue back and forth with you and your emotions. Be sure to allow your emotions to speak in the first person. Do not edit the answers.

Start your journey by opening your records. Begin an honest expression of how you're feeling. Identify the emotion or emotions that are expressing themselves.

Choose to work with one emotion at a time.

Write down everything this emotion is telling you about yourself and your life. Don't edit! Keep writing until you feel you've captured everything that the emotion wants to share. What you're hearing and sensing are threads of beliefs related to these emotions. They will feel very real. But again, do not edit or analyze them.

Once you're finished, begin with your questions, and dialogue with that emotion. Shift into that emotion and let it have its own voice. The question is:

Dear (Emotion), what are you really telling me?"

Be still and listen for the varied answers. Keep writing until you feel you have recorded everything that wants to be said. This time, you are communicating to your emotions and they are responding to you.

When you feel you're finished, ask the next question.

Dear (Emotion), how are you serving me?

When you feel you're finished, ask the next question.

Dear (Emotion), who are you really?

Take a moment to breathe into your emotion. Allow it to expand into your sacred space. This is very similar to the Sacred Heart Meditation, in which you breathe into heavy feelings of energy to allow them to expand and transform.

Once you have understood who or what this emotion really is, then ask the next question:

Dear (New emotion, essence, or spirit guide), what are you really telling me?

What you're hearing and sensing in this part of the dialogue are new perceptions of yourself and your life.

Observe the difference between your reactions to your emotions and this new awareness brought to you by your expanding emotions.

Once you feel you're finished with this question, ask the next question.

Dear (New emotion, essence, or spirit guide), who are you in my Akashic Records?

When you're done, close your records. Put the journal down for at least a day before you return to it. Wait 24 hours before you work with this emotion again. Remember—do not judge, analyze, or force your answers with preconceived expectations. This work is a journey.

How Does This Work?

The natural inclination of our emotions is to expand into their highest essence. Your emotions will expand until they reach the vibration of your Soul. Your injured unconscious Self may block them from reaching their destination. Once you unblock them, your emotional energy will complete their destined journey.

Your Soul learns from your emotions. When we repress feelings, we deny our Soul the journey it came here to this life to experience.

The expression of your feelings and emotions will lead you to an expansion into a higher vibration. This expansion will lead to integration of your emotional energies with your conscious heart. Once this integration happens, your Soul has access to the experience. Healing on a Soul level can now take place. Your sense of well-being and peace will begin to return.

Exercise 9

Opening Your Circuit to Infinity and Beyond

Set up: A quiet place where you won't be interrupted

Time: 20 - 30 minutes

You will need:

- your Akashic prayer
- your journal and pen

This exercise is for working energetically with closed circuits.

This visualization exercise can be done standing up or lying flat on a comfortable surface. Once you learn this technique, you can do it in any position, anywhere, and any time.

Open your Akashic records and say a prayer and intention for healing.

Start this visualization by imagining the infinity symbol, which is a continuous Mobius strip that overlaps in the middle. This strip represents the flow of infinite energy that moves through the universe to you and supplies you with continuous sustenance and guidance.

Using your intuition, locate within your body where the emotion you are working with resides. Every emotion we feel has a physical presence in our body. Bring your breath into that place. Locate the chakra (energy center) nearest this place in your body.

Imagine that the place the strip overlaps is centered over the physical location of your emotion and the nearest chakra.

- Now, imagine traveling from this location up the front of your body to three feet above your head into the star above your energy bubble. We mentioned this star during the Akashic attunement in Chapter 3 - Begin the Journey. (You may also envision this end of the strip as

 Divine Love Affair

going into the Akashic Field of energy, or into heaven)

- Once you pierce the star, imagine traveling down the strip behind your body and piercing your heart.

- Continue traveling down the front of your body. Travel down until you are three feet below your feet into the chakra that reside deep in the earth.

- Follow the strip as it turns to travel up the back of your body and back into the center of your heart.

- The strip will then continue up the front of your body until it reaches the star once again.

Once you get the feel of the motion of this energy, add a prayer.

Breathe in, pulling the earth's energy into your heart with your breath. Let the earth's energy fill your body as it travels upward.

Pray – Mother

Release your breath slowly. Repeat until you feel full.

Breathe in again, pulling in heaven's light, or beautiful sunlight, into your heart. Imagine your heart's energy center expanding with each breath.

Pray – Father

Your heart's energy center continues to expand with each breath.

Pray – God, Creator of all that is, and the Akashic Energy of compassion

Now, imagine again the energy of your Mobius strip traveling through your heart, up and over your head, back through your heart, and down your front to the earth. From there travel up your back, coming through your heart once again. Each new circumference shifts a little to the right (clockwise) until the Mobius strip has woven a complete sphere around you.

Pray – Divine unconditional love fills me and surrounds me in a sphere of protection and guidance that sustains me throughout my life. I acknowledge this presence of Love is the source of all creation.

Continue to envision the infinite energy running through your body. Affirm that all is one. all is connected, and that you are filled and surrounded with Divine, nurturing energy.

Once you feel the energy of this area begin to soften and shift (this is intuitive work; use all your senses), breathe into the emotion in continuous, deep breaths. Imagine this emotional energy is expanding. Imagine as it expands it begins to flow into the Mobius infinity strip. The emotion and stuck circuit are now following the path of the Mobius strip up into the upper Akashic Realm and then back down into the earth. Stay with this flow for several rounds until you sense the circuit is open and flowing without your help.

You can do this with all your chakras for an amazing tune up.

At the end of the session, shift your focus to your heart center and imagine the flow of the Mobius moving through your heart. Sense the flow for a few cycles. Affirm to yourself that the flow of the Creator's energy runs through you cleanly and clearly, bringing unconditional love and Akashic Energy to you and through you.

Close your records.

You have now been introduced to three exercises that you can use to open the closed parts of your consciousness. These closed parts are the result of trauma. They are created by the beliefs you developed because of that trauma. The actual trauma may be forgotten, but the energy and pattern built from your inner reaction to it has not been forgotten. As you look back on the "threads" of reaction you wrote on your emotion map in relation to your circled emotion, you may discover some new inner voices that need to be heard.

Remember, this is the journey of a lifetime, and this journey will continue throughout your lifetime. This is what your Soul came here to do. As you do this work, you will feel lighter. You will feel your sense of well-being deepen. Your creativity will begin to flower because the energy you were using to maintain your closed circuits and belief systems is now free to be spent on your gifts and talents.

Your Soul's Journey

The journey of your Soul through space and time is as important as your journey through life from birth to death.

Your Soul's journey is accessed through your Akashic Records and Soul book. Past life journeys can reveal your Soul's personality, its strengths, and its weaknesses. Your Soul is magnificent.

Whatever you do in your life, whichever healing journey you take, it will impact your Soul. In turn, whatever impacts your Soul, impacts all the lifetimes your Soul has lived.

We often misunderstand our Soul's mission and plan for our lives. Your Soul desires love, peace, joy, and well-being. In the chapter on Soul Contracts, you'll learn to discern what your Soul's message and plans are from what is just extra baggage you picked up along the way. When you heal your life on a Soul level, you open your path for magnificence in this life, in past lives, and in future lives.

Chapter 10

Your Soul's Journey Through Past Lives

Many years ago, when my children were preschoolers (or, should I say, *Once upon a time* . . .), I gave them a bucket of colored pieces of chalk. They busily went to work on the asphalt driveway. I watched, hidden from their sight.

My daughter loved fairy tales. When she was four years old, her favorite movie (made for TV) was *The Twelve Dancing Princesses.* The movie was played several times, so I recorded it on my VCR so she could "always have it." She watched this movie at least once a day. I jokingly thought about getting some kind of intervention for her. There was no other movie, TV show, or activity that would hold her attention like this movie did. Maybe playing with her Barbie princess doll did for a while, but for her it was all about the princesses—and the dancing! I even signed her up for dancing classes, which she loved.

So there we were, my four year old daughter and three year old son, ear-deep in chalk. They colored away. My son did the typical three-year-old circles and lines. But my daughter had something more epic going on. As I watched, I couldn't quite figure out what she was doing. She drew a huge arch (about as tall as herself) that looked like a quarter circle. Next, she drew some lines connecting the arch to some sort of horizontal line. Then she drew more horizontal lines extending from the base of the arch, but that stopped and lined up with the top of the arch. She added a circle next to the arch, with some more vertical lines that connected to horizontal lines. Then she drew an oblong shape that went from just below her horizon line to just below the arch. Her work reminded me of one of my dad's architectural drawings.

Suddenly, she burst into tears and came running to find me. "I can't finish my castle!" she sobbed. I walked her back to the drawing and tried to figure it out. Then it dawned on me. She had drawn the exact half of a building that was remotely familiar to me.

I completed the arch by turning it into a half circle, and I added another circle in line with the first circle, but on the opposite side of the arch. Then I finished the horizontal lines and extended then past the circles. I drew vertical lines on either end to close the horizontal off in a box. She gasped. I kept drawing.

"Were there towers here?" I asked as I drew three more oblong shapes in perspective to the almost completed castle. "And is there a pool here in front of the building that reflects the castle in it? She stood perfectly still.

"How did you *know?*" she whispered, with round amazed eyes. She then started jumping up and down, laughing and clapping her hands. "That's where my sisters and I played! Only I was a baby and they were older."

Later that afternoon, I dug out my old art history books from college. The Asian art history volume had a beautiful picture of the Taj Mahal with a quick description about when and why this mausoleum was built. I showed my daughter the photo and she recognized her castle immediately! I felt a shiver run though her. She started telling me more about her sisters, how they took care of her, and played with her. She knew she didn't have a mother.

The Taj Mahal was built by Emperor Shah Jahan, in India. The construction lasted from 1631 to 1643. He commissioned this amazing complex to be built as a tribute to his beloved wife, Mumtaz Mahal (Arjumand Banu Begum). Mumtaz died giving birth to their 14th child, a daughter named Gauhara Begum. Gauhara had six sisters and seven brothers.

Another odd thing that I noted at the time was that I kept referring to her as my sister rather than my daughter. My own mother had a baby when I was sixteen years old, and I spent a lot of time taking care of her. I wondered if that was the source of my confusion, unless—was *I* also one of the fourteen children of Shah Jahan and Mumtaz?

Meanwhile, back at the driveway, something else was stirring. My three-year old son came up to me and told me, quite earnestly, that he too had been somewhere else. "I used to work in a bomb factory," he proudly told me.

My son was a late talker. His sister often spoke for him, translating what she thought he was saying. She wasn't always that accurate. He was often frustrated at not being able to get his whole idea out as clearly as he wanted to. He had more going on in his head than he had access to words. To my amazement, his words for this particular story rolled right out of his mouth. He explained to me that he had worked in a bomb factory. One day, one of the bombs went off and he was injured. He was rushed to the doctor for help. Once there, they gave him a new head!

"What kind of new head did they give you?" I asked him. (I was expecting a silly answer, like a dinosaur head.)

He placed his hands on his ears. "This head!" he said, while shaking it side to side.

About an hour later, he repeated his story one more time, exactly as he had told it to me before. After his bath I asked him to tell me the story one more time. It was so nice to hear him speak. But he shook his head and buried his face in a pillow. Then he tried to stand on his head, and he was my three-year boy old again. ♡

 Divine Love Affair

I don't have a clue as to *why* my children had these spontaneous past-life memories that day. What I do know is that after that day, I started to consider the possibility of past lives, and began to read up on them!

I have learned that children often have past-life memories when they're as young as my children were, and sometimes even younger. They're young enough to not have any of adult distractions. Young children are still connected to the One Mind and the Akashic Field of energy. They hear their Soul as an energetic flow. They're too young to have an analytical discussion with themselves, so they're able to freely see and accept their past lives. Some children are still relating to their memories from the last time they were alive. Interesting dynamics can occasionally happen when a child can relate to a past-life Self when *she* was a *he*—a girl in this lifetime might have been a boy in a past life. Therefore, in her early years, she may still see herself as the boy she used to be, until she reaches a certain maturity within herself and her current life.

Our Souls are gender free. Souls choose to incarnate as either gender throughout time. Souls design specific dynamics to promote the learning and growing they need to move forward. Don't be surprised if you see yourself as a man or woman in a past life. A Soul may have had many lifetimes as a domineering male, and then choose to have a lifetime as a subservient woman to get a balanced point of view from a Soul level.

What Does Your Soul Look Like?

Before we go on a past life journey, let's have a look at how your Akashic Records see you now.

Meditation 4

The Mirror of Your Soul and Yourself

Set up: A quiet place were you won't be interrupted

Time: 20-35 minutes

You will need:

- your Akashic prayer

- your journal and pen

- a timer

This is a meditation with visualization.

Begin by opening your records with your prayer.

Once your records are open, ask your angels, masters, teachers, and loved ones to help you have an experience of seeing yourself as your Soul. Ask that you see yourself from your Soul's point of view.

Take three deep breaths, in through your nose, hold for three to four counts, and gently and deeply release your breath through your mouth. Your first breath is to relax your body. Your second breath is to soften your mind and drop your focus into your heart. Your third breath is to bring you fully into the present moment, releasing the last bit of distraction in your mind.

Relax your breathing to a natural pace. Breathe deeply in, hold; exhale deeply out, hold. Repeat this cycle until you are breathing deeply. When you're breathing in a slow, rhythmic way you're telling our physical, mental and emotional bodies that all is well. You are now free to be completely in the present moment.

Focus on your mind and let it soften. Drop your awareness into your heart center.

Breathe golden light into your heart. Imagine this light expanding your heart's energy center with each breath, until you're finally sitting in the middle of your own heart's space.

Imagine a crystal door in the center of your heart. Open this door; it's the door to the heart of the universal and unconditional love of the Creator. Invite this energy of the Akasha in. Invite your teachers, guides, and the angels to be with you.

Allow your heart to open to receive the Heart of the Akasha; the Heart of the Divine.

Imagine that you're standing in the center of your heart at the crystal door, which is open to the universe of unconditional love. There's a path for you to step onto that will lead you to your sacred room. Walk gently up this path, counting backwards from thirteen to one. As you ascend, you are relaxing more deeply with each step.

You find yourself stepping into a great room. This room is a hall that has been lovingly prepared for you. A comfortable chair has been placed in the center of the room for you. Walk over to the chair and sit in in it.

As you sit in the chair, the walls around you begin to fade. You can clearly see the night sky all around you. You are now surrounded by stars and are sitting in the Akashic Field of energy within your Akashic Records.

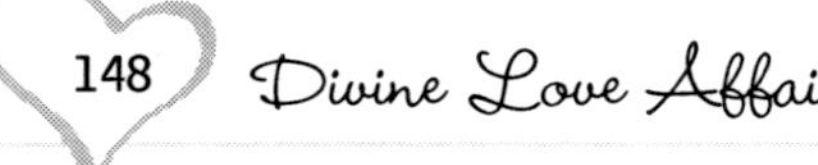

A light, white vapor begins to form around you. You sense a consciousness to this light. You feel a warm and loving presence.

This is the essence of your Soul. Allow yourself to blend with this essence. Feel your Soul's personality blending with yours. What are the traits you sense? Do you recognize any of them within yourself?

Ask your Soul to reveal itself to you. Now ask your Soul to tell you what it's working on at this time.

Continue to blend with this energy as your conversation unfolds. This may take a few minutes, and can go on as long as you like.

As you sit with your Soul you are also sitting in the Akashic Field, inside your records.

This is *YOU* in *YOUR* records. Your awareness of your own Self in your records opens a new dimension of consciousness. Allow yourself to feel the plane of the records around you. As you enter your own records, begin to energetically scan the space around you—left to right, top to bottom and then bottom to top—make a slight movement with your physical body to get a sense of the body of light that surrounds you in your own records.

Ask to see yourself as your Soul and as the Creator sees you.

Feel your etheric body; imagine you can see your etheric hands and feet.

What are you wearing? What does you essence feel like? Take some time to sit in this awareness.

As you sit in your own etheric body, register the presence of your angels, masters, teachers, and loved ones. Who can you sense? Can you focus on a guide or an angel? What are they like? Look at their feet; what are they wearing? Sometimes their presence shows up as a feeling like love, peace, or stillness. Sometimes it's a sensation of warmth and softness. Sometimes it's a quality of illuminating light. And sometimes it's a quality of support, which can be either strong or subtle.

Allow some time to be in this space.

When you're ready, begin to return to your aware state. Imagine the white vapor begins to lift. You can see all the stars around you. The walls begin to return. When you're ready, leave the chair and follow your path back to the center of your heart. Come back into your room.

Journal This ♡ Write down your observations. ♡

Close your records.

You have two sphere shaped energy centers above your crown chakra. These are stacked about eighteen inches above your crown chakra, with eighteen inches between them. The sphere closest to your crown chakra, or the top of your head, contains your personal Akashic Records. You will have a sense of familiarity with this chakra when you work with it.

The second sphere, farthest from your crown and closest to the edge of your etheric body, contains more non-personal information. The information and connections are global in essence.

Meditation 5

A Journey to your Soul's Energetic Center

Set up: A quiet place were you won't be interrupted

Time: 15-25 minutes

You will need:

- your Akashic prayer
- your journal and pen
- a timer

This is a journey meditation with visualizations.

Your awareness of your own Self in your records opens a new dimension and expands your connection to your Soul. In this journey you will travel to the two Soul energy centers above your head.

Begin by opening your records with your prayer.

Once you records are open, make this intention—ask your angels, masters, teachers, and loved ones to help you have an experience of seeing yourself as your Soul. Ask that you see yourself from you Soul's point of view.

Take three deep breaths, in through your nose, hold for three to four counts, and then gently and deeply release your breath through your mouth. Your first breath is to relax your body. Your second breath is to soften your mind and drop your focus into your heart. Your third breath is to bring you fully into the present moment, releasing the last bit of distractions in your mind.

Relax your breathing to a natural pace. Breathe deeply in, hold and exhale deeply out, hold. Repeat this pattern until you are breathing deeply. When you're breathing in slow, rhythmic cycles, you're telling you're physical, mental, and emotional bodies that all is well. You are now free to be completely in the present moment.

150 Divine Love Affair

Focus on your mind and let it soften. Drop your awareness into your heart center.

Breathe golden light into your heart. Imagine this light expanding your heart's energy center with each breath, until you are finally sitting in the middle of your own heart's space.

Imagine a crystal door in the center of your heart. Open this door to the heart of the universal and unconditional love of the Creator. Invite in the energy of the unconditional love of the Akasha. Invite your angels, teachers, guides, and loved ones to be with you.

Allow your heart to open to receive the Heart of the Akasha, the Heart of the Divine.

Imagine that you're standing in the center of your heart, at the crystal door that is open to the universe of unconditional love. Inside this door is a line, or tube, which is your life-line. Allow your consciousness to follow that line up through your body to your crown chakra. Pass through your crown chakra, traveling up your life-line to a sphere eighteen inches above your head. Walk into this sphere; observe how it expands as you enter. This sphere vibrates at a higher rate than the chakras in your physical body. Allow yourself to adjust your vibration to the vibration of this chakra.

Now, look all around you.

his is the energy center of your current records, your memories of this lifetime. This sphere is directly connected to all that is, and all that is about you. What do you see? What do you feel? This space holds your beliefs, your agreements, and your dreams. This is a place of both pain and joy. This is a local, personal energy directly related to your current life. This center is also the portal to your past lives. Each past life holds a Soul truth and a gift to help us in this lifetime.

What images are you seeing? Can you influence these images?

The highest potential for your healing lies in this sphere. The key to this sphere is expression and forgiveness. As you're able to feel and heal all that is here, you can also fill this sphere with the higher energy of the Akasha for healing. Some of your Soul contracts lie in this chakra. This is where you personalize and try to understand your Soul's journey and how it's affecting your life now.

This is also the home of your personal template and the design for your highest potential. You may activate this template, and through visualization, bring the template down into your physical body for a type of "rebooting" and revitalization of your Self.

Ask: What do I need to be aware of in my life right now? What is the path I am to take? Is my life style aligned with my Soul at this time? If not, how so? What is the best course of action for me to take at this time in my life?

Ask your guide to help you remember what you see, hear, and feel here when you return from your journey.

Now it's time to travel to the next energy sphere, above the sphere you are now in. Follow your life-line. Enter into the sphere that resides about eighteen inches from the sphere you are currently in, about three feet above your head. This sphere vibrates at a higher rate than the sphere below it. Allow yourself to adjust your vibration to the vibration of this chakra.

What does is feel like? What do you see and imagine?

This is the energy center of the higher and larger consciousness of humanity. This is the place where your and others' Souls hold their beliefs about universal love, global needs, and how to care for others. This is the One Mind. Simply put, this is the center of compassion. This is a portal for spiritual truths. This sphere contains the ability to anchor your Soul and Soul's journey more firmly into your physical body and consciousness. This sphere shows you how you can, and how you have, carried spiritual truths into action. This portal is non-local and is not personal to your life now.

Invite in a past life. Imagine these two spheres merging together. Seat yourself comfortably within these energetic centers. Ask that a past life Self be revealed to you. Imagine a door opening, and someone coming through the door. Observe this person as you welcome him or her into your sacred space. Ask them who they are. Listen to the story of their life. What were the biggest challenges? What was the greatest joy? What is the greatest learning and gift from that lifetime? Can you feel the details of the story? The emotion? How does this story relate to your life now?

Spend a few minutes in this space. Look around and observe the details. Ask your visitor questions.

When you're ready, say good-bye to your visitor and thank them for all they have shared with you.

As your visitor leaves, become aware of a pathway that leads beyond and above the sphere you are sitting in now. With your guide, follow that pathway out of your sphere. As you leave the sphere, notice that you're reaching the edge of a universe and are about to step into a new field outside of your etheric body. You have now left the edge of your Self. As you travel on this silver path that is your external life-line, you are traveling through five more star-like spheres. Each is refracting the white light into multiple rainbows. Each sphere is lighter and more brilliant than the previous one. What do these spheres feel like?

The path leads to a brilliant white field of light. Step into the field. What does it feel like? What is the essence of this place?

Bask in the light, and let it fill you and cleanse you. Fill yourself up with this light. Know you can take this light with you. Feel the feeling of being in the I AM. You are perfectly loved here (pause and stay in this space for a while).

It's now time to return. The silver path is in front of you. This silver path will always be in front of you, wherever you journey, and whenever you come to this field of white.

Travel through the five spheres, into your energy field, through the two spheres, into your physical body. Enter into your heart through the crystal door.

You are home.

Wiggle your toes and fingers. Rub your hands together. Return your awareness to your room. Open your eyes.

Journal This ♡ Record your experience in your journal. ♡

Close your records with your prayer.

Healing through Accessing Past Lives
Past Life Exploration

In this section there are three different ways of accessing a past life. All of them start with opening your Akashic Records. You will be in a sacred space when you view your past life, using the principle that whatever you observe in sacred space heals to a higher vibration. During each sacred past life journey you will have an opportunity to meet your past life Self, and any others participating in your journey. You will have the chance to see if any of the participants are in your life now.

When viewing your lives, you can bring healing to yourself then and to yourself now. You may also access the gifts and talents from these lifetimes and activate them in your life now.

At the end of each lifetime session, you must seal the lifetime closed to keep it in the past. You may heal, learn, and grow from a past life experience, but remember when the journey is complete, you must fully and completely return to the present moment in order to fulfill and actualize the healing and activate the gifts.

Meditation 6

The Flying Ship Past Life Journey

Set up: A quiet place were you won't be interrupted

Time: 25- 40 minutes

You will need:

- Your Akashic Prayer

- A journal and a pen

- A recorder, if you wish

- Someone to read the following meditation to you
  (or you may use a recording of it)

You may do this with a partner as your facilitator, or on your own. If you are doing this on your own, take a moment to identify your internal sacred witness. Imagine placing your witness above your right shoulder.

\Read the meditation. Allow yourself to relax as you count down. Allow yourself to see your past life. Afterwards, write your answers in your journal. During the part for Facilitator shift into your sacred witness Self and follow instructions.

Open your Akashic Records

Set your intention to visit a past life appropriate for you in your life now.

Sit upright with feet flat on the floor.

Begin breathing in through your nose, hold for one, two, three . . . and out through your mouth, one, two, three.

Establish rhythmic, deep breathing. Allow yourself to be calm and relaxed.

When we establish a rhythmic, deep breathing pattern, we are telling our body, our mind, and our emotions that all is well. When we feel all is well, we are free in body, mind, and spirit to be in the present moment. All awareness, healing, and deep creativity happen while we are in the present moment.

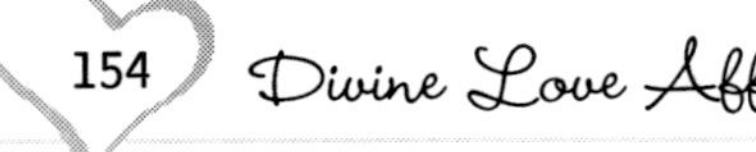

Imagine a stream or wave of warm, nurturing energy coming up from the earth.

This energy is coming up through the soles of your feet, warming and relaxing your body. This energy is pure, relaxing, healing, and it nurtures us as it travels up into our feet and ankles. Breathe this energy up into your calves and shins, allowing them to relax. Allow it to travel up into your thighs, hips, and hip joints, relaxing your muscles, tendon, and ligaments.

If you have any area that is in pain or discomfort, allow the energy to penetrate and linger to bring deeper healing to that area.

The warmth now travels into your lower back, relaxing all muscles and ligaments and tendons. (Pause . . . one, two, three, four.)

Allow the warmth to move up and relax your mid-back, adjusting your posture if needed.

Feel the warmth move to your upper back and spread across your shoulders like angel's wings. Now move this warmth down your arms—your upper arms, lower arms, into your wrists and the palms of your hands to the tips of your fingers. You may feel tingling in the palms of your hands. Breathe deeply into your relaxed back and arms. (Pause -one, two, three, four.)

Move your attention to your upper back, relaxing the muscles there. Imagine the warmth moving to the back of your neck as you relax it deeply. Now allow this warmth to move into your skull, relaxing the connection between neck, spine, and skull.

Allow the warmth to travel up into the back of your head, over your scalp, into your forehead. Relax and release tension in these areas. Now relax your forehead, eyes, eyebrows, and eyelids. Relax your cheeks and jaw around your ears.

Let the warmth move into your neck and throat. Relax your throat and neck completely.

Allow this warmth to travel into your chest and then to all your inner organs. Relax your chest.

The warm energy travels into your abdomen. Relax your abdomen completely.

The energy now travels back into your legs, your feet, through your soles, and back into the earth. Relax your hips, legs, and feet.

Now open your mind to all the thoughts within. Soften your thoughts and quiet them. Allow your awareness to drop down into your heart.

With each breath, your heart center is growing and expanding until it encompasses your entire body. As your heart center expands, become aware of a doorway appearing in your heart's center. Allow that doorway to open. This is your doorway to the universal love and intelligence of the Creator. As you sit in this heart center, imagine that you're sitting in the center of the heart of universal love and awareness.

Invite your guardian angels, spirit teachers, loved ones, and masters to be present with you in this heart space.

Now imagine that you're standing on a dock that leads to a fast flowing river. A ship is tied to the end of the dock. Observe the ship and its crew. The ship is waiting for you.

Walk to the ship and step onto the gangplank. Allow yourself to enter the ship. Watch as the gangplank is pulled up.

The ship pushes away from the dock and is pulled into the strong current of the river. The river is going so fast that the ship is launched into the air and begins to sail on the air currents.

You find yourself sailing high into the sky, watching the land move further and further away from you.

You sail through the stratosphere of the earth. Feel the air getting colder.

You move through the blue sky into the milky way of star studded darkness.

You pass the planets and continue on past other solar systems as you travel deep into a starless darkness.

Your ship passes into light as you see a white island in front of you. The island is surrounded by a pink river. Your ship navigates the pink river until it comes to a dock jutting out from the white island.

Your ship docks and the gang plank is lowered. It's now time to journey to your Temple and the Hall of Records.

You walk down the dock to the shore. As you step onto the shore, you see a gravel path.

Your guardian angel is waiting for you on the path. Greet your guardian and speak your intention for your journey.

Together with your guardian angel, follow the path to a structure in the distance. Observe the building as you approach it. Notice the many steps that lead to a large porch area. On the porch, there is a large door that leads into the temple.

Walk up the steps. As you climb, you become more and more relaxed and are able to go deeper and deeper into your journey. Counting seven, six,

five, four, three, two, and one . . .

The door opens to you. The Lord of your Akashic Records greets you. Tell him of your intention to journey to a past life, and allow him to lead you down a long hallway of doors. Each door is unique in size, color, and shape. When you feel that you are at the correct door, ask that it be opened to you.

(Note: The facilitator will ask the participant to acknowledge when they've reached their door.)

The door swings open. You must now step down three steps—three, two, and one. Each step takes you further on your journey.

Step into the landscape of your past life.

(Note: The facilitators will ask questions and pause to hear the answers.)

Look down—what are you wearing?

Look around—where are you?

Begin to travel through your life. Ask to meet people who were significant to you in this lifetime. Ask to be taken to an important event.

Observe what's going on. Observe how you feel about it.

Share your observations with your facilitator.

Continue to journey through this life until you come to your final moments in this lifetime.

Once you have passed, follow the Spirit of that lifetime to a golden room or space filled with light. This is a place of peace and calm. It can be filled with whatever you desire; a place in nature or a beautiful room filled with whatever you choose.

As you sit in your sacred space, invite your guardian angel to sit with you.

Invite your past life Self to join you in this sacred space. Discuss what you experienced. Ask if there is anything else to add to the understanding of this lifetime.

(The facilitator will pause to ask what was seen and to listen to the answers. If you're doing this on your own, write down you're perceptions in your journal.)

Review your struggles and desires over that lifetime. Next, review gifts and accomplishments. Share your current life's gifts and abilities with your past life Self. You are now making a quantum exchange, integrating your gifts and abilities from both lives, and healing yourself in both lifetimes.

Ask your guardian angels to bring balance, compassion, and healing for both of you.

Invite in anyone who played a role in your past life. Let them show you what they were there to teach you, and what you taught them. Let them show you where they are in your life right now.

(The facilitator will pause to ask what was seen and to listen to the answers. If you are doing this on your own, write down you're perceptions in your journal.)

Ask your guardian angel to bless, balance, and heal these relationships.

Thank them and release them.

As you stand to leave your healing sacred space, a door appears. It is the same door you entered to visit this lifetime in your Akashic Temple.

Walk three steps down and out of that lifetime. The Lord of the Records now seals the door shut.

Allow yourself to be led down your hall of doors to the entrance of your temple. Step out into the white light, saying good-bye to the Lord of the Temple.

With your guardian angel, walk down the temple steps to the gravel path. Follow the path to the dock. Say good-bye to your guardian and step onto the ship.

The ship launches into the pink river, then sails into the darkness and up into the lighted sky. The ship passes through other solar systems until it reaches ours. The earth gets closer and closer. You can see the river. The ship drops into the river and pulls up to your dock. The gang plank drops down. It's now time for you to disembark from your journey and come back into the room.

Journal This ♡ Record your experiences in your journal. If you are with a facilitator, discuss for a moment and then jot down your notes along with your facilitator's observations. ♡

Close your records with your prayer.

Follow a String of Pearls

The following past life journey is designed to enable you to view your life with a specific life issue in mind. For instance, maybe you have trouble with speaking up. Or maybe you have trouble with finances. You'll do a life review, while watching for a trail of clues woven throughout your life that will show you how this issue or trait plays out in your life.

A String of Pearls Past Life Journey

Set up: A quiet place were you won't be interrupted

Time: 25- 40 minutes

You will need:

- Your Akashic Prayer
- A journal and a pen
- A recorder, if you wish
- Someone to read the following meditation to you
  (or you may use a recording of it)

You may do this with a partner as your facilitator, or you may do this on your own. If you're doing this on your own, take a moment to identify your internal sacred witness. Imagine placing you witness above your right shoulder.

Now, read the meditation. Feel yourself relax as you count down. Allow yourself to see your past life. Afterwards, write any answers in your journal. During the part for Facilitator, shift into your sacred witness Self and follow instructions.

Open your Akashic Records

Set your intention to visit a past life that will help you with a particular life issue. State the issue out loud.

Sit upright with feet flat on the floor.

Begin breathing in through your nose, hold—one, two, and out through your mouth, one, two.

Establish a rhythmic, deep breathing pattern. Allow yourself to be calm and relax.

When we establish a rhythmic, deep breathing pattern we're telling our body, our mind, and our emotions that all is well. When we feel all is well, we are free in body, mind, and spirit to be in the present moment. All awareness, healing, and deep creativity happen while we are in the present moment.

Imagine a stream or wave of warm, nurturing energy coming up from the earth.

This energy is coming up through the soles of your feet, warming and re-laxing your body. This energy is pure, relaxing, healing, and it nurtures us as it travels up into our feet and ankles. Breathe this energy up into your calves and shins, allowing them to relax. Allow it to travel into your thighs, hips and hip joints, relaxing your muscles, tendon and ligaments.

If you have any area that is in pain or discomfort, allow the energy to penetrate and linger to bring deeper healing to that area.

The warmth now travels into your lower back, relaxing all muscles and ligaments and tendons. (Pause and count to yourself – one, two, three, four.)

Allow the warmth to move up and relax your mid back; if necessary, adjust your posture.

Now it's moving to your upper back and spreading across your shoulders like angel's wings. Now, move this warmth down into your arms; your upper arms, lowers arms into your wrists and the palms of your hands, to the tips of your fingers. You may feel tingling in the palms of your hands. Breathe deeply as you relax your back and arms. (Pause and count to yourself – one, two, three, four.)

Move your attention to your upper back, relaxing the muscles there. Imag-ine the warmth is moving to the back of your neck, as you relax it deeply. Now, allow this warmth to move into your skull, relaxing the connection between neck, spine, and skull.

Allow the warmth to travel up into the back of your head, over your scalp, and into your forehead; relax and release tension in these areas. Now, re-lax your forehead, eyes, eyebrows, and eyelids. Relax your cheeks and jaw around your ears.

Let the warmth move into your neck and throat. Relax your throat and neck deeply.

Allow this warmth to travel into your chest, and all your inner organs. Relax your chest.

The warm energy travels into your abdomen. Relax your abdomen and all your inner organs.

The energy now travels back into your legs, your feet, through your soles, and back into the earth. Relax your hips, legs, and feet.

Now open your mind to all the thoughts within. Soften your thoughts, quiet them down and allow them to drop into your heart. Imagine your thoughts changing and becoming more heart-centered as they drop into your heart.

With each breath your heart center is growing and expanding, until it encompasses your entire body. As your heart center expands, become aware of a doorway appearing in your heart's center. Allow that doorway to open. This is your doorway to the universal love and intelligence of the Creator. Affirm that as you sit in this heart center, so you also sit in the center of the heart of universal love and awareness.

Invite your guardian angels, spirit teachers, loved ones, and masters to be present with you in this heart space.

Adjust your point of view to a non-judgmental observing point of view. We will now begin a life review.

Ask yourself these questions after each journey back in time:

What are my dreams?

What are my frustrations? What do I wish for?

What is important to me? Who are my friends and family?

Think back to what your life was like six months ago.

Observe, and then ask yourself the questions.

Now, journey back to how your life was one year ago.

Observe, and then ask yourself the questions.

Also ask, "What have I accomplished?"

Now go back further still, to your life two years ago.

Observe, and ask yourself the questions.

Journey back to the life you were living five years ago.

Observe, and then ask yourself the questions.

Also ask, "Who is with me? What am I doing? How am I feeling?"

Journey back to the life you lived ten years ago.

Observe, and then ask yourself the questions.

Also ask, "What are the milestones in my life?"

Now remember yourself at 21 years of age.

Observe, and then ask yourself the questions.

Also ask, "What are my skills? What kind of jobs have I done? What is my family like? What are my struggles, wishes, and desires? What was my favorite thing at this age?"

Journey back to the last year you were in high school.

Observe, and then ask yourself the questions.

Now think back to the time when you were just entering high school.

Observe, and then ask yourself the questions.

Journey a little further back to when you were in the sixth grade.

Observe, and then ask yourself the questions.

Journey back to when you were a child in first grade.

Observe, and then ask yourself the questions.

Also ask, "Who is my best friend?

Now see yourself in kindergarten.

Observe, and then ask yourself the questions.

Journey back to your preschool years, ages three and four.

Observe, and then ask yourself the questions.

Journey back to when you were a toddler, ages one and two.

Observe, and then ask yourself the questions.

Lastly, journey back to yourself as an infant.

Imagine that you are a baby in your parent's arms.

Who took care of you? Who is your family? How do you feel?

Observe yourself.

What are you dreams and hopes for this lifetime (from your Soul's point of view, and then from your parent's point of view)?

Pick out a theme of pain or difficulty that has reoccurred throughout your life as you have just observed it.

Observe your tiny infant Self and see a string of pearls stretching out from the baby's crown chakra. Each pearl represents a lifetime. Ask to be led to the lifetime when you first faced these difficulties.

(You can also ask that you be led to a lifetime in which you had the skills, abilities, and experience that you wish for in your current lifetime.)

Follow the string of pearls until you feel an intuitive pull to stop. Imagine yourself entering into that pearl and into that lifetime.

Step into the landscape of your past life.

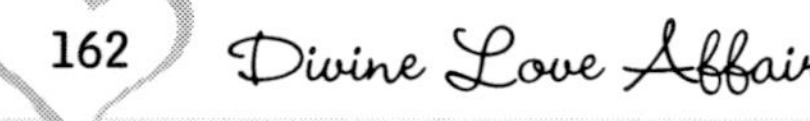

 Divine Love Affair

(The facilitator will ask questions and pause to hear answers.)

Look down. What are you wearing?

Look around. Where are you?

Begin to travel through your life. Ask to meet people who are significant to you in this lifetime. Ask to be taken to an important event.

Observe what is going on. Observe how you feel about it.

Share your observations with your facilitator, if you have one.

Continue to journey through your life until you come to your final moments in this lifetime.

Once you have passed, follow the Spirit of that lifetime to a golden room or space filled with light. This is a place of peace and calm, and can be filled with whatever you choose. It can be a place in nature, or a beautiful room.

As you sit in your sacred space, invite your guardian angel to sit with you.

Invite your past life Self to join you in this sacred space. Discuss what you experienced. Ask if there is anything else to add to the understanding of this lifetime.

(The facilitator will pause to ask what was seen, listen to the answers. If you are on doing this on your own, write down you're   perceptions in your journal.)

Review your struggles and desires during that lifetime. Review your gifts and accomplishments. Share your gifts and abilities from your current lifetime with your past life Self. You are now making a quantum exchange, integrating your gifts and abilities from both lives, and healing yourself in both lifetimes.

Ask your guardian angel to bring balance, compassion, and healing to both of you.

Invite in anyone who played a role in your past life. Let them show you what they were there to teach you, and what you taught them. Ask them to show you where they are in your life right now.

(The facilitator will pause to ask what was seen, and listen to the answers. If you're doing this on your own, write down you're perceptions in your journal.)

Ask your guardian angel to bless, balance, and heal these relationships.

Thank them and release them.

Begin to lift up and out of the pearl. Travel back through time along the pearls until your see yourself as a baby.

Follow your lifetime milestones towards your current time. Observe your life. Knowing what you know now, do you see anything differently?

Observe your current life. Begin to re-enter the room you are sitting in now. Once you're fully aware, share what you experienced with your facilitator, or write notes in your journal.

 Record your experiences in your journal. If you are with a facilitator, discuss for a moment and then jot down your notes along with your facilitator's observations. ♡

Close your records with your prayer.

A Quick Past Life

There are times when we need to quickly access information for a healing. It may be that you're in a reading with a client or in a situation where you need to get a quick grasp on what's happening. Do is this Quick Version which uses our innate ability to access information through story telling.

This technique is based on accessing a past life through a feeling or series of feelings that are active in your life now. You may find that you're overreacting to something, or you're experiencing the same event for the billionth time in your life. You may have a sense of déjà vu; "I've here before."

To begin this journey, set up your sacred witness as before. Intend to see yourself in a past life having the same issue you are having now. As you journey, you will get snippets of details. Do not edit them. During this journey, you will have plenty of time to explore the subtle sensations of your feelings as a story emerges. Use your imagination. Once you start the story the characters will take on a life of their own. Trust the flow.

You can take this journey alone or with a partner.

Meditation 8

Quick Version - Past Life Journey

Set up: A quiet place were you won't be interrupted

Time: 25- 40 minutes

You will need:

- Your Akashic Prayer
- A journal and a pen

- A recorder, if you wish

- Someone to read the following meditation to you
  (or you may use a recording of it)

Open your Akashic Records with your prayer.

Set your intention to visit a past life that will help you with a particular current life issue. State the issue and your feelings about it out loud.

In your journal, discuss a difficult feeling or situation in your life. This could be a   circumstance that has a strong emotional pull for you, or an unexplained fear that is out of proportion to any real threat in your current life. Set the intention to journey to an earlier time in your life, or another lifetime where you have experienced this same challenge before.

Begin your relaxation method for this part of your journey.

Sit upright with your feet flat on the floor.

Begin breathing in through your nose, hold, one, two, three; and out through your mouth, one, two, three.

Establish a rhythmic, deep, breathing pattern. Allow yourself to be calm and relaxed.

When we establish a rhythmic, deep breathing pattern, we are telling our body, our mind, and our emotions that all is well. When we feel all is well, we are free to be in the present moment. All awareness, healing, and deep creativity happen while we are in the present moment.

Imagine a stream of warm, nurturing energy coming up from the earth.

This energy is coming up through the soles of your feet, warming and relaxing your body. This energy is pure, relaxing, healing, and nurturing as it travels up into your feet and ankles. Breathe this energy up into your calves and shins, allowing them to relax. Allow it to travel up into your thighs, hips, and hip joints, relaxing your muscles, tendon, and ligaments.

If you have any area that is in pain or discomfort, allow the energy to penetrate and linger to bring deeper healing to that area.

The warmth now travels into your lower back, relaxing all muscles and ligaments and tendons. (Pause . . . one, two, three, four.)

Allow the warmth to move up and relax your mid back, adjusting your posture as necessary.

Feel it moving to your upper back and spreading across your shoulders like angel's wings. Now, move this warmth down into your arms; your upper arms, your lowers arms into your wrists, the palms of your hands to the tips of your fingers. You may feel tingling in the palms of your hands. Breathe deeply into your relaxed back and arms. (Pause one, two, three, four.)

Imagine now the warmth moving to the back of your neck. Relax the back of your neck completely. Now allow this warmth to move into your skull, relaxing the connection between neck, spine, and skull.

Allow the warmth to travel up the back of your head, over your scalp, and into your forehead; relax and release tension in these areas. Now relax your forehead, eyes, eyebrows, and eyelids. Relax your cheeks and jaw around your ears.

Let the warmth move into your neck and throat. Relax them deeply.

Allow this warmth to travel into your chest and all inner organs. Relax your chest.

The warm energy now travels into your abdomen. Relax your abdomen and all your inner organs.

The energy now travels back into your legs, your feet, through your soles, and back into the earth. Relax your hips, legs, and feet.

Now open your mind to all the thoughts within. Soften your thoughts; quiet them and allow them to drop down into your heart.

With each breath, your heart center is growing and expanding, until it encompasses your entire body. As your heart center expands, become aware of a doorway appearing in your heart's center. Allow that doorway to open. This is your doorway to the universal love and intelligence of the Creator. As you sit in this heart center, you also sit in the center of the heart of universal love and awareness.

Invite your guardian angel, spirit teachers, loved ones, and masters to be present with you in this heart space.

Bring to mind your intent and feelings. Ask out loud, "Where have I experienced this before?" If these feeling remind you of something—a place, a smell, a movie, a book—go with it. Build your story from your impressions.

Allow yourself to see another version of yourself.

Describe what you see (or write it down).

What are you wearing?

What does your environment look like?

What are you doing?

Who is there?

What is happening?

Follow the events so you can see that life's situation unfold.

End by journeying to the end of this life.

Whatever details you get are fine.

Now repeat the story you have just observed. Focus on your emotions to help you grasp more of the details. Tell it all the way to the end. If you remember more details, say them out loud or write them down. Be sure to include everything you see. Don't edit.

Take a deep breath and repeat the story one more time. Intuitively fill in any details you feel are missing. By now you will be in the flow of the story. Study the scene around you. Let it expand in your third eye.

You have now told your story three times. You can repeat it again if you feel there is more, or you can stop now and go on to the next stage.

Once you have completed your review of this life through your stories, you will begin an in between life review.

Travel to the last moments of this lifetime, to the time of death. Observe the circumstances of the death. Who is around you? What is happening? Pass through this life to Spirit. Follow the Spirit of that lifetime to a golden room or space filled with light. This is a place of peace and calm, and can be in nature, or a beautiful room filled with whatever you choose.

As you sit in your sacred space, invite your guardian angel to sit with you.

Invite your past life Self to join you in this sacred space. Discuss what you experienced. Ask if there is anything else to add to the understanding of this lifetime.

Review your struggles and desires over that lifetime. Now review gifts and accomplishments. Share your current gifts and abilities with your past life Self. You are now making a quantum exchange, integrating your gifts and abilities from both lives, and healing yourself in both lifetimes.

Ask your guardian angels to bring balance, compassion, and healing for both of you.

Invite any people who played a role in your past life. Let them show you what they were there to teach you, and what you taught them. Ask them to show you where they are in your life right now.

Ask your guardian angel to bless, balance, and heal these relationships.

Thank them and release them.

 ♡ Record your experiences in your journal. If you are with a facilitator, discuss for a moment and then jot down your notes along with your facilitator's observations. ♡

Close your records and close your past life.

Note to Facilitators and Your Sacred Witness

Here are some things to consider if you choose to facilitate a past life journey for others.

Your job is to be open and sensitive to your client's journey.

Feel the ebb and flow of the energy. Sometimes you may see what they see, or have a sense of where they're going in their memories.

Encourage the participant to stay in the story or memory, even if they doubt what they see.

Encourage them to see the story through. Guide them to dig deeper into the details they have observed. If the participant can't see or sense anything, guide the to go into the silence or "nothing" and ask them to describe it. Silence and "blank" can be details, and information can be retrieved from "nothing". What color is it? Ask if the sensation of not seeing anything looks black, grey or maybe white? What is the feeling of this inner place? Frustration? Doubt? Remember the exercise in chapter 9 where arising emotions are surrounded by reactions. Once the reactions are acknowledged, the true emotion or "picture" often emerges. This exercise often feels like you are making it up as you begin. The repetition of the story calls in the higher conscious part of self to activate and fill in the story.

Allow yourself to sense and visualize along with them, but do not interpret or add information that will influence them. This is their journey. Do ask questions to help them explore.

Remember that information comes in many packages—emotions, flashes of images, colors, silence or absence of information, daydreams, symbols— the list is endless and as unique as the person you're sitting with.

Example facilitation questions:

Client: I see a dog.

Facilitator: Can you describe the dog? How is the dog related to you? How do you feel about the dog? Why is the dog here?

Use your intuition to create questions that will help the participant to become curious and want to explore what they're sensing. (While you do want to ask questions that help with exploration, be careful not to lead the participant to a particular space, thought, or conclusion.)

After Viewing a Past Life

After you've had a past life viewing, the session is done, and you've closed your records and sealed your past life, you may still have questions. Refrain from going back to the same past life for at least a few days.

Let the past rest. Once you have viewed a lifetime, it's a good idea to allow your conscious and unconscious mind time to mull it over. Trust that you have what you need. Go about your life as usual. If your past life included trauma, remind yourself that you're in this life now. Affirm that you're healing the traumas from your past. Do not recreate them in your mind.

When you are ready, you can open your records to ask questions about your past life. Spend some time thinking about what you want to know. You may want to ask about individuals from your past life and who they are now to you. Write down the questions and then open your records. Have your journal handy with a deck of tarot or inspirational cards. Relax and begin to listen to what the records have to say.

Write down all the people and places you remember in a list.

One at a time, say each person or item out loud. Write down the first word, feeling, or sensation that comes to you. Next, pick one card for that person. (Pick a card for each person, place, or thing.) Now you have the past life person, how you react to them, and the card you picked. "Read" this layout intuitively to get the information you are looking for.

Sometimes a past life reveals beliefs that we still hold in this lifetime. An example of this would be viewing a past life in a religious order where you took a vow of poverty. You may correlate this with your current lifetime struggle with finances and accepting money.

In the next chapter, we'll look at Soul Contracts and agreements we make on a Soul level that are active in our lives now. You will learn how to recognize them, heal them, balance them, and then finally, clear them.

Chapter 11

Soul Contracts in Your Akashic Records

Healing and bringing my Soul into balance through contract work is very powerful. My first marriage had turned into a very painful place. I strongly believed in my marriage vows; *'til death do us part*. After doing contract work, I was able to see the situation with new-found clarity and make better decisions for myself and my children in a way that I hadn't been able to do in years. Later, in my job and career, I was able to identify why I chose the work I did, and identify what wasn't working for me. I discovered that I had more potential and ability held within my Soul than I ever realized.

Meanwhile, during my divorce days, I found myself constantly plagued with self-doubt. I worked with the *Holy Mother* through prayer and meditation. I also worked with a therapist and spiritual counselors. I learned about my chakras and how to clear and balance them. I learned to remove energetic cords. I trained in Reiki energy healing and eventually became a Reiki Master. (The second level of Reiki was very powerful for me.) I experienced how deeply and personally powerful energy healing could be.

Even with all I had learned, my life was still a rollercoaster of pain and grief over what I perceived as a failed marriage. Fear and anxiety followed me as I built my new life. I experienced a stark contrast between my anxiety and my exhilaration about connecting with energy and Spirit and the Divine presence of my Soul. I didn't know how to reconcile one with the other. I needed to integrate both experiences.

Through shamanic journeying, I realized my life had led me to a symbolic wall that was built from many different beliefs about life and myself. Even though I talked in therapy and did many reiki sessions, my anxiety and grief remained. I couldn't get passed the feeling that I had broken some horrible rule—had betrayed something huge—and I was (unconsciously) waiting to be punished.

My shamanic healer took me on a journey to visit my wall of pain and shame. The wall actually looked like a book. The shaman told me I was in my Akashic Records; I was looking at my own life book. (I could relate to that—I *love* books!)

In my book, I was able to "read" about the agreements I had made in my life. These agreements had developed into beliefs that held a lot of power over me. They were the source of my "stuckness." My guide told me that I had made these agreements and devised these beliefs. Since I authored them, I could change or release them. I had never even thought of changing a belief like that. I had accepted my beliefs as carved in stone; these were just the cards in life I was dealt. I didn't even realize they were my beliefs—I thought they were what I was *supposed* to do—learned and enforced from the day I was born. Some deep, personal changes were now about to take place.

Breaking my marriage vows was difficult for me. I could clearly see as I looked at this book that I hadn't broken my vows energetically. I was punishing myself for being disloyal.

With my shaman's help I gently and systematically began to acknowledge and clear the personal beliefs that trapped me in pain. As I cleared my self-doubt around loyalty to another, I found a compassionate realization that I could now be loyal to myself in a new, liberating way.

As I read the Soul level agreements from my book, I learned to discern which ones were aligned with my Soul, and which ones were not. I cleared and released the ones that were not.

I still do this Soul contract practice. It's a lifelong journey. As I release false beliefs and contracts I am able me to live in my authentic Self in partnership with my Soul. ♡

What is a Soul Contract?

Soul contracts are energetic devices used to move us in certain directions in our current incarnation; possibly to fulfill our life's plan. They represent thoughts or beliefs where we, on a Soul level, perceive ourselves to be out of balance. They're meant to be the balancers in our Soul, but are they working? Or are they serving only to keep us out of balance?

Do you feel like there are certain issues in your life that keep coming up?

Did you know that decisions you made in your past lives (or even between lives) can affect your life today?

Throughout history, and around the world, vows and promises have been taken very seriously. People who are in love may pledge to love each other for all eternity, or to never love another. Religion often inspires people to take vows of poverty, celibacy, or repentance. One may pledge a life of service to a cause or a leader, and then find that pledge still influencing them many lifetimes later.

These vows and promises may have made sense at the time, but what about when you're a new person in a new place with a new life and body? Even in the life you're living now you may have made promises that are causing you to suffer in some way. Sometimes it's appropriate to release yourself from the oaths of your past.

We have a multitude of Soul contracts and agreements. Some are not working for us anymore, and some had been paid in full, yet we continue to be bound to them. Here you'll learn how to journey to the Hall of Records to read your contracts and learn to rewrite them with the help of your angels, masters, guides, and loved ones.

In this lesson, you will make meaningful changes in your life by working with Soul Contracts in your Akashic Records. This work gives you clarity, healing, and a clean spiritual closet ready to be filled with inspiration, connection, and LOVE!

Understanding Your Soul Contract's Journey

The Soul contract's journey to your records will help you discover what is informing you from your unconscious mind, and what is informing you from your higher mind. We'll do a series of journeys that will lead you to the Soul level contracts you have agreed to. We'll explore the difference between these contracts, and your Soul's true plan. You'll observe your belief patterns and the emotions that hold them in place. You will also learn to recognize your own patterns, and understand how they could be impacting your life. You will then be able to assess your beliefs and patterns as either helpful or limiting.

As you continue on your Akashic journey, you will learn how to change and restructure personal limiting belief systems. You'll be invited to connect with the Higher Power of the Akasha and the archangels to help you with this healing journey. They'll help you to recognize and restructure your limiting agreements, vows, and beliefs.

When you create sacred space in the Akashic Field of compassion, you will be sustained in a loving presence to heal the emotional and mental patterns that hold old contracts and beliefs in place. You'll be working for your highest good; better then you can imagine now. While working in the Akashic Field and your records, you will be in a circle of protection. You'll learn how to clear energies and create energetic protection on all levels—spiritual, emotional, mental, and physical.

We're all influenced in many ways (good and bad) by subtle forces in our unconscious Self. These influences began to touch us from our birth to now. Yet as we become more and more aware of who we are and where we come from, we're free to shake loose from the influences that bind us. To make a real change in our lives, we must acknowledge the "problem" (or drama or pattern in our lives), how it serves us, and what the message and essence of

 Divine Love Affair

it is. You already know suppression doesn't last; it only delays the inevitable work that needs to be done.

When we are suffering and want to heal, we often superficially get rid of the symptoms of our ailments and diseases. We don't truly heal until we realize the root cause. Resolving the cause from our energetic records, whether it comes from this life or a past life, is true freedom and healing.

The influences we are discussing here can also be energetic templates that have been placed within our energetic essence. Some have been created as part of our life's plan before we were born. According to Carolyn Myss, our Soul and spiritual teams place patterns, or templates, within our psyches that act as maps home to our Soul. They can also be ancestral traditions embedded in us, or early childhood experiences we have interpreted, or lessons we have learned from our parents, schools, and peers. Once we begin deciphering the code of our struggles and begin a journey to consciously sort out our behaviors, fears, and foibles, we can find the higher meaning and the hidden gifts in our lives. As we become more conscious of our true essence of Self and our spiritual make up, we are free to grow and change who sits in the driver's seat of our lives.

Energetic templates, or maps, are created on a Soul level in response to each lifetime's experiences. They are embedded in your personal Akashic Records and sit in the eighth chakra within your energetic body. This eighth chakra sits about eighteen inches above your head and crown chakra.

The Function of the Patterns and Beliefs in our Lives

The first task of these templates is to ensure our survival in our human form once we're born. The next task is to lead us back home to our spiritual Self, and ultimately to our Soul as we live out our lives. The more conscious we are about these patterns and beliefs, the more spiritually empowered we become to grow and heal at a faster rate. You become the "author" of yourself; your own authority for the progression of your life. When you advance to that level of Self-knowing you become co-creator with your Soul and the Creator of all that is. You become your magnificent Soul-filled Self.

Observe yourself. What are the patterns acting out within your conscious Self? How are they impacting your life? What is activated in your life? What is laying fallow and unrealized in your life? Is it time to grow these patterns up? This process is about taking your life's patterns to a higher level and a higher power. This means allowing these patterns to connect and integrate with your Higher Self and Soul.

How Does This Soul Stuff Work?

The theory is that there are three positions in our energy bodies that house our Soul. The over-Soul (non-personal) is connected to our ninth chakra about three feet above our crown chakra. A personal and more local sense of our Soul, as well as our past lives memories, reside in the 8th chakra, about eighteen inches above our crown chakra. The Soul is also positioned within our bodies as an energetic essence in our belly, half way between our navel and the base of our spine (the sacral chakra). This area contains the Soul's map and the "appointments" we are meant to keep, as they are there to guide us on our Soul's desired journey.

From our Soul's point of view, we are created energetically, like nesting dolls. The over-Soul is the largest doll, which holds the next largest doll and all the other dolls within it. Our Spirit, the next largest doll, contains our essence, will and personality for this lifetime. These inner parts of our self are represented by the many little dolls nested within it and resonate with each other on a personal level. The largest doll or our over-Soul is non-personal and resonates with us on a universal level. Both are important to sustain life, and grow and evolve as the Creator intended.

A Soul's essence, while manifest on earth in a specific life, is held by a collection of bodies, one wrapped into the other. The body is made up of an etheric energy body, which envelops your physical body and houses the emotional and mental bodies. Our Spirit is created from the Soul's essence and is imprinted with the Soul's design and the physical body's functioning design (being human) on earth. The living, functioning part of being human contains its own programmed intelligence known as our ego. The Soul also imprints itself on our ego consciousness, leaving patterns and impressions which form a personality that suits the Soul's purpose. The ego's job is to survive; your Spirit's job is to live, grow, learn, and return all your experience back to the Soul. Both ego and Spirit are given the map that leads us back to our spiritual Self and Soul.

A Soul can have a theme, or dharma, that is a series of experiences consistent throughout lifetimes. This is a theme that the Soul longs to experience and learn about. These themes, as we explore our past lives, will give us clues about our Soul's personality and essence. Our Soul is the essence of the Creator, and our Soul is huge. The more we are able to integrate our Soul into our lives, the more magnificent our lives become.

At the time of the inception of your life, your Soul made a deeply considered plan with a team of advisors and helpers. The Soul designed a life and series of circumstances that would bring the knowledge, experiences, and opportunities the Soul needed and desired for growth. In the long run, the growth and development of a Soul is about becoming closer to God, communicating with the God essence, and becoming God-like in every way—a full communion with God as Self. Your lifetime is a journey toward connection with your own divinity and inner gifts. As you learn to use and master your gifts you're growing your Soul and enabling your Soul to grow in its own divinity (which is also *your* divinity).

Healing on a Soul level is about integration. Integration is about bringing together all the parts of our Self in order to blend them and work together as a whole. The definition of healed is to become whole. The definition of becoming whole is to integrate our life on all levels—mental, physical, and spiritual—within our Soul.

The Agreements and Contracts in Your Soul's Records

Soul Plan

On the way to becoming human, your Soul drew up a plan of what it wanted to experience. The plan included the Soul's own desires and needs for growth. The details were carefully chosen as to who your parents would be, the circumstances of your life, and how they might affect you. Your Soul also made a timetable for your life; who you would meet, and the potential impact they would have on you; the illnesses you would have; the prosperity and jobs you would land and when they would end. This plan included personality profile, DNA, and ancestral patterns from your family. Your Soul chose your talents and inclinations. It also gave you its own personality. While the plan was precisely made, your Soul also knew you would make other choices and have ideas of your own. As a matter of fact, your Soul is counting on it.

Soul Level Agreements and Contracts

Once your Soul seated itself in your body, it imprinted its plan into your Spirit and into your ego. "You" or your awareness of "*I*" began to develop.

The "*I*" consciousness begins to interpret information from the Soul. You (your unconscious Self) filter memories from the Soul, past lives, preferences, and desires and wishes, and filter it into your visceral body. Significant experiences of joy, ability, pain, loss, and more are re-interpreted through the intelligence of your consciousness—in your heart and emotions. Your unconscious begins to build defenses and reaction patterns to events as if you had actually experienced them.

Soul level agreements are made in the unconscious part of your Self. These agreements feel as if they are the Soul's purpose, and often they're not. But they can be healed and redirected. This is called Soul level healing.

Ancestral patterns are also downloaded into your unconsciousness. Soul groups come together to create projects of awareness that continue on over generations. Abilities and gifts are passed on through DNA. But the gifts and talents can be disrupted over generations, and fears and beliefs can be imprinted into family DNA, overriding and hiding the gifts. Soul level healing can be accomplished through your records which help you to remember and activate those gifts buried in your DNA. Ancestral healing can happen as you observe your family's stories. You can heal the patterns as you observe them and feel them operating in your life.

Beliefs and Contracts from this Lifetime

Once a baby is born, the imprint of the outside life and the influence of the inner life begin. The Self begins to interpret the information and experiences as he or she develops into maturity.

Systems of beliefs based in mental logic and emotional knowing develop. These systems are built from experiences in early childhood; what was learned through relationships, situations, and experienced through our senses; joy, trauma, happiness, or pain. The flight or fight patterns are activated in the "old brain" which sends messages of fear and survival. Abilities, inclinations, and personalities also contribute to the building of these personal belief systems. Beliefs and thought patterns can lead to more pain emotionally and   mentally, and can also cause illness in our bodies when out of balance.

As we live our lives, we make agreements and promises for many reasons. These promises can carry over from past lives, or can be made in our current life. These agreements, vows, and promises can hold us hostage and keep us from living complete and full lives. The ultimate Soul plan is always to live a complete and full life. These types of "rules of engagement" can complicate our lives, leaving us with less than what we started with, *until* we choose to observe, acknowledge, and assess what's really going on.

Complicating these relationship and agreements is our need to survive. We can unconsciously limit our Self when we're convinced we won't survive. Our fight or flight mechanism is activated, and so we're misinformed about the danger in our lives. We believe we can't live without something (whatever that *something* is) so we unconsciously choose to live a limited life in order to survive.

The Records

All of these contracts, patterns, and beliefs are recorded in our Soul contract book in our Akashic Records.

The journey to our Soul is through our emotions. Our emotions carry the map back to the origin of our understanding. The chaos of all our reactions to our emotions can take us off track in our journey to our Soul. Our reactions can, however, show us where and how we are operating in our Soul contracts book. A reaction of "I am not good enough" to an emotion of fear can show us a belief system that's driving us and possibly misinforming us. (See Chapter 9 Feel It and Heal It.)

In your Akashic Record you will learn and understand the difference between your Soul's contracted life plan, and a Soul level contract and agreement that is limiting your life. You will learn to clear and remove what is limiting you. You will learn to grow-up spiritually, mature, and heal the underdeveloped parts that are your Soul's gifts, and part of your Soul's purpose and plan.

Prepare for your Journey

As you prepare for this journey, you'll need to call in your highest helpers in Spirit. As you open to the Akashic Field of energy where your records are stored, you will find that they are energetic, with all the properties of energy, including neutrality. As you approach this energy from the emotional state we mentioned, the energy will reflect your state of heart and mind. That's okay. Your highest helpers will guide you while working with the Akashic Records and powerful life force. Each guide has a specialty and individual connection with the God-conscious awareness within the Akasha.

Your spiritual helpers can include your master teachers, your spirit guides, your guardian angel, the archangels, and your loved ones in spirit.

Additions to Your Spiritual Team

The archangels we will call upon in the journey are Archangel Metatron, Archangel Michael, Archangel Gabriel, Archangel Raphael, Archangel Uriel and Archangel Zadkiel. Feel free to also invite all the angels and Archangels that you are familiar with to help. Include an invitation to your Guardian Angel, always!

Archangel Zadkiel as you recall frrom Chapter 6, Zadkiel brings with him the violet flame of alchemical and energetic clearing and focuses on qualities of freedom and the alchemy of transformation. His name also means "the Righteousness of God." Zadkiel will teach you, when you ask, us to use the violet flame to clear our heavy psychological energy. Ask him for the secret of freedom, happiness and forgiveness when you feel weighed down and unclear about your life. He will help dissolve painful memories and negative traits. Ask him to clear your old contracts and patterns and belief systems with his violet flame.

The Violet Flame is a healing clearing essence held by Archangel Zadkiel and at times, Archangel Uriel. The properties and instructions of this flame was revealed by the master St Germaine, channeled to Guy Ballard in 1930. The violet flame works with all the bodies, etheric, physical, mental and emotional to clear them and change their rate of vibration. This flame dissolves, dislodges and transmutes heavy negative energy, including trauma and painful memories so that you are able to open a flow of Akashic God energy. This flow of energy nurtures and builds our personal capacity, and helps us realize the full potential we can reach when we're united with our souls.

St Germain You met St Germain in Chapter 6. In this chapter you will use his gift and guidance for using the violet flame. If you haven't attuned yourself to him, take some time to do that before you do the Contract work in this chapter. St Germain teaches that every experience in life can be expanded and transformed into a higher vibration that will guide and teach you. You can find divine experience in all you encounter in your life. .

Mother Mary represents the archetype of Mother. She can teach you to nurture and care and love yourself, even when you haven't experienced that in your life. Ask her for the knowledge, training and experience to love yourself, she will teach you. Mother Mary works with your fourth chakra and solar plexus. She works with spiritual DNA templating with Archangel Raphael.

Your Loved Ones that are in Spirit now serve as witnesses for your healing. They are sacred witnesses of your Soul Contract work. They will receive the benefits of your healing work. They will continue to support you in your work after your session in the records closes.

Going on Your Soul Contract Journey

When to Do Soul Contract Work:

- When during a session you come across a closed circuit or stuck emotion
- After an inner voice session
- After a past life session
- While clearing a traumatic experience
- During or after the break-up of a relationship
- During or after a job change or a change in life circumstances
- When you sense an entity is affecting you or your client
- Any kind of "stuck" situation in your life

Journey to Your Soul Contracts

The Soul contract journey is done in three parts. The first two parts are meant to help you identify what in your soul contracts you are working on. In some cases you already know what you want to work on. In that case, you can start with part three of the journey.

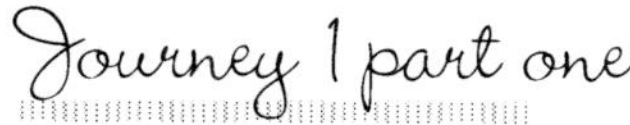

Life Review

Set up: A quiet place were you won't be interrupted

Time: 15-25 minutes

You will need:

- your Akashic prayer
- your journal and pen

This meditation is preferably done with a partner to help you walk you through the life review. You can do it alone successfully by reading each time increment, considering it, and then writing your memories in your journal.

Begin by opening your Akashic Records with your prayers.

Meet your guide for the journey to the Hall of Records

Journey to your sacred space, using the crystal door in your heart. As you center your self in your space, Invite your guide to be with you.

When you sense your guide, repeat the following:

Guide me and show me the themes and information that will help me the most today. I am looking for specific things in my life that will guide me to my Soul's contracts. What are the things in my life today that you want to show me?

Begin to discuss your Sacred Soul books and your journey to your Soul Contracts with your guide. Allow some silent time of reflections to receive the energy of your guide. Prepare yourself for your life review.

Start your life review:

Imagine going back through your life in small increments of time, all the way back to your life between lives.

As you journey back through your life, ask your guide to travel with you. Request that they point out situations and events that are significant, based on the specific themes you're working on. You may have someone read this to you while you close your eyes. Alternatively, you may contemplate each period of your life you're visiting and write what you sense is important about it in your journal.

Start with today, the present moment.

Who is in your life now? Who is important to you? Who is influencing you the most? What are you doing with your time? Do you want to spend that much time doing it? How much freedom do you have? How are you feeling about your life, your health, your well-being? What are your goals? What are your responsibilities?

In your mind, move back one year and ask the same questions.

Now move back five years. What were the most important events at that time? Who were the most important people in your life?

Move back ten years now. What were the most important events at that time? Who were the most important people in your life?

Move back to the time you landed your first significant job, or when you became independent of your parents. What were the most important events at that time?

Move back to the time you were in college or were college age. What were the most important events at that time?

Move back to when you were in high school. What was your life like? Did you have a job? Did you get along with your parents? What were the most important events at that time?

Move back to the 5th, 6th, and 7th grade. What did you like about school? Who were your favorite teachers? Who where your best friends? Who did you hate? What was your family like?

Now move back to elementary school. What did you like about school? Who were your favorite teachers? Who where your best friends? Who did you hate? What was your family like?

Move back to your seven year old Self. You were in second grade. What was important to you at that time?

Move back to your five year old Self. You were in kindergarten. What was important to you at that time?

Move back to your three year old Self. Imagine your first taste of independence. Remember what your parents or guardians were like. Did you have siblings?

Move back to your one year old Self. Remember your first steps. Think about what your parents or guardians were like.

Move back to your infant Self. Imagine being in the arms of your parent or guardian. What was that like? What was birth like?

Move back to being in utero. Imagine hearing voices out in the world.

Now you are back in Spirit. You are with your Soul, planning and creating the life you will soon enter.

While you are in the "tween" space, travel with your guide to your hall, your table, and the Soul book of your life. Go to the first page. Inscribed there is a description of the purpose and intent for your current life. You may see it in symbols, or realize it through words or a specific memory. Observe the information but don't edit it. Remember what you have seen. Hold it close to your heart.

Now, ask your Soul book to review your life as it's written. Journey forward in time, looking at your life through the eyes of the records. Observe how your life is unfolding. Ask to be shown what parts of your life that have repetitive patterns and situations that need healing.

Watch for themes, and also for specific memories to pop up at you. Ask to be shown important events slowly. Observe yourself and how you felt at that time.

When you're done, slowly come back to the room and write down what you observed.

Journal This ♡ Use the following questions to help you remember what you saw. Write your observations in your journal:

- Where else have I experienced this or felt this way?
- What do I know about myself based on what I saw?
- What do I believe about life based on what I remembered during this journey
- What healing intention do I want to make?
- What do you want to add about your life's purpose based on the events in your life??♡

Close your records with your prayer, or continue to part two.

Journey 1 part two

Claiming Your Healing

Set up: A quiet place were you won't be interrupted

Time: 10 - 15 minutes

You will need:

- your Akashic prayer
- your journal and pen

You may do this with a partner as your facilitator, or you may do this on your own. Read the instructions and write your answers in your journal. If you're doing this on your own, take a moment to identify your internal sacred witness. Imagine placing your witness above your right shoulder. During the parts for F, shift into your sacred witness Self and follow the instructions.

(**P** = participant **F** = facilitator or your internal sacred witness)

Begin by opening your records. If you left your records open at the end of part one, follow instructions below.

P: Describe what you learned from your Soul book. Describe what you observed in your life review.

F: Write down any key words and statements the participant says. Describe what you heard the participant say out loud.

P: With facilitator's input, identify your feelings, beliefs, and any patterns you've discovered. Don't try to fix anything. Only observe what you see. You may see a concept, experience, or point of pain. Invite your inner voices to speak up as the present themselves..

F: Keep notes on what P says and describes.

P: Write down (with the facilitator's help and observations) what you *FEEL* and think to be true about yourself in your life now. (This statement will take you to your current agreement in your Soul contract book in the Akashic Records.)

P: Next, based on your understanding of your life's purpose discovered in your Soul book, write an intention for healing you would like for yourself.

P: Write a statement of the positive behavior and actions you would like to incorporate into your life.

You should now have two clear statements for healing in your life.

Close your records with your prayer or continue to part three.

Journey 1 part three

Journey to Your Sacred Book of Contracts

Set up: A quiet place were you won't be interrupted

Time: 20-30 minutes

You will need:

- your Akashic prayer

- your journal and pen

You may do this with a partner as your facilitator, or you may do this on your own. Read the instructions and write your answers in your journal.

If you're doing this on your own, take a moment to identify your internal sacred witness. Imagine placing your witness above your right shoulder. During the parts for F shift into your sacred witness Self and follow the instructions.

(**P** = participant **F** = facilitator or your internal sacred witness)

Begin by opening your records. If you left your records open at the end of part two, follow instructions below.

F: Begin with participant opening up to their personal guide. This guide is the same one that helped in part one of this journey. Give P a moment to feel the presence of her guide. Ask them to signal to you when they are in contact with their guide.

P: Signal when you sense your guide.

F: Pray and lead this guided meditation. (If you are doing this on your own, follow this prayer and visualization.)

> *I call upon the Archangels Michael, Metatron, Raphael, Uriel, Zadkiel St. Germaine, the violet flame, Mother Mary, and your guides to travel with you on this journey.*

Begin your journey to the Hall of Records. Enter through the crystal door in your heart. See a path. Travel along this path as it leads you to a temple-like structure. There is a set of stairs leading up to the temple's door. Walk up the stairs. Touch the door and open it.

Enter into a great hall. You are greeted by the Lord and guide of the Akashic Records.

F: Ask participant to let you know when they are in the Hall of Records.

P: Signal your facilitator when you are in the Hall of Records.

F: Once participant says yes, ask them to describe what they sense and feel.

P: Describe what you sense.

F: Once you both have a sense of where the participant is continue:

> *Request that your Soul contract book be brought to you. You are now being lead to a reading table. Seat yourself as your guide retrieves your book.*

> *When the book arrives at your table, observe what it looks like.* (Encourage the participant to tell you what they see. Observe the book. What shape is it in? How many pages does it have?)

Ask the Guide of the Records to find the pages that concern your request.

> *"We are looking for the page in this book that has the contract that addresses (read aloud the first statement you wrote in part two).*

> *In your imagination, allow the book to open to the correct pages. Trust that what you sense is the exact information you need at this moment. Allow the information to show up in whatever way it needs to. It could be a memory, a statement, a symbol, or a simple feeling. Allow the information to come as it will.*

F: When the participant sees the page, ask them to describe it.

P: Describe what you see to the facilitator, or write it in your journal.

F: Ask if there is anything else written on that page. Ask if there is anything else attached to the contract.

If the participant is stuck, re-read the statement written before the journey (the first statement in part two.) Ask if they are in the space of that energy as they are viewing the book. If yes, continue on. If no, then call in Archangel Gabriel to shed light on the pages. Ask the book and the light to shift until the participant can sense it. The sense of the records can be subtle. Encourage participant to use their imagination to describe what they are sensing. If they say they see nothing, ask them to travel into the nothing to explore what is there.

Questions to Ask about the Contract in Your Records

Facilitator – ask the following questions:

- Observe the page it opens to. What kind of paper? What colors?
- What is on the page?
- What does the contract say?
- Do you see any images or symbols on the page?
- How do you feel about the pages? Are there words on the page or are they moving images?

Assessing your Contract

Facilitator - ask the following questions.

Participant - answer each question quickly and intuitively.

- What did you agree to do in this contract?

- How are you using this contract?

- What are you receiving from this contract?

- What is the status of this contract?

- Is it completed and fulfilled?

- Ask to see the contract play itself out like a movie.

- Who is this contract for? Why?

- What am I being called to do to complete this contract?

- What is the bottom line of this contract?

- Is this contract for my highest good?

- What is the purpose of this contract?

- How is this contract serving me?

- When was this contract written? (This question may lead to a past life or a current life memory.)

- What do you need to learn and know about this contract? (Later, you may want to ask your higher power team to retrain you regarding this contract.)

- Is this contract serving you? If yes, how is this contract serving you?

- Is this contract written to support your Soul's journey? How?

- Is this part of your Soul and Spirit plan for my life now? How?

- Does this contract help me in my life now? How?

- Is this contract necessary? Why?

- Does this contract need to be rewritten or cancelled?

P: Decide what to do next with the contract.

If the contract is re-written:

F: Ask the participant what they would like it to say.

P: (Say this prayer and then say what you want in your contract.)
  I ask Archangels Metatron, Raphael, Uriel, and Zadkiel to help me re-write this contract (in your own words say what you would like).

Does this bring you into balance? How does it feel?

F: Note the participant's new wording of the contract (or write in journal).

If the contract is to be cancelled:

F: say this Prayer:

> *I Ask Archangels Michael and Metatron to take complete control of the contract, close it, and restore you and your book to balance.*

Clearing the Contract

Whether you keep the contract, rewrite it, or close it completely, the energy and thoughts around the contract now need to be cleared.

Your facilitator will guide you to do the clearing.

Contraptions and Disincarnate Energies that Hold Contract in Place

F: Are there any energetic contraptions connected to this contract, beyond your will, that holds it in place?

P: Answer intuitively. Describe what you see and feel. Use your imagination to create and see symbols representing the energy.

F: Are they in the highest good for you and the contract?

P: Answer yes or no (Clue: usually the answer is no, if you want contraption or energies to remain in place, understand your co-dependent role and personal responsibility regarding this issue you are working on.)

F: Would you like to clear them?

P: Give permission to clear your contracts.

Facilitator Prayer:

> *I call on Archangel Michael, St. Germaine, and the violet flame to come and clear this contract, taking complete control over any energetic contraptions serving this contract in any way, removing them from this Soul book, from all energy fields belonging to (participant's name), sending them to the heavenly realm of balance and correction. I am calling forth the violet flame to clear and transmute any energies past, present, and future, that lay claim to this contract in any way. Clear this temple with your light and violet flame and free (participant's name) spiritually, physically, mentally, and emotionally in this life, past lives, in DNA, in Mother's mitochondria, family heritage, and all future incarnations.*
>
> *I call Archangel Raphael and Mother Mary to gently and completely train (participant's name) towards their Soul's magnificence, removing*

any harmful habits that keep this lower vibration in place. I ask that a clear and restored template be placed in their conscious and unconscious Self, that they can now use to support and guide them on their path to magnificence.

F: Are there any disincarnate entity ruling, influencing, or connected to this contract?

P: Answer intuitively. Describe what you see and feel. It's okay to use your imagination to create and see symbols representing the energy.

F: Are they in the highest good for you and the contract?

P: Answer yes or no (Clue: usually the answer is no, if you want contraption or energies to remain in place, understand your co-dependent role and personal responsibility regarding this issue you are working on.)

F: Would you like to clear them?

P: Give permission to clear your contracts. (Clue: don't leave any disincarnate entity anywhere. Once you see it, you need to have the angels remove it. They will need your permission to do the removal)

Facilitator's Prayer:

I call on Archangel Michael, St. Germaine, and the violet flame to come and clear this contract, taking complete control over any energetic entities and intelligences serving this contract in any way, removing them from this Soul book, from all energy fields belonging to (participant's name) sending them to the heavenly realm of balance and correction. I am calling forth the violet flame to clear and transmute any energies past, present, and future that lay claim to this contract in any way. Clear this temple with your light and violet flame and free (participant's name) spiritually, physically, mentally, and emotionally in this life, past lives, in DNA, in Mother's mitochondria, family heritage, and all future incarnations.

I call Archangel Raphael and Mother Mary to gently and completely train (participant's name) towards their Soul's magnificence, removing any harmful habits that keep this lower vibration in place. I ask that a clear and restored template be placed in their conscious and unconscious Self, that they can now use to support and guide them on their path to magnificence.

Final Prayer:

Archangel Michael, St. Germain, the violet light, the Archangels Metatron, Gabriel, Uriel, Raphael, Mother Mary, all guides and protectors serving (participant's name), we call on you and command you to totally and completely clear this contract and all its contraptions and entities that hold it in place. Be our sacred witnesses as this energetic contract is released and be our holy guides as (participant's name) is retrained in their new awareness of life.

We bring down the Akashic light of clearing, clarity, and love to marked

paid in full, releasing this Spirit and Soul into balance.

We now call in the highest source—Mother, Father, All That Is—to reset and teach this Soul and Spirit, (participant's name) to function at their highest level, and clear any habits, thoughts, and beliefs as a result of this contract and all of its influences.

It is done.

So be it and so it is.

Thank you Mother, Father, God, Creator of All, and the Akashic Energy of love and compassion.

Amen

F: Read out loud the participant's intention for healing.

P: Create a statement or affirmation based on the new you! Incorporate and expand the healing intention to create new behaviors, actions, and choices.

Close your records with your prayer

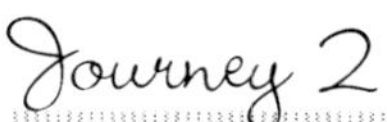

Journey 2

A Journey to Reclaim and Develop Latent Talents

Set up: A quiet place were you won't be interrupted

Time: 15-25 minutes

You will need:

- your Akashic prayer
- your journal and pen

What in your life, as you have observed it, would you like to be able to do? What do you have trouble with or just can't do right now?

Begin by opening your records

Journey to your life book and explore where this ability could be. Ask to see this ability in this life or in a past life.

Ask: What is holding me back? What is blocking me from being the best I can be? What have I taken on that is affecting me now? What things have been imposed on me that are now binding me? Trust your initial sense of things; what do you see? How do you feel? *Journal your answer using intuition as your guide.*

Ask Archangels Michael, St. Germain, and the violet flame for a cleansing and clearing.

> *I call on Archangel Michael, St Germaine, and the violet flame to come and clear this contract and binding energy, taking complete control over any energetic contraptions and entities serving this limiting contract in any way, removing them from this Soul book, from all energy fields of "_____" sending them to the heavenly realm of balance and correction. I am calling forth the violet flame to clear and transmute and energies past present and future that lay claim to this contract in any way. Clear this, my Temple with your light and violet flame and free "_________" spiritually, physically, mentally and emotionally in this life, past life, in DNA, in Mother's mitochondria, Family heritage and all future incarnations.*

Imagine yourself obtaining the training and abilities you desire. You may again travel to a past life where you were brilliant and masterful with this gift. Imagine you are learning from this master Self.

Ask for the training to be given to you in both your conscious and unconscious mind:

> *I call Archangel Raphael and Mother Mary to gently and completely train me towards my Soul's magnificence, removing any harmful habits that keep this lower vibration in place. I ask that a clear and restored template be placed in my conscious and unconscious Self which I can now use to support and guide me as I develop my gifts on my path to magnificence.*

$\mathcal{Journal\ This}\ \heartsuit$ What will your gift look and feel like as you develop it in your life? Journal your answer. $\heartsuit$

Final prayer:

It is done.

So be it and so it is.

Thank you Mother, Father, God, Creator of All, and the Akashic Energy of love and compassion.

Amen

Close your records with your prayer

Note to Facilitators and Internal Sacred Witnesses

Your job is to be open and sensitive to the energetics of the participant's journey. Feel the ebb and flow of the energy. Intuitively know when to allow them to explore, and when to encourage them to speak.

It's important to stay in the moment and capture what is observed and felt. Stop the participant when they try to analyze, fix, or edit what they are perceiving.

Allow yourself to sense and visualize along with them, but do not interpret or add information that will influence them. This is their journey. Do ask questions to help them explore.

Remember—information comes in many packages, emotions, flashes of images, color silence or absence of information, daydreams, and symbols, to name a few. The list is as endless and as unique as the person you are sitting with.

If your participant gets stuck, pray out loud that higher helpers from Spirit intercede. Archangel Gabriel is the light bringer. Ask him for help to see your way on this journey. Then encourage the participant to dive deeper into the fog or space of nothingness to explore what is there. You will usually hear responses of frustration, fear, and doubt. Encourage the participant to look more deeply into these feelings. Encourage them to be curious and brave in this journey.

You may also find your own doubts creeping in. if that's the case, repeat this prayer:

"Holy Spirit of God, I ask for protection as I open my heart and myself to the work at hand and I release all distractions of ego, thought, worry, and delusion."

Use your intuition to create questions that will help the participant to be curious and explore what they are sensing.

Using a Pendulum with Soul Contracts

Pendulums can be aligned to the guides and energy of the Akashic Records. Hold the pendulum in your hand and open the records. Intend that the pendulum be aligned to the flow of the Akashic Energy and its angels and guides.

Hold the pendulum with your arm out, dangling it from the chain or string. Ask the pendulum to show you the motion for *yes*. Then ask the pendulum to show you its motion for *no*. Use the pendulum while you're clearing your contracts. When the contracts are clear, the pendulum will swing *yes*. If it's not cleared, the pendulum with swing *no*, and you'll need to dig a little deeper.

The same is true when you create healing prayers and affirmation. If it's right, you will see it swing *yes*. If it swings *no*, you'll need to go deeper.

Soul contract work is a lifetime journey. As you do this work, you'll find yourself not only clearing things in this lifetime, you will also clear past lifetimes. Consider clearing your path for future lifetimes!

Chapter 12

Conversations in the Akashic Energy and Records

Change your Questions–Change your Listening

Diving into your Akashic Records can be daunting. Students often ask me how they can know if they're *really* in the records and not just making it up.

A big part of learning how to read your records is learning to trust your intuition. The way to do that is to practice using your intuition on small things. Pay attention to little "twinkles" or intuitive pulls throughout your day. Follow where those intuitions take you.

Continue to do the meditations in this book to further open up your abilities. Spend time in the meditations to let the Akashic Energy build up within you. Allow the healing energy of the Akasha to flow through you and connect with you. These meditations are rewiring you for reception. You're being attuned to the vibrations of Akashic Wisdom when you meditate in your records.

Practice reading your own records and writing your intuitive answers down in your journal. The more you write the more information will come up that is beyond what you would normally sense.

Ask trusted friends and loving family member to allow you to practice on them. When you read, feel the texture of the information you are giving. Be willing to listen to feedback. The feedback from your participants will tell you how to discern your senses and feelings around the information you are *getting* and *giving.*

Always keep your heart open to your guidance as your read the records. Practice opening your records during daily tasks and asking your guides to speak to you. For instance, open your records while shopping and ask to be shown the best products at the best prices. Then allow yourself to be lead through the store using your Spirit guidance. What did you find in the store? Open your records before a meeting at work. Ask for guidance regarding the meeting. Jot down some notes from your records before the meeting. Observe your inner guidance as you attend the meeting. What did you learn?

We often get stuck when reading our records because we insist on receiving certain information in certain ways. The information may not be available to us in the way we want it come to us—on *our* terms. When you interact with the Akashic Records, you are learning to speak the language of your Soul. Your Soul speaks the language of love. What does that mean? When we approach Akashic work in fear, we block ourselves from hearing the Wisdom of the Akasha. That is why this book is filled with Self-healing modalities. Go back to the inner-Self exercises and do them again. Your inner work will help you hear the language of your Soul and the One Mind of the Akashic Energy.

One day I opened my records and asked the dreaded question, "How do I know that I'm in my records and not just making it up?"

I received this answer from the guides of the Akashic Records:

Dear Ones,

The journey to knowing and receiving guidance and information is multi-layered.

Building intention is the first part.

Realizing your logical mind is now opening into a higher plane of receiving guidance is the other part.

Trust that you're making the journey, and practice letting go of your local understanding.

A hallmark of knowing you're in the records receiving higher awareness is that the flow of information that is NOT familiar and is beyond what you know now. Learn to recognize the texture and signature of the energetic flow from the Akashic Field of energy.

The inner voice will often feel and sound like "you" as the information is flowing into your consciousness. The difference will be that the concepts and relationships of ideas and realizations will not always be familiar to you.

I suggest using writing as a tool to sort out the information coming into your conscious mind.

Know yourself; learn about your inner tendencies. Observe yourself and how you operate in your conscious mind. Learn to quickly identify who

 Divine Love Affair

is at the heart of your consciousness. Are you in the operator's seat, or has a faction of yourself stepped into the control panels?

Practice being in the conscious and aware seat in the center of your heart. Observe yourself—how long can you stay there before you let go and the noise in your head starts up?

When you're in your conscious, aware mind, you then have the power to release and surrender to the flow of the Akashic Wisdom.

Fear, doubt, and the need to do it your way take you out of the power seat. When you're in fear and doubt you are no longer able to surrender to the flow of this higher Wisdom.

~All our love, your Akashic team

Exercise 10

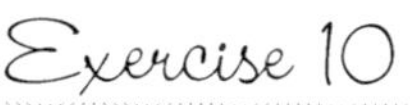

Asking Questions in Your Akashic Records

Set up: A quiet place were you won't be interrupted

Time: 15-25 minutes

You will need:

- your Akashic prayer
- your journal and pen

Begin by writing a list of question you would like to ask in your Akashic Records.

You will receive information from your records that is about what, when, how, and where. They are records of what has come to pass. Once you receive information, you can get help from your guides working with the information.

When you're finished with your list, open your records.

One by one refine your question in the records. Ask what is the best way to ask your question. What do I need to know about this question? Allow the guides of the records to talk to you about your question. When you feel you have gone as far as you can, ask the revised question. Write down what you perceive.

Close your records.

Sometimes, diving deep into a concern can help you get meaningful information from the records.

When you're stuck with a life issue, open your records and ask:

- What belief is operating in my life that causes me to live and experience life the way I do?
- When did this start; where is its root?
- What am I holding onto that is keeping me stuck?
- Is there anything else I need to know?

Working successfully in your Akashic Records takes curiosity and courage. Be willing to look down different roads within your records to discover what you're seeking. This is a journey. You are well guided. The lords and guides of your records are willing to work with you, as long as you're open and willing to receive.

Inner Guidance versus Intuition—A Question from a Student

Here is an example of a conversation about developing intuition:

Student: How do I know if it's my intuition? Is my inner guidance different from my intuition?

The Records: *We have an inner guidance system; an inner voice that's embedded within us. It's been developing in our unconscious since we were born. Sometimes our inner guidance system can be right on target for our life, sometimes it's limited by certain fears or rituals we have developed. Your guidance system is based in your lymphatic brain. This is the part of us that is causal; I feel this way, therefore I should do this, or I did this, therefore I'm going to create this belief system around this whole stuff. And it's limited to your own life experience.*

When you're looking to open up to more awareness in your life—when you're working towards a more enlightened kind of awareness beyond the same old, same old, been there, done that—you will need to go beyond your inner guidance system. You want to use your intuition, and access your higher guidance and higher Self.

Student: Explain how our intuition is our higher guidance, and our inner voice is our inner guidance system.

The Records: *Your inner guidance system is your inner voice, which comes from your unconscious and is based on being alive, being human, and on all the experi-*

ences that you've had in your life. Let's say you've had a lot of trauma your life, maybe you're struggling with addiction, or you are always involved in bad relationships. You look for a way to resolve your struggle. You will use your inner guidance system. BUT it's your inner guidance system that got you into your struggle in the first place. You may feel comfortable with your inner guidance system, you may think 'Oh, finally I have an answer, I figured this out.' The problem is your guidance system is using faulty data. You will arrive at the same old "place" every time. At some point you will hopefully to realize "I need to know more than this. I need to rise above this."

This dynamic happens because your inner guidance system is developed through all the feedback and input you've received since you were born. They are static and full of old news. Consider a GPS system in a car. If the GPS system isn't updated, it will always be giving you directions based on old information. To be effective in our lives, our inner voices, our inner guidance systems, we need continuous updates, and the most accurate updates come from our higher Self, our Soul.

To make changes in your guidance system, you'll need to learn to have a different dialogue with yourself. You want to be aware of when your inner guidance clicks on. Your inner voices need interaction with your Soul to get the updates needed to raise your consciousness.

Your intuitive system is heart based. You must consciously choose to hear and respond to your intuition. Your intuition arises from your emotions, your creativity, and your higher Self, your Soul. Meditation enhances your intuition. Your intuition doesn't always have that comfortable feeling of recognition. The information coming from your intuition can cause a frantic inner dialogue in which you're at odds with yourself. Intuition is a calm, cool voice, while your inner guidance system varies in its tone. If you have to choose between the calm, cool voice and the fearful voice, go with the calm.

Student: How do you allow that system to grow and learn?

The Records: *When your intuition and your higher guidance are activated you are automatically educating and updating your inner guidance system. You are upgrading to a new map—a new set of coordinates. Guiding your life by intuition means you're paying attention to the signs and signals of your Soul, and listening to a new set of voices. The best way to get intuition into your life is by utilizing some of the many meditative and awareness practices available to learn and use.*

When you use meditation to bring yourself to a calm and peaceful state, you connect to a flow of energy that is a little bit beyond where you are. The flow of energy has a higher vibration; allow that vibration to impact you. Here's the deal with vibrational stuff—the physical property of water is that water always wants to balance itself at the lowest level, with some help from gravity. The physical properties of vibration (and all things vibrate at the atomic level), is that vibrations want to match each other at the highest level. The higher vibration entrains the lower vibration. When you're letting yourself grow and change, you really have to let go of those inner voices, the ones that feel like your inner guidance system. Purposefully focus to open up your consciousness and align with the higher vibrational guidance system that comes through meditation and awareness practices.

Your intuition kicks in through your feelings, emotions, imagination, and creativity. Intuition doesn't work or communicate with us the way we think it should. I can't tell you how many times I've heard someone on a spiritual path say, "It's not what I thought it was." They're amazed and frustrated at the same time. Wait for the click to happen when your vibration starts to connect into a higher vibration. That's when the information and high level download starts to grow your inner voices and guidance systems.

Student: I know the way inner dialogue works, but what actually happens when you talk to a piece of yourself? Are you bringing that energy, awareness, and emotional healing to that piece? You're calling it out in the light and asking, "What do you need?" but how does that take place energetically? You're always talking about how when you look at something, it changes.

The Records: *There are a couple of principles at work when you allow yourself to listen and connect to inner pieces or yourself. The first principle is, "As above, so below." What's true in the microcosm is true in the macrocosm. The other principle is the natural inclination for vibrations to want to meet and vibrate together at the highest rate. Listening to your inner voice in sacred space, even if it's angry, feeling victimized, or expressing a negative presence, won't bring your vibration down. By observing in sacred space with your records open, the higher vibration of your Soul and the Akashic Energy is going to affect your inner voice. First of all, you allowed it to talk. You let that part of yourself bring all its concerns to the table. You're not suppressing anything. That doesn't mean you have to agree with them, but bring them to the table and allow them to express themselves. This way your observer Self, your inner witness, can see and realize what's in action right now. Then you can see what you need to do to heal; what you need to do to feel better about what you're doing.*

When you ask your inner personality, "How are you serving me right now?" and the personality shares its rationalizations, your inner dynamics will be out in the open where they can be observed. Your Soul and the Akashic Energy also observes the dynamics. You have a chance to feel the vibrations of your whole Self. When you observe yourself in action, you can decide with your consciousness how you want to respond. This is an awareness practice that will heighten your intuition and entrain your inner personalities to align with a higher vibration. Your unconscious Self will entrain to the vibration of love that flows from your Soul and the Akashic Energy of the Creator. This is the nature of awareness and healing. As above, so below.

Relationships in the Akashic Records

One of the most frequently asked questions I get during readings are about partnering and romantic relationships. One day, a client with particularly bad luck with relationships came for a relationship reading. The Akashic Records opened up and gave a healing and energy training around relationships. This information, even though focused on heterosexual relationships, seems to also apply to same sex relationships. She agreed to let me share the reading here. A year later my client reports she is happily involved in a long-term relationship with a man she dearly loves.

Question: How can I achieve a healthy relationship in my life? I tend to fall in love quickly, and the relationships don't work out. Will I ever be in a long-term relationship? The men I attract don't stick around; they all seem to be leading me on, and then they disappear.

The Records: *Did you know you can ask for healing AND training within the Akashic Records? In this session, we're going to give you an energetic training on being with a partner; in this case, a man.*

This training will override the previous patterns in your life that aren't working for you or serving you. The Akashic healing today includes an energetic training followed up with a verbal training. This training is now imbedded in your physical, emotional, and spiritual body, in your past, present, and future of your life. The training will embed in your past and future lives, in your spiritual DNA, and in your ancestral family.

We will now retrain and clear all previous understanding you have around all relationships. This includes how you understand who you are in relationship to men.

You will be able to refer back to this training throughout your life in all your relationships, including family, friends, and romantic partners. You are now preparing for the relationship you are dreaming to be in.

The new template and energetic training are now set in place.

The Akashic Teaching of Relationship Development Begins

During courtship or the romantic or sexual chase, you can be fooled by those who only want to take something from you. Their interest is to feed off of you. The thrill is the chase and then the energetic sexual feeding. They have no desire to reciprocate what they have taken. You often won't know that until the thrill is over and you're left emptied out. There are ways you can "check in" with yourself during these exciting encounters to assess where you are energetically during the thrill of the encounter.

In all relationships you must have a sense of yourself and your boundaries. Build your personal and spiritual boundaries and put them in place to protect and support you when attracting and building a new relationship. Give yourself the freedom to say NO to any relationship, friendship, romance, or marriage if need be to keep yourself safe and intact.

If you're in a relationship in which you feel that you can't say no, then it's not a healthy relationship. We often believe that if we disagree or fight with a partner that it must not be a good relationship. The truth is that in a healthy relationship you negotiate the terms of the relationship because you're constantly growing and developing. Healthy relationships aren't symbiotic, with one person feeding off of the other. Your personal growth is best supported when it parallels your partner's. Working on your own personal growth does not mean you will grow away from your partner. It simply means you're supporting your own growth, and then hopefully and purposefully you will both support each other's growth cycles.

Some people play a good game of convincing you that they can have a relationship with you. Then you find out they can't; they either aren't able to emotionally or they had no intention of carrying out a relationship in the first place. Some people disguise their expectations and controlling behavior. Being attentive to your own reactions, needs, and boundaries will tip you off quickly if you're entering into this kind of agreement, rather than a loving, growing relationship.

Retraining and Understanding How to Build Relationships

The first phase of a relationship is the thrill and excitement of the new connection. While you may be having lots of fun, don't get invested emotionally at this phase. Have your fun, joke around and flirt all you want, but remain emotionally separate.

The emotional, vulnerable part of you needs to stay grounded and not get too attached during this early stage. No matter the circumstances, remember that this phase is still simply a meet and greet.

This phase is very Self–focused, even selfish. The primary focus is, "Who am I?" The attraction to another triggers you to leave your enclosed Self to engage with another human being. You ask yourself, "Who am I as a woman?" or "Who am I as a man?" and "Who am I as a sexual being?" The answer to these personal questions can only come from within you. The folks you are attracted to and flirt with are showing you a mirror of yourself. You are basking in that mirror. That's okay, it's part of the dance, but don't get too caught up it.

Sometimes the conversations, promises, and answers people are giving you are manipulative. They're looking to get the response from you that they want. They aren't, and possibly you aren't, offering anything to recognize, support, or nurture you. You're both attempting to make the other person feel good to get what you want. Remember this and remind yourself often of this fact while you're in this first phase. When you questioning the relationship your are in, remember there is nothing substantial between you and the other because you haven't built "it" (the relationship) yet. The nature of a good relationship is that it is built overtime.

Don't abandon yourself while you're in this phase. Ask yourself, "How can I be in the feel good stage of flirting and not abandon myself?"

The second phase of a relationship usually begins between the 3rd and 5th date. This is the research phase when you're both asking, "Who is this person and what will I get from them? What do I want to give them?" You begin to explore the capacity and limitations of them. You explore your compatibility with the other. You'll feel a sense of curiosity about this person.

If you have fallen in love at first sight, you may not be allowing yourself to see this person as they really are. You may be romanticizing them, projecting your dreams and wishes for your own happy life on them without seeing the reality of who they are. If you have remained emotionally separate, you will feel the true attraction and see the real person.

This second phase of research is still a very self-focused and selfish stage. You're seeking to find out what's in it for you. Be careful not to fall in love with your own dreams and desires at this point. If you feel like you're falling in love, whatever that means for you, do a check in. Ask yourself, "Who is this person? What do I know about this person, separate from what I desire from them?"

In this phase you begin to develop a rapport with each other. (If you don't develop this kind of connection during this stage, you will both go your own way.)

The third phase of the relationship is the development phase. You both begin to take an interest in each other's life. You will begin to give back and forth to each other in unselfish ways. You begin to take more risks with each other by sharing vulnerabilities. You let the other person see you as you are. Both of your auras drop the flirting energy for the real you.

As you give in a reciprocal way during this stage, trust develops. You have interacted enough times to have a sense of how the other person operates. You'll also have a sense that you and the other person both want to hang out in this relationship. You have made a soft agreement to be with each other for the time being.

You're both building bridges of understanding between you. A flow of support and compassion for the other begins to grow. You're slowly moving from the Me stage to the We stage.

This is not the time to move in together or get married. You still have work to do! You need more developmental time to get to the merging part of your relationship.

The commitment phase is about the merging of two ideals, two separate people. You are now a couple. In the early part of this commitment stage, you'll still be experimenting with compatibility. The different is that you're more focused on building a relationship together than you are on testing each other. Don't jump the gun and move in together yet! Experiment with compatibility projects like long weekends away.

Many couples spend more time together at this point. Share a space for periods of time, but still maintain a separate space away from each other. This is the time to get into the details of living. What foods do you both like? What are their eating habits compared to yours? What keeps you both healthy and happy? What is the other person asking you to give up or take up? Is this something you want to do?

You are exploring fulfilling each other needs now. What are your partner's needs? As you fulfill your needs, can you fulfill the other's needs? Where is the balance going to be? Support materially, emotionally, and timewise is also considered here. What are the different ways you show love and support for each other?

Money and financial matters are discussed here. How does your partner handle money fiscally and emotionally? Are there any hang-ups around this

topic? Do you want to work with them? Are you able to talk about money? A good way to understand how someone works with the flow of energy in their life is to observe how they work with their money. Don't move in with your partner until you get the money questions answered.

As you work through your understanding of each other and what you want to create together, you will naturally grow into a deeper commitment. The two of you will decide together what that will be.

When is a good time for sex to become part of the relationship?

The best time for sex depends on where you are in your personal, emotional, and spiritual development. Sex usually starts in the second phase of a relationship. However, many people start sexual relations in the first phase.

Some people want to get sex questions out of the way in the first phase. They want to know if they are a good match sexually. Sex can be the answer to the meet and greet flirting, and the pressure that it builds. Many people use sex as a way to vet out possible relationship partners. The sex in this phase is self-focused. If you view sex differently, or want a different kind of sexual experience, then wait.

If your potential relationship is nipped in the bud because you put off introducing sex, then the relationship would never have developed well in any event.

The research part in the second phase of a relationship is where most people choose to have their first sexual connection. Both have begun to develop a deeper rapport with each other. They have a sense of comfort or deep attraction to each other. They feel they know enough about the other to dive in to something deeper. This phase is still a very Self-focused phase for each person. Questions of sexual compatibility are addressed in this phase; sex is part of the research. It's about attraction and performance. Fail that test and you could be out. So the sex has a flavor of risk to it.

Sexual boundaries and Self-care are important considerations in this phase. Actually, Self-care is important in every phase, but in this second phase you must be clear with yourself that this is still not a committed relationship. Ask yourself if that matters to you.

Most people can't wait long enough for a sexual encounter to make it to the developmental stage of the relationship. Trust is part of the developmental stage. This is probably the most secure time to share in sex in the beginning of a relationship. If you have already shared in sex, this phase may add a deeper connection to your sexual relationship. The nature of your sexual interactions will give you clues about what phase your relationship is in.

Men and women experience sex differently. In the records, sexist thinking is understood as limiting. Having said that, men and women are often very different in how they experience the sexual union; even about the same act of sex. The records do acknowledge same-sex experiences and validates this union as being a powerful way to deepen a bond between two people. The male and female energetic principles play out differently for each individual person.

For some, sex is an act that is a release and a connection that assures them it is okay to move forward in a relationship. Sex HAS to happen before they can commit to a relationship.

For others, sex is a sense of conquering, and they will acquire as many partners as they can until a partner "conquers" them and makes them wait for it. Then they're willing to enter into a longer relationship. Many women feel that if they make the man wait and insist that the man court them before sex, they have a better chance at securing the relationship.

Some people can't use sex as a way to vet people early in a relationship. The act of sex is an act of love. For them it's a spiritual exchange. Others may feel deep pain after being tried out for sex and then rejected.

If you're looking for a viable relationship, it's best not to allow sex to be used as a hostage situation or as a tool for manipulation. You will be better off if you don't use sex to manipulate another. Ideally, the best time for having sex is when both people are emotionally ready.

Know who you are and what is important to you when deciding to share sex. Don't send mixed messages. If sharing your bed too soon puts you in an emotionally vulnerable position, then respond to yourself and take care of your needs. If your potential partner is hesitating, respond with respect and compassion. Move forward only after you're assured that you are joining together in mutual agreement, mentally, emotionally, spiritually, as well as physically.

Compassion is a powerful way to build a lasting bridge between you and your partner. And that's what it's all about.

Chakras, Energy, and Relationships

Energetically, we're built with Twelve chakras. Our physical body is constructed around seven chakras. These seven chakras are our core essence. Then there are two chakras above our heads, one chakra below our feet, and

one in the palms of our hands and soles of our feet. Each of these chakras is connected to a life-line, or Hara line, that reaches from the Akashic Field of energy to deep within the earth. Lastly, an energy system called the twelfth chakra connects the meridian points of your body to your auric field, or what I call your energy bubble or the energy sphere that surrounds you.

The twelfth chakra extends all the way to our energetic edge or bubble. There are filters on the edge of your energy bubble. These filters allow information through to your twelfth chakra which then carries the information to your physical body and your other chakras. This energy passes through etheric layers before reaching our core Self. It's made up of a mental layer, an emotional layer, and a physical layer, with the physical layer being the closest to your body.

The seven chakras make up the core of our energetic Self. This core is the energy that runs our ship (our body and consciousness). This core is unique to you; it's precious to you. If your core melts down, the ship is going down.

We're meant to interact through our energy bubble and the twelfth chakra that surrounds us. If there's a break, breech, or tear in this energetic system, we become vulnerable to outside influences. We're affected in many subtle ways before we even realize it.

Breaks can come from trauma and unresolved issues in our lives. Other people can make tears in our energy systems. They can throw energetic tentacles into our energetic systems to drain us, connect to us without permission, or control us for any other number of reasons. We can also do the same to others when we're acting unconsciously.

When our chakras are out of balance for any number of reasons, we can also cause tears or vulnerabilities in our own energetic fields and auras.

When we're in a relationship, or beginning a relationship, these out of balance energies affect us, and also affect the way we interact with the another person. They can skew your perception. Sometimes you engage with the wrong person for you because of your out of balance energy.

If someone's energy gets into our core energy, or we enter another's core energy, it can be toxic to us. Addictive relationships are indications that the core source of our personal energy has been breached.

In a healthy relationship, we blend our energies with another—we give and take energy in the form of communication. We do this through our energy bubble and twelfth chakra. This information flows to our core. The person's personal core energy stays with them and yours with you. You're connected, but you're not draining vital force energies.

What happens in an addictive personality is that the energy bubble and twelfth chakra are compromised and the core is cracked. You allow others direct access to your vital force energy; usually someone with a similar energetic distortion. This direct connection of these energies is thrilling at first, like a high, but detrimental in the end. You will find yourself quickly depleted.

You can change that pattern through personal work and by engaging with an energy healer.

Understanding yourself energetically is immensely helpful in the early phases of relationship. "Who am I?" resonates within your solar plexus chakra. This is the energy center between your ribcage and your navel. "Who am I sexually?" resonates in your sacral chakra. This energy center is just below your navel. When your energy centers get entangled with another's, it's like an explosion. You broadcast (unconsciously) from these centers, and so magnetize and attract partners to you. What if these energy centers are broken and not functioning at their highest level? Who would you be attracting then?

When you find yourself running out of personal power, pull back. Open your Akashic Records and connect with your angels and guides. Make your intention to be in the healing mode in the Akashic Field of energy. Begin the session. Disengage any core chakras that are involved in the relationship. To disengage your core essence chakra, imagine pulling your core essence close to your body. In all areas of your body or essence, be aware to a pull or a tug. Imagine disconnecting from the force that is pulling at you. Ask your higher guidance to assist you. Ask them to build a layer of protection and healing around your core essence. Ask for assistance and training from your spirit team on how to engage from your twelfth chakra and energy bubble.

Now you can re-engage with your twelfth chakra. This will help you get some distance. Invite your sacred witness Self to observe the relationship. This quiet observation will help you clearly discern what is going on. Observe the difference in your viewpoint of this relationship when you engage your energy differently.

Red Flags

When you're in that first phase of a relationship, the partying can be a blast. You need to check in with yourself often. Do you see any red flags? Any signs? Do you feel safe? It's hard to know where you are or how you feel when you're drunk on love.

Have a handy checklist to remind you to ground yourself and look around at what is going on in your early encounters. The list could include things like:

- Am I happy?
- Do I feel safe and respected?
- Am I being heard?
- Do I really listen to what this person is saying?
- Am I glossing over anything?

Look at where you are in the relationship by examining the talk and behavior you're exchanging. Remind yourself of what you intend to find in a relationship. Compare it to what you're experiencing in the moment. Relationships don't always come in the packages we imagine. On the other hand, sometimes what's in front of us isn't what we're looking for at all.

Take a moment or two to reread your check-list. If a few things in the new relationship are missing, begin to test the relationship out as part of your research. You can revise the check-list if you want, but be daytime sober and in your own space when you do. Many people, especially women, feel that they're just lucky to even have someone interested in them, so they accept whatever they get and don't look deeper. With that belief, you may end up molding yourself around another's personality and forget who you really are. There is a saying that applies here—Pay now or pay later.

Have some fun. Find out if the missing items from your checklist are possibly going to show up later. Give the relationship enough time to show you its full potential. Relationships have a life of their own. They grow at their own rate. In any event, don't put a ring on it until you know what the relationship is.

When you're interacting with someone and find you're feeling numb or anesthetized, that's your clue that you may be in a draining situation. Listen to yourself closely and observe any other signals your body may be sending out. Imagine that you're sitting in your energy bubble and pull it in tight to you. Then ask your guides and angels to place protection around you. Ask them to close off any energetic invasions that may be happening. Remove yourself from the situation as fast as you can.

When you're in a bizarre situation that you don't care for, and yet you still allow yourself to be drawn in, something is wrong. And it's something within you. This is the time to remove yourself from the relationship, get some energy healing, and work on your personal boundaries and belief systems.

If you use this relationship phase concept as part of your check-list, ask yourself, "Where am I now in this relationship?"

It's a red flag if there's a push to move to quickly to a stage you're not ready for yet. For instance, discussing a wedding during a first encounter can be fun or silly, but if one of you is dead serious, there's a problem. The problem is that you're not in the present moment. How can you develop a viable relationship if you aren't in the present moment? Projecting into the future sets you both up for playing roles for each other. You're no longer acting from your authentic selves. You're not developing the relationship—you're building a fantasy. The end result of playing roles with each other is that you'll have no flippin' idea what's "under the hood" of your partner because you aren't interacting with who they really are.

Relationships are designed to help us grow and learn. They can be healing and can inspire us to be better people. They are mirrors in which to see ourselves more clearly. In these mirrors we see our behaviors, our faults, our priorities in life, and our gifts. Soul level relationships activate our connection to our Soul path. Soul mates can be fantastic or they can be a nightmare depending on how we view, love, and accept ourselves. We learn compassion when we're in an intimate relationship. It's a Soul's journey to learn compassion for yourself and others.

Learning to give to another person so that they may flourish in life is a wonderful gift to your partner and yourself. Abandoning yourself for an-other's wishes and dreams can be incredibly self-destructive. As you grow in your relationship with each other, be sure to find that balanced flow between you.

May your relationships be gifts to you filled with love, growth, inspiration, and joy.

 Divine Love Affair

In an Akashic Nutshell

This small section is a summary of the Akashic concepts presented in this book.

The Big Picture

The Akashic Field of energy is the Creator's essence. The essence of this energy is what we recognize as unconditional love and compassion. We are created from love and we return to this love.

The Akashic Energy of the Creator is with us throughout our lives. It protects, supports, and guides us from birth to death and beyond. This energy has been scientifically measured as a constant brain wave that pulses within us. We can access this pulse through meditation; by becoming quiet, calm, and receptive.

The Akashic Records are the Library of all Creation, including your life. This library is a dynamic, ever renewing source of information in an energetic form.

An energetic consciousness, called the Lord of the Records, has the keys to grant us access to the Akashic Records. They also work as librarians to help us negotiate to the records we are asking for. Your prayer to the Akashic Records connects you with these beings who then allow you conscious access to the records.

Angels, guides, teachers, masters, and even our loved ones help us integrate the information we receive from the records. They teach us and guide us throughout our lives in alignment with the Akashic Creator's energy and our Soul's purpose.

The Personal Picture

Our energetic essence and conscious system is a model of the Akashic system, only at a lower vibration and in a much smaller scale. "As above, so below."

Your soul is made of the Creator's essence.

Your unconscious ego Self is a dynamic recording of your current life since you were born. In your unconscious Self you will find all the influences, reactions, and beliefs that your unconscious Self has built to help you navigate your life. The personal records within you are not neutral; they have a mission to keep you alive at all costs. The Akashic Records exist at a higher vibration and are neutral observations of all creation.

Your conscious Self, your heart, navigates and bridges your unconscious Self with your Soul. Without this bridge, your unconscious Self will not have Soul direction. Your conscious Self needs both Soul and roots for a fulfilled and joy filled life.

The organizational principles in this book are designed to help you on your Soul's journey through life.

We are Soul's having a human experience. Love your life, respect your life, and make the most of this life that you can. You are here for such a short time compared to infinity. Then you go *home* to spirit and heaven with all the rich and wonderful experiences and growth from this life.

You are not alone. You are loved deeply and completely.

Make the most of your life.

Free yourself from fear.

Embrace the miracle you are living right now.

And always let love be your guide.

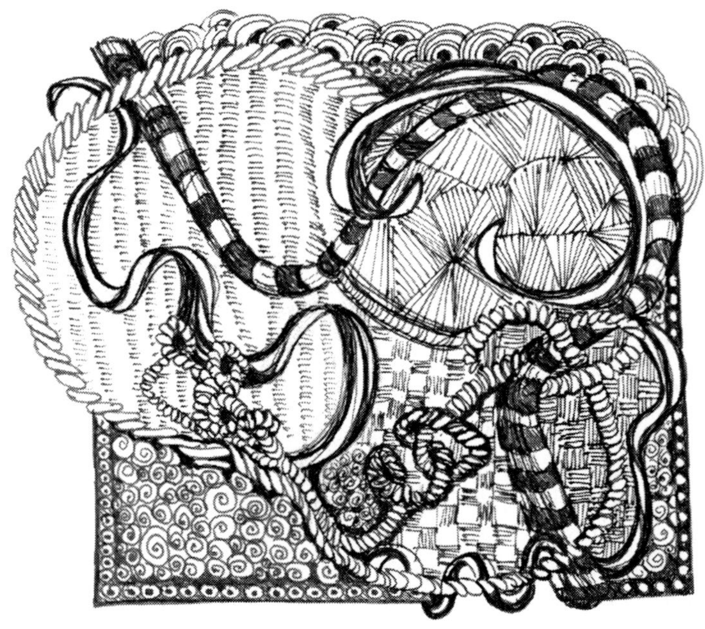

Index of Exercises, Meditations and Journeys

Bibliography

Chapter One: Creation Stories

Mayell , Hillary Did *First Americans Arrive By Land and Sea?* for National Geographic News November 6, 2003   http://news.nationalgeographic.com/news/2003/11/1106_031106_firstamericans.html

Mann, Charles C. *1491 New Revelations of the Americas Before Columbus* Alfred A. Knopf 2005.

Sturluson, Snorri, *Biography of the Edda,* Every Man Publisher Copyright JM Dent 1995

Doniger O'Flaherty, Wendy *Excerpt from Hindu Myths: A Sourcebook translated from the Sanskrit,* London: Penguin Books, 1975. Pages 27-28.

Palmisano, *Creation according to Buddha,* Thai Language Blog, December 18, 2012; http://blogs.transparent.com/thai/creation-according-to-buddha/

Caduata, Micheal J., Brushac , Joseph *Native North American Myths: Keepers of the Earth* Copyright 1988 published by Fulcrum, Inc

Metareligion, *Incan and Quechua creation Myths:* http://www.meta-religion.com/World_Religions/Ancient_religions/South_america/inca_creation_myth.htm

Cumes, Carol and Lizarraga Valencia, Romulo *Pachamana's Children,* Copyright 1995 published by Llewellyn Publications

Smithsonian National Museum of the Amercan Indian, *Creation Story of the Maya* https://maya.nmai.si.edu/the-maya/creation-story-maya

Cooper, Rabbi David, 2373 *Creation According to Kabbalah,* November 7, 2010 *God is a Verb Kabbalah;* http://www.rabbidavidcooper.com/cooper-print-index/2010/11/7/2373-creation-according-to-kabbalah.html

Parsons. John J., Hebrew4christians, The Kabbalah of Creation, *Tzimtzum-Creation "Out of Nothing"* http://www.hebrew4christians.com/Articles/kabbalah/Creation/creation.html

Baruch, Bnel, *The Wisdom of the Kabbalah,* Chapter 6.1 – *The Seven Days of Creation;* http://www.kabbalah.info/eng/content/view/frame/4516?/eng/content/view/full/4516&main

O'Connell, Robert, *African Creation Myths,* July 24, 1999, Untangle Incorporated, Toronto, public Domain stories; http://www.mythome.org/creatafr.html

Crystal, Ellie, Compiled by: *Egytian Creation Myths, Aboriginal Creation Myths, Mongolian Creation Myths*; http://www.crystalinks.com/egypt-creation.html; http://www.crystalinks.com/dreamtime.html; http://www.crystalinks.com/mongoliacreation.html

Janey, *Slavic Creation Myth: Translated from "Songs of the Bird Gamayun"*; Russophilia, September 12, 2008; https://russophilia.wordpress.com/2008/09/12/slavic-creation-myth-translated-from-songs-of-the-bird-gamayun/

Chapter 2: Akashic History

Goodsmith, Barbara, *Other Powers: The Age of Sufferage, Spiritualism, and the Scandalous Victoria Woodhull,* Harper Perennial March, 1999

Blavatsky, Helena P. , *Isis Unveiled: Secrets of the Ancient Wisdom Tradition, Madame Blavatsky's First Work,* Theosophical University Press, *The Secret Doctrine: The Classic Work,* Abridged and Annotated, TarcherPerigee; First Edition edition (July 23, 2009)

Laszlo, Ervin, *Science and the Akashic Field: An Integral Theory of Everything,* Inner Traditions; 2nd edition (May 3, 2007) *The Akashic Experience: Science and the Cosmic Memory Field,* Inner Traditions; Original ed. edition (February 12, 2009)

Larry Dossey, M.D. *One Mind: How Our Individual Mind Is Part of a Greater Consciousness and Why It Matters,* Hay House, Inc.; Reprint edition (October 7, 2014); *Healing Words: The Power of Prayer and the Practice of Medicine,* HarperOne; 1st edition (January 19, 1995)

Todeschi, Kevin J., *Edgar Cayce on the Akashic Records, The Book of Life,* A.R.E. Press; Second Printing edition (April 1, 1998)

Tesla, Nikola, *Man's Greatest Achievement, Institute for Ethics and Emerging Technologies,* Giulio Prisco; http://ieet.org/index.php/IEET/more/Prisco20151211

Chapter 3: Akashic Principle of Love

Dowling, Levi H, *The Aquarian Gospel of Jesus Christ,* Devorss & Co. (June 1, 2007)

Fromm, Erich, *The Art of Loving,* Harper Perennial Modern Classics; 15 Anv edition (November 21, 2006)

Dossey, M.D. Larry *Healing Words: The Power of Prayer and the Practice of MedicineHarperOne;* 1st edition (January 19, 1995)

Dale, Cyndi, *The Subtle Body: An Encyclopedia of Your Energetic Anatomy,* Sounds True; 1 edition (February 1, 2009)

Chapter 4: Prayer and Meditation for Akashic Connection

Penczak, Christopher, *The Temple of Shamanic Witchcraft: Shadows, Spirits and the Healing* Journey (Penczak Temple Series) Llewellyn Publications; First Edition edition (July 8, 2005)

Herrera, Jose Louis. The Rainbow Jaguar Institute

Howe, Linda *How to Read the Akashic Records: Accessing the Archive of the Soul and Its Journey,* Sounds True; Reprint edition (September 1, 2010)

Nairn, Rob, *Diamond Mind: A psychology of Meditation,* Shambhala; New edition edition (March 27, 2001)

Chapter 5: Creating Sacred, Personal Healing in the Akasha

Chodron, Pema, *The Places that Scare You; A Guide for Fearlessness in Difficult Times,* Shambhala; 1 edition (August 13, 2002)

Marciniak, Barbara, *The Bringers of the Dawn: Teachings form the Pleiadians,* Bear & Company (December 1, 1992)

Myss, Carolyn, *Why People Don't Heal and How They Can,* Harmony; 1 edition (September 23, 1998)

Chapter 6: Your Personal Team in the Akashic Records

W, Bill, *The Story of Bill W,* You Tube and Wikipedia

Marooney, Kimberly, *My Angel Connection: The Guidebook to Interactions with Angels,* Angel Blessings; 2nd edition (June 1, 2013)

Marooney, Kimberly, *The Angel Blessings Kit: Cards of Sacred Guidance and Inspiration* Fair Winds Press

Grant, Robert J., *Edgar Cayce on Angels, Archangels, and the Unseen Forces*, A.R.E. Press; Revised ed. edition (May 2005)

Prophet, Elizabeth Clare, *Talk with Angels: How to Work with Angels of Light for Guidance, Comfort and Healing*, Summit University Press (November 7, 2014)

Webster, Richard, *Encyclopedia of Angels*, Llewellyn Publications; Original edition (January 8, 2009)

Davidson, Gustave, *A Dictionary of Angels: Including the Fallen Angels*, Free Press (October 1, 1994)

Chapter 7: The Three I AMs

Dossey, M.D. Larry *One Mind: How Our Individual Mind Is Part of a Greater Consciousness and Why It Matters,* Hay House, Inc.; Reprint edition (October 7, 2014)

Three Initiates, *The Kybalion - Hermetic Philosophy* - Revised and Updated Edition, White Crane Publishing; Rev Upd edition (February 8, 2011)

Nix, Steve, *Trees and the Process of Photosynthesis*, about education, http://forestry.about.com/od/Treebiology/g/Trees-And-The-Process-Of-Photo-synthesis.htm

Newton, Michael, *Journey of Souls Journey of Souls: Case Studies of Life Between Lives*, Llewellyn Publications; 1st edition (July 1994)

Jung, Rex, rexjung.com

Chapter 8: Meeting Your Team of Experts

Joy, Brugh W., *Joy's Way A Map for the Transformational Journey: An Introduction to the Potentials for Healing with Body Energies*, J. P. Tarcher, Inc.; 1st edition (February 1, 1979)

Stamboliev, Robert, *The Energetics of Voice Dialogue*, Liferhythm; Revised edition (June 1, 1992)

Stone, Sidra, *The Shadow King: The Invisible Force that Holds Women Back*, iuniverse1997

Stone, Hal and Sidra, *Embracing Our Selves: Inner Voice Dialogue Manual*, Nataraj Publishing 1989

Chapter 10: Your Soul's Journey Through Past Lives

Tucker, Jim B., *Life before Life: Children's Memories of Previous Lives*, St. Martin's Griffin; 1st edition (April 1, 2008)

Weiss, M.D, Brian, *Many Lives, Many Masters*, Fireside (July 15, 1988)

Chapter 11: Soul Contracts

Myss, Carolyn, *Sacred Contracts: Awakening Your Divine Potential Harmony;* 1 edition (January 28, 2003

Prophet, Elizabeth Clare, *St Germaine: Master Alchemist: Spiritual Teachings from an Ascended Master,* Summit University Press (January 1, 2004)

Prophet, Elizabeth Clare, *Violet Flame To Heal Body, Mind And Soul (Pocket Guide to Practical Spirituality) ,* Summit University Press (January 1, 2004)

Other Books and Authors of Interest

Janet Conner, *Writing Down your Soul,* Conari Press (January 1, 2009)

Alice Bailey, *The Light of the Soul,* Lucis Publishing Company; New edition edition (April 1, 1983)

The many writings of Charles Leadbeater

The writing of Henry Steele Olcott

Rudolph Steiner, *How to Know Higher Worlds: A Modern Path of Initiation (Classics in Anthroposophy)* Anthroposophic Press (November 30, 1993)

Amit Goswami, *Physics of the Soul: The Quantum Book of Living, Dying, Reincarnation and Immortality,* Hampton Roads Publishing (September 2001)

About the Author

Nancy Smith lives in Massachusetts with her husband and dog, Rose. She has been working in the Akashic records with Spirit for over 17 years. She owns and runs two spiritual businesses called *Angelscapes and Angelscapes Publishing*

Nancy Smith is a practicing spiritual medium, Akashic practitioner and energy worker in the New England area. Akashic sessions can include Akashic healing, past lives, soul contracts, and soul connection readings.

Nancy is also a spirit artist. As medium, she delivers the message of love from spirit through her artwork by drawing the likeness of the communicating spirit.

Nancy has developed and teaches a program called *The Akasha Journey to Soul Mastery,* a series of classes about the higher energy of the Akasha that holds the mystery of your soul. Nancy lectures, teaches and demonstrates mediumship and Akashic records at Spiritualist churches and holistic centers throughout New England as well as at her studio in North Andover.

Nancy is an author and illustrator. Nancy wrote and illustrated a children's book called *Make a Magic Wish,* also published by Anglescapes publishing. She is an author in the book *"No Mistakes, How to Change Adversity into Abundance"* published by Heirophant Publishing as well as *The Inner Circle Chronicles* published by Inner Vision Publishing. Nancy's Spirit Art is also published in *"Right of Passage, What the Dead say about Reincarnation"* by Deborah Richmond Foulkes.

You can reach Nancy at: *nancy@angelscapes.net* or contact her through *www.angelscapes.net* where you can also book an Akashic session.

CPSIA information can be obtained
at www.ICGtesting.com
Printed in the USA
BVOW00s2340271016

466248BV00003B/4/P